African Development, African Transformation

Africa is home to many of the world's fastest-growing economies. This powerful book traces new continental institutions for development and their capacity to affect economic growth, regional integration, and international cooperation in Africa. It also assesses Africa's ability to achieve the Sustainable Development Goals and the African Union's Agenda 2063. As the continent's most ambitious development initiative since independence, the African Union Development Agency (or AUDA, previously known as the New Partnership for Africa's Development or NEPAD) provides an excellent case study for examining how an African-based, continent-wide development institution emerged. Inspired by the ideas of Pan-Africanism and the African renaissance, NEPAD was created to bring Africa into the globalizing world, to close the gap between developing and developed countries, to enhance economic growth, and to eradicate poverty. Almost two decades after NEPAD's creation and given its transformation into AUDA, this brilliant book examines AUDA's role in achieving these goals.

PROFESSOR LANDRY SIGNÉ is a David M. Rubenstein Fellow at the Global Economy and Development and Africa Growth Initiative at the Brookings Institution, Distinguished Fellow at Stanford University's Center for African Studies, Andrew Carnegie Fellow, Chairman of the Global Network for Africa's Prosperity, Professor and Senior Adviser to the Chancellor at UAA, Special Adviser to Global Leaders, and was a Woodrow Wilson Center Public Policy Fellow, and Visiting Scholar at the University of Oxford. He is the author of numerous key publications in the political economy of development with a focus on Africa and has a special interest in the politics of economic reform, regional integration, institutional change, business in emerging and frontier markets, global political economy, governance, state capacity and fragility, political regimes, public service delivery and the fourth industrial revolution. He is the recipient of more than sixty awards and recognitions from four continents. He has been recognized as a World Economic Forum Young

Global Leader for "finding innovative solutions to some of the world's most pressing issues", as an Archbishop Desmond Tutu Fellow who "drives the transformation of Africa," and was named one of the "Top 10 Outstanding Young Persons in the World." He has authored numerous key publications, including *Innovating Development Strategies in Africa* (Cambridge University Press, 2017). His work has appeared in *The New York Times, The Washington Post, Foreign Affairs,* and *Harvard International Review.*

Advance Praise for African Development, African Transformation

"Professor Signé has made an outstanding contribution to the understanding of the evolution of inter-state cooperation and regional economic integration and strategies in Africa, through the lens of studying new pan-African institutions on the continent. He provides a unique insight into the African Union Development Agency, and also covers critical initiatives such as the Sustainable Development Goals, Agenda 2063 (a shared strategic framework for inclusive growth and sustainable development), the Programme for Infrastructure Development in Africa, and the newly created African Continental Free Trade Area. This enlightening book is written with a deep knowledge of economics, international relations, and political science put at the service of Africa at a critical time in our history."
— H. E. Quartey Thomas Kwesi, Deputy Chairperson of the African Union Commission

"Professor Landry Signé, a well renown global political economist, has applied fresh and thought-provoking perspectives to some of Africa's most pressing development challenges, the emergence of regional institutions and their ability to positively shape (or not) international cooperation, intra-regional integration, and Africa's economic transformation. His book has a remarkable richness of details, including on the African Union Development Agency, and is a must-read for global development scholars and leaders from African governments, intergovernmental organizations, and cooperation partners."
— Dr. Vera Songwe, United Nations Under-Secretary-General and Executive Secretary of the United Nations Economic Commission for Africa

"In this illuminating book, Professor Signé brings his unique and prominent African voice to enrich the debates on development, and Africa's transformation, challenging the existing narrative. He is definitively one of the world's most authoritative development and African voices. I commend the book to experts and practitioners interested in global development and Africa."
— Dr. Donald Kaberuka, African Union High Representative on Financing and the Peace Fund, and former President of the African Development Bank

"Professor Landry Signé, in this strong contribution on new institutions on the African continent and their impact on economic growth, regional integration, and development, has shown why he is one of the intellects to watch on the continent and beyond. This book shows why it matters for Africa to build continent-wide institutions and use them to drive the development of physical and human infrastructure so needed on the continent. A welcome contribution to the discourse on how to build the new Africa."
— Dr. Ngozi Okonjo-Iweala, Chair of the Board of Gavi; former Nigerian Finance Minister; former Managing Director, World Bank Group; and Distinguished Visiting Fellow at the Center for Global Development

"This incredible book combines a deep expertise in global development with an impressive perspective on Africa's economic development, continental integration, and interstate cooperation for development. This important analysis by Professor Landry Signé seeks to advance knowledge on Africa in the global sphere, through drawing on his close links with the continent and his understanding of the people of Africa. Professor Signé challenges and reconciles perspectives often considered contradictory, such as the ones from Dambissa Moyo, Paul Collier, Jeffrey Sachs, William Easterly, and Steven Radelet. He is one of the world's most prominent and dedicated experts in this area, making this book a worthy read for anyone interested in Africa and its public affairs."
— Professor Tawana Kupe, Acting Vice Chancellor, University of the Witwatersrand, Johannesburg, South Africa

"Through the lens of the African Union Development Agency experience, Professor Landry Signé provides a refreshing new take on the critical role of institutions in Africa's economic development. His very insightful analysis makes this book a must-read for anyone interested in the unique role of institutions in shaping economic development in general, and in Africa in particular."
— Dr. Brahima S. Coulibaly, Senior Fellow and Director of the Africa Growth Initiative at the Brookings Institution; former Chief Economist and Head of the Emerging Market and Developing Economies Group, Board of Governors of the US Federal Reserve System

"In this uplifting and intellectually rich book, Professor Landry Signé, one of the seminal thinkers on Africa's development, offers a masterly and endlessly interesting analysis of the African Union Development Agency (formerly NEPAD) and Africa's transformation in the twenty-first century."
— H. E. Olusegun Obasanjo, former President of the Federal Republic of Nigeria, co-founder of NEPAD (renamed the African Union Development Agency or AUDA)

African Development, African Transformation

How Institutions Shape Development Strategy

LANDRY SIGNÉ
Stanford University

FOREWORD BY HIS EXCELLENCY PRESIDENT
OLUSEGUN OBASANJO
Former President of the Federal Republic of Nigeria,
Co-founder of NEPAD

CAMBRIDGE
UNIVERSITY PRESS

CAMBRIDGE
UNIVERSITY PRESS

University Printing House, Cambridge CB2 8BS, United Kingdom

One Liberty Plaza, 20th Floor, New York, NY 10006, USA

477 Williamstown Road, Port Melbourne, VIC 3207, Australia

314–321, 3rd Floor, Plot 3, Splendor Forum, Jasola District Centre, New Delhi – 110025, India

79 Anson Road, #06–04/06, Singapore 079906

Cambridge University Press is part of the University of Cambridge.

It furthers the University's mission by disseminating knowledge in the pursuit of education, learning, and research at the highest international levels of excellence.

www.cambridge.org
Information on this title: www.cambridge.org/9781108470575
DOI: 10.1017/9781108575041

First published 2019

Printed and bound in Great Britain by Clays, St Ives plc, Elcograf S.p.A.

A catalogue record for this publication is available from the British Library.

Library of Congress Cataloging-in-Publication Data
Names: Signe, Landry, author. | Obasanjo, Olusegun, writer of foreword.
Title: African development, African transformation : how institutions shape development
    strategy / Landry Signe ; foreword by His Excellency President Olusegun Obasanjo.
Description: Cambridge ; New York, NY : Cambridge University Press, 2018. |
    Includes bibliographical references and index.
Identifiers: LCCN 2018021923 | ISBN 9781108470575 (hardback : alk. paper) |
    ISBN 9781108456203 (paperback : alk. paper)
Subjects: LCSH: New Partnership for Africa's Development. | Economic development–Africa. |
    Africa–Economic conditions–1960-
Classification: LCC HC800 .S5374 2018 | DDC 338.96–dc23
LC record available at https://lccn.loc.gov/2018021923

ISBN 978-1-108-47057-5 Hardback
ISBN 978-1-108-45620-3 Paperback

Contents

Figures

Tables

Foreword

In the twenty-first century, Africa has become one of the world's fastest-growing continents economically, defying the forecasts of the best specialists, who used to consider it a "hopeless" and poorly performing continent.

In 2001, when I was President of the Federal Republic of Nigeria, I cofounded the New Partnership for Africa's Development (NEPAD), along with my colleagues, who were then presidents of South Africa, Senegal, Algeria, and Egypt. Our goal was to reverse the historical trend of the continent's marginalization in global affairs, to put Africa on the path to sustainable economic prosperity and development, and to make Africa a strong and influential partner in world affairs, claiming the place we deserve in the twenty-first century. NEPAD became the official development program and agency of the African Union, and NEPAD's Secretariat was transformed into the NEPAD Planning and Coordinating Agency. In July 2018, the African Union decided to transform NEPAD into the African Union Development Agency (AUDA).

Almost two decades after the creation of NEPAD, Africa has reversed the trend of poor economic performance, hosting some of the world's fastest-growing nations, so that it is now considered a "hopeful," "emerging," or "rising" continent. Although these results cannot be attributable to NEPAD alone, the partnership brought an individual and collective commitment from African leaders to accelerate growth and development, improve governance, and extricate their countries from extreme poverty.

One of the seminal thinkers on Africa's development, Professor Landry Signé, offers, in his uplifting and intellectually rich book, a masterly and endlessly interesting analysis of the African Union Development Agency (formerly NEPAD) and Africa's transformation in the twenty-first century. Professor Signé tackles a key issue in the policy and academic development communities: understanding

the complexity involved in bringing about positive structural transformation in Africa. His incisive and provocative analysis is so good, in
so many ways, that I despair listing them all.

With his provocative and enormous undertaking of reviewing four
decades of Africa's development, he offers a most compelling and
readable book on continental development almost two decades after
the creation of NEPAD, including an assessment of the origin, evolution, and impact of NEPAD as well as its transformation into the
African Union Development Agency and the new international relations of Africa. Finally, the book offers sound and powerful policy
advice on how to implement the African Union Development Agency
and African development strategies successfully.

His Excellency Olusegun Obasanjo
Former President of the Federal Republic of Nigeria
Cofounder of NEPAD
(Renamed African Union Development Agency)

Preface

How do new continental development institutions and paradigms evolve in Africa, and what do their evolution and performance mean for understanding the emergence and effects of regional organizations, interstate cooperation, and development outcomes?

How This Book Came About

"Landry, you should not write your PhD dissertation on a new continental institution such as the New Partnership for Africa's Development (NEPAD). NEPAD could disappear before you have the time to finish your dissertation, and this would be embarrassing." This was the recommendation of one of my mentors in 2004, as I was exploring topics for my PhD dissertation. My mentor was not the only person who was skeptical about NEPAD's survival. In 2002, some civil society figures announced its anticipated failure: "NEPAD will fail. (It) will have a catastrophic effect on South Africa and an equally detrimental effect on the rest of the African continent."[1]

Almost two decades after its emergence, however, NEPAD (renamed the African Union Development Agency, or AUDA, in July 2018) has survived and thrived, evolving into a specialized development agency of the African Union, in charge of coordinating continent-wide implementation of the United Nations Sustainable Development Goals (SDGs) by 2030 and the African Union's Agenda 2063. Against all odds, AUDA has persisted and innovated by influencing the parameters of interstate cooperation and continental integration in Africa, contributing to the slow-moving harmonization of development

---

[1] This quote is attributed to Richard Pithouse, who was a spokesperson of an anti-NEPAD demonstration during the World Economic Forum on Africa in Durban, South Africa (www.fin24.com/Economy/Protesters-Nepad-will-fail-20020605, accessed April 27, 2018).

policies across numerous sectors. Contrary to the claims of its founders, however, its development initiatives are not entirely endogenous and innovative, as they are generally similar to the ones previously developed by international institutions such as the International Monetary Fund (IMF), the World Bank (WB), the Food and Agriculture Organization (FAO), and the United Nations (UN) – largely due to the fact that AUDA relies heavily on foreign aid. Moreover, AUDA has yet to make substantial progress in implementing key elements of its initial agenda, despite some success stories and the encouraging economic performance of the continent since its creation. As a close observer of AUDA since its inception, and having written numerous pieces about it since I was recommended not to select it as my dissertation topic, I have decided that now is the right time to write a comprehensive book on it. This endeavor is particularly timely and important, as many leading development thinkers such as William Easterly, Dambissa Moyo, Paul Collier, Steve Radelet, and Nicolas van de Walle have overlooked some of the enigmas that this book seeks to demystify, the solutions to which are critical for Africa's future development.

Studying AUDA is particularly important to enrich the development debate, as it suggests that some of the key arguments against aid from Moyo's *Dead Aid* (2009)[2] or Easterly's *White Man Burden*'s (2006)[3] are partially wrong, while Collier's *Bottom Billion* (2007), Sachs's *End of Poverty* (2005), van de Walle's *Overcoming Stagnation in Aid Dependent Countries* (2005), and Radelet's *Primer on Foreign Aid* (2006) critical but favorable perspectives about aid are mostly right.

Don't get me wrong; indigenous and entrepreneurial solutions with "searchers" (Easterly 2007), private investment, trade, and entrepreneurship (Moyo 2009) are of critical importance and should not be substituted by foreign interventions. However, despite many failures and "horror stories about aid bureaucracy" (Collier 2007, 101), AUDA's case illustrates that if aid is appropriately structured with

---

[2] Rejecting aid as suggested by Moyo, if systematic, would lead to the deaths of millions of the most vulnerable people in the poorest countries, including newborns, children, women, the disabled, and people suffering from hunger and malnutrition, who depend on aid.

[3] Although the "planners" are far from being perfect, rejecting them as suggested by Easterly, if systematic, would leave many poor countries that lack policy and macroeconomic management competencies, as well as the ability to negotiate with some of the searchers taking advantage of the weak and sometimes inappropriate rule of law and state capacity, in trouble.

better policies and accountability (Radelet 2006; van de Walle 2005, 79–101), the world's poor require more aid, not less (Sachs 2005). Rightly done, "aid makes private investment more attractive and so helps to keep capital in the countries." Aid is therefore "part of the solution rather than part of the problem. The challenge is to complement it with other actions" (Collier 2007, 123). A well-targeted, tailored, and structured aid program is good both for the poorest and for business, especially when integrated in a broader pro-growth, pro-business, pro-poor agenda with accountable and effective governance with responsible and competent political leadership. AUDA aims at achieving such goals, and Chapter 6 evaluates its achievements.

What This Book Is About

This book is about the emergence and persistence of new continental development institutions and paradigms in Africa and their capacity to affect development outcomes and interstate cooperation under conditions of near-anarchy.[4] I explore questions related to these themes through a detailed study of AUDA. The subject of intra-African state relations has been largely neglected in the discipline of international relations, and many of the region's potential contributions to the field remain underexplored. AUDA, formerly NEPAD, provides an excellent case study for examining how a continent-wide, African-based development institution emerges and can affect international relations and development outcomes.

This book has two main goals. First, I examine whether AUDA does, in fact, represent an innovation as claimed by its founders, or whether, instead, it is merely a continuation of the development initiatives created by the IMF and the WB. This book helps understand how and to what extent new regional development institutions, ideas, discourses, and norms evolve in a context dominated by entrenched and persistent development paradigms and, further, shape actors' behaviors and substantive development policies and outcomes. Second, I analyze the emergence of AUDA and its evolution to the present,

---

[4] In international relations, anarchy means a lack of supreme and sovereign authority with overarching and coercive power and legitimacy in the international system – here at the continental level.

including its contribution to Africa's transformation and positive economic performance. This book provides insights about cooperation among African states when near-anarchy reigns and the ways in which this cooperation has evolved since AUDA's emergence. Thus, I propose a selective assessment of some of AUDA's key programs and analyze the major challenges the institution faces in terms of political and economic governance, agriculture and food security, regional integration, infrastructure, and resource mobilization. I also discuss academically informed policy options for using AUDA in the future to achieve the Sustainable Development Goals and the Agenda 2063, explore the newly created Africa Continental Free Trade Area (AfCFTA) and Single African Air Transport Market (SAATM), and conclude the book with a discussion of theoretical, methodological, empirical, and practical implications.

Tackling Africa's Developmental Challenge

In 2000, the *Economist* considered Africa a "hopeless" continent, listing several reasons to despair for the future of the continent, including war, disease, famine, and poor economic performance (Economist 2000). By 2011, the *Economist* adopted a new tone, presenting Africa as a "hopeful" continent and the world's second fastest-growing region (Economist 2011b). Between 2001 and 2010, six of the ten fastest-growing markets in the world were located in Africa (*Economist* 2011a, using IMF data), and from 2018 to 2022, five out of twelve of the world's fastest-growing economies are projected to be in Africa (International Monetary Fund, 2017).

NEPAD, known as AUDA as of July 2018, was created in 2001 and was envisioned to be an ambitious development initiative that would propel the region to greater heights of economic development in the twenty-first century. An important objective of NEPAD was to bring Africa into the globalizing world, to close the existing gap between developing and developed countries, to contribute to economic growth, and to eradicate poverty. The creators of NEPAD considered the project to be completely different from previous development policies and from strategies implemented in Africa by international financial institutions (IFIs).

In 2010, NEPAD was integrated into the African Union and became its technical development body – the NEPAD Planning and

Coordinating Agency (NEPAD Agency or NPCA).[5] In 2016, NEPAD celebrated its fifteenth anniversary, one year after the United Nations Millennium Development Goals (2000–2015) were replaced by the Sustainable Development Goals, to be implemented by 2030. NEPAD is also the lead development agency of the African Union, in charge of implementing its newly adopted (in 2015) Agenda 2063, a "strategic framework for the socio-economic transformation of the continent over the next 50 years" (African Union). On July 1, 2018, the AU announced it would be renaming NEPAD the African Union Development Agency, or AUDA.

In this book, I seek to answer the following questions: How and why did AUDA emerge and evolve, and what does it teach us about the creation and evolution of new continental development institutions and paradigms in Africa? Almost two decades after its adoption, what critical assessment can be made of its institutional development and the implementation of certain key programs, and what changes, if any, have manifested in interstate relations? In other words, why do African states cooperate for development through AUDA when near-anarchy reigns? To what extent does AUDA constitute an innovation or a continuation of earlier IMF and WB initiatives, and what are its functions and effects? By answering these questions, this book also offers a critical assessment of the ability of African states and the continent as a whole to achieve the Sustainable Development Goals, as well as the African Union's Agenda 2063, and discusses the newly created Africa Continental Free Trade Area (AfCFTA) and Single African Air Transport Market (SAATM).

Why Study AUDA Instead of Other Regional Institutions

The reader might ask why I have chosen to focus on AUDA. I have done so for four reasons.

First, AUDA is the only continental organization that specializes in planning and coordinating Africa's development at the continental level. Other continental institutions have broader political missions;

---

[5] The term NEPAD in this book refers to the NEPAD Secretariat during the period 2001–2010 and to the NEPAD Planning and Coordinating Agency (NEPAD Agency or NPCA) from 2010 to the present.

the African Union, for example, aims to ensure regional integration, peace, and security. Some institutions have broader financial missions, such as the African Development Bank, which is a regional multilateral bank and financial institution. Additionally, some continental organizations have been established but are not yet operational, namely the African Central Bank, the African Investment Bank, and the African Monetary Fund.

Second, what was then known as NEPAD became an official specialized agency of the African Union in 2010 and officially renamed the NEPAD Planning and Coordinating Agency (NEPAD Agency). This change in itself is worth examining in order to track the evolution of interstate cooperation in Africa. AUDA is also the main African Union continental development agency and is in charge of the implementation of the Sustainable Development Goals and the African Union Agenda 2063. Thus, by studying AUDA, I am in fact studying the specialized development agency of the African Union and, by extension, the African Union itself. In 2018, the African Union officially decided to transform NEPAD and name it the African Union Development Agency (AUDA).

Third, one could ask why I have not focused on one of the sub-regional institutions: the Community of Sahel-Saharan States (CEN-SAD), Common Market for Eastern and Southern Africa (COMESA), East African Community (EAC), Economic Community of Central African States (ECCAS), Economic Community of West African States (ECOWAS), Intergovernmental Authority on Development (IGAD), Southern African Development Community (SADC), or Arab Maghreb Union (AMU). I answer, not only have these organizations already been extensively studied in the past, but as they are sub-regional organizations, they do not have continental jurisdiction as AUDA does.

Fourth, AUDA evolved within a unique context: after the mixed results of endogenous initiatives, such as the Lagos Plan of Action for the Economic Development of Africa (1980–2000), and exogenous ones, such as structural adjustment plans, the reorientation of IFIs in Africa began to allow more room for endogenous participation. NEPAD (now AUDA) itself was established only a year before the Organization of African Unity (1963–2002) transformed into the African Union (2002). Moreover, since AUDA's creation, African countries have experienced their best economic performance in more than four decades. Whether this growth is expressly related to AUDA can be determined only upon actual examination of the claim.

Finally, I have been monitoring African regional institutions since the early 2000s, and AUDA has proven itself to be the most enigmatic of all. AUDA puzzling history provides researchers the opportunity to demystify and explain its function, to further understand the emergence and evolution of a continental development organization in Africa, and to determine the extent to which it affects economic development outcomes and interstate cooperation in Africa.

An Eclectic and Heuristic Perspective

In answering the research questions raised earlier here, I favor an eclectic approach. AUDA encompasses both ideational and material components: ideology, shared vision, strategy, programs, and institutions, some of which appear contradictory. AUDA emerged through competition among actors and nations with different strategies, interests, and plans, and it has evolved into a complex institution exhibiting asymmetric implementation of its programs. The factors explaining its ideational components may not be those explaining the material ones, and the factors explaining its origins may also differ from those explaining its institutional evolution, its effect on interstate cooperation, and its variation in implementation across its member states. Instead of trying to explain everything dogmatically with a single theory, I explore the best perspectives from various approaches to better explain specific aspects of AUDA.

Eclectic theorizing (Katzenstein and Sil 2008), or the "assemblage approach" (Abrahamsen 2017), allows the researcher to combine relevant perspectives and analytical tools – in this case from international relations, comparative politics, and African studies – that are analytically suited to the specific object of study. This approach follows the footsteps of Keohane (2008, 714), who considers, for example, that ideational and material approaches are "complementary rather than alternative." This method allows researchers to maneuver with flexibility and in a timely fashion, outside the usual dogmatic approach. As Abrahamsen (2017, 1) points out, the eclectic perspective "offers a productive way of negotiating this encounter between IR [International Relations] and African Studies, making it possible to study Africa simultaneously as a place in the world and of the world, capturing the continent's politics and societies as both unique and global."

My own eclectic analysis takes place at the intersection of international relations, comparative politics, and Africa studies, although my dominant approach proceeds within the framework of neo-institutionalism, following in the tradition of works by Peter Hall and Rosemary Taylor (1996) and Paul Pierson (2004), who have all proposed using the three branches of the neo-institutional approach – historical institutionalism, rational choice institutionalism, and sociological institutionalism – to strengthen one another. Thus, the overall theoretical framework fits within the school of historical neo-institutionalism, although I also draw on the concepts of interest, strategy, and power taken from both realist schools, as well as those of ideas and paradigms from constructivism and sociological institutionalism. This eclectic approach makes it possible both to increase the explanatory strength of the neo-institutional approach and to better understand AUDA, its origins, and effects. The variables to be studied include the visions and strategies of actors, programs, and institutions. The method I have chosen is qualitative, inductive, and interpretative, using the past to better understand the present, and focusing in particular on the "critical junctures" and "bifurcations" that have contributed to AUDA's emergence, as well as on the "path dependence" that explains its evolution. My method is also comparative, for it is only by analyzing similarities and differences that phenomena of continuation or change can be explained.

Findings in Brief

The use of the above-noted theoretical and methodological framework to meet the two main research goals makes it possible to bring to light the historical phenomena that comprised the "critical juncture" at the origin of AUDA: the adoption and contested results of structural adjustment programs, paradigm changes among IFIs and African leaders, and favorable national and international dynamics. It would initially appear that AUDA's political will, its idea of partnership, and its mechanism for implementation are all indicative of substantive regional innovation. However, AUDA's development policies and strategies are, in fact, consistent with those established by the IMF and the WB, as shown through an examination of the discourses, strategies, and programs it has adopted. AUDA's "bifurcation" – its new institutional trajectory – depends on an earlier institutional path, and the solutions it proposes are similar to those prescribed by IFIs following a modification of their discourses during the 1990s.

Almost two decades after its creation, AUDA has yet to make substantial progress in implementing other key elements of its initial agenda, despite some success stories and Africa's encouraging economic performance. Although recognized by its international partners and accepted in Africa, AUDA struggles to ensure the effective implementation of its programs by member states and subregional organizations and to mobilize adequate international financial resources. The current CEO since 2009, Ibrahim Mayiki, has reinvigorated the organization, but much more remains to be done by national, regional, and international actors. In terms of institutional evolution and development, AUDA underwent a significant transformation in February 2010, when it was further integrated into the African Union and what was then called the NEPAD Secretariat was replaced by the NEPAD Agency, a technical body of the AU. In July 2018, then, the African Union decided to transform NEPAD into the African Union Development Agency (AUDA), straightening its role on the continent. AUDA is now in charge of the continental implementation of the SDGs in Africa and the African Union Agenda 2063, with the support of its strategic partners.[6] AUDA faces many challenges, including the fact that some African states and the public sphere have little stake in it. Despite some notable success stories, many of its programs still exhibit limited implementation by state actors and others. Thus, AUDA should strengthen its mobilization, coordination, and delivery mechanisms and its institutional capacities to realize its visions, missions, and programs and deliver on its promise. AUDA's integration into the AU as its lead development agency is a step in the right direction.

---

[6] The most important partners of AUDA have been the United Nations System (especially the Economic Commission for Africa and the Office of the Special Adviser on Africa), the African Development Bank, the German Agency for International Cooperation (GIZ), the Spanish Agency for International Development, the Department for International Development (DFID) of the United Kingdom, and the Swedish International Development Cooperation Agency, the Bill & Melinda Gates Foundation (BMGF), the European Union, and the World Bank-managed funds, among others.

This analysis of AUDA shows the importance of integrating ideational and material perspectives in order to understand the complexity
of interstate cooperation in Africa, and it helps explain the origin and
effect of African development organizations. It also sheds light on the
complexity of policy coordination, planning, and delivery at the continental level, and in a context where it lacks overarching continental
and sovereign authority enforcing and coercive power. Under these
circumstances, the contrast between the countries that hold themselves
accountable to their regional commitments and the ones that do not,
without fearing penalties, is quite intriguing.

Finally, the analysis better links African studies, international relations, and comparative politics in a context of mutual learning. The
goals are to avoid the extremes of both exaggerated ethnocentric
particularism and excessively decontextualized generalizations, and,
rather, focus on the most heuristic tools available, whether disciplin-
ary, interdisciplinary, or pluridisciplinary – in other words, theoretical
and methodological perspectives are not chosen dogmatically. The
unique and global contributions of Africa then have the potential to
be heuristically highlighted. Although using a predominantly neo-
institutional approach, the theoretical perspective is enriched by realist,
liberal, and idealist/social constructivism in international relations.
I have shown that each of the perspectives complements the others,
possibly mutually reinforcing one another. For example, there is no
systematic antagonism between rationalism and idealism regarding
African countries' desire to end their marginalization and underdevelopment and to achieve their destiny as independent, respected partners
in the global sphere – in fact, these ideas and interests are mutually
constitutive (Wendt 1999).

Who Should Read This Book

As an African, I wrote this book bearing in mind Africanists, African
policy makers, and friends of Africa from all over the world, in order to
offer a unique, although potentially controversial perspective, on the
emergence, evolution, and effects of AUDA. This book is therefore,
first and foremost, analytically grounded. Yet, as AUDA's goals are
now aligned with the United Nations Sustainable Development Goals
to be achieved by 2030 and with the African Union Agenda 2063,
the book offers academically informed policy options for national,

continental, and international leaders. Bearing in mind the goals of transforming Africa by 2030/2063, it examines avenues for resource mobilization, financing, and capacity-building strategies for effectively achieving the SDGs and Agenda 2063, and further explores the newly created African Continental Free Trade Area. Thus, this book should prove enlightening for a broader audience interested in the future of Africa and developing countries.

Acknowledgments

This book is the culmination of fifteen years of research, from AUDA's creation in 2001 to the present, which inspired a series of publications that form the foundation of this book. The book has been made possible by the assistance of several individuals and institutions, to whom I express my sincerest gratitude. Any and all shortcomings are my responsibility. I am indebted to Vartan Gregorian, president of the Carnegie Corporation of New York, and to his fabulous team, for making this project possible. I am also indebted to David M. Rubenstein, cofounder and coexecutive chairman of the Carlyle Group, John Allen, president of the Brookings Institution, and Karim El Aynaoui, managing director of OCP Policy Center, and their respective teams for their extraordinary support.

Special thanks to His Excellency Olusegun Obasanjo, former President of the Republic of Nigeria and Cofounder of NEPAD (now AUDA), who has graciously written the Foreword for this book. Without his early visionary efforts to join with other African leaders to found NEPAD, there would have been no reason for the book.

I also would like to thank the institutions that have hosted me or funded parts of this research (per alphabetical order): The Brookings Institution (Global Economy and Development Program, Africa Growth Initiative), Cambridge University Press, the Carnegie Corporation of New York, Cornell University (Institute for African Development), German Marshall Fund of the United States, the OCP Policy Center, *Revue Canadienne d'Études Africaines*, Stanford University (Center for Democracy, Development, and the Rule of Law and Center for African Studies), the University of Alaska Anchorage (UAA), the University of Montreal, the University of Oxford (Centre for the Study of African Economies), and the Woodrow Wilson International Center for Scholars (Africa Program).

I am extremely grateful to the Cornell University Institute for African Development (IAD), along with their extraordinary team, including

Director Muna Ndulo, Evangeline Ray, and Jackie Sayegh, for their outstanding support. I am also thankful to Daniela Ginsburg and Ashleigh Imus, who have similarly made priceless contributions.

I am indebted to two visionary university leaders who are making a huge difference: Chancellor Tom Case and Provost Samuel Gingerich, both of the UAA. Their extraordinary support and commitment to excellence, diversity, and equity are transforming the United States' coldest state into the warmest workplace.

I would particularly like to thank influential scholars who have played a significant role in the development of my views: Nicolas van de Walle and Muna Ndulo of Cornell University; Paul Collier and Anke Hoeffler of the University of Oxford; Laura Hubbard, Larry Diamond, Richard Roberts, Francis Fukuyama, Stephen Stedman, and Jeremy Weinstein of Stanford University; Mamoudou Gazibo, Anne Calvès, and Robert Dalpé of the University of Montreal; Émile-François Callot of the University of Lyon; and Rita Abrahamsen of the University of Ottawa.

I have never seen a person as extraordinary at community building as Laura Hubbard. Under her leadership, I have seen Stanford University's Center for African Studies (CAS) growing and becoming the heart of Africa in the Silicon Valley, one of the best globally. She has created a community that embodies the spirit of academic and research excellence, community engagement, cultural vibrancy, love, and passion for Africa. Because of her, I am fortunate and grateful to call CAS home since 2010.

There are no words to express my gratitude to James W. Muller, my highly esteemed Department Chair, outstanding proofreader, and great friend, for his incredible support. I am also thankful to my colleagues Forrest Nabors, Dalee Dorough, Guy Burnett, and Kimberly Pace, as well as Assistant Vice Provost Marian Bruce. I am grateful to the College of Arts and Sciences and its leadership, Dean Stalvey and Associate Dean Petraitis, for their support as I completed this project.

Many others have provided valuable feedback on some aspect of the book: Nadine Kwebetchou, Elsabeth T. Tedros, Abdoul Salam Bello, Ben Idrissa Ouedraogo, Tamekou Raoul, and Leonardo Arriola and his University of California, Berkeley African Research Seminar's graduate students, among others. I also owe thanks to Bonnette Ishimwe, Matthieu Ostrander, Caroline Streff, Samantha Mack, Wilfried Youmbi,

Gandhi Dhruv, and Zezhou Cai for excellent research assistance, and to my extraordinary postdoctoral fellow Chelsea Johnson.

I am deeply grateful to the Africa Program team at the Woodrow Wilson Center: its inspiring director, Monde Muyangwa, and her wonderful team, Elizabeth M. Ramey, Grace Chesson, Jeremy Gaines, and Hannah Beckett. Together they have made the Wilson Center a second home for me and my research.

My new colleagues at the Brookings Institution have also created a unique environment for success, especially Homi Kharas, Kemal Derviş, Brahima S. Coulibaly, Carol Graham, and Christina Golubski.

Last but not least, I am very grateful to my many friends and my wonderful family: my mother Joséphine, my father Michel, my sisters Nadège, Carine, and Marcelle, and my brother Gaël. This book has benefited from the outstanding support of Maria Marsh at Cambridge University Press and her fabulous team, including Abigail Walkington and Matt Sweeney.

I dedicate this book to the "Cheetah generation," the fast, visionary, and transformational generation committed to the prosperity of the cradle of humanity.

This book was made possible in part by a grant from the Carnegie Corporation of New York. The statements made and views expressed are solely those of the author.

Abbreviations

AAP	African Action Plan of the AU/NEPAD
ACP	African, Caribbean, and Pacific countries
AfCFTA	African Continental Free Trade Area
AfDB	African Development Bank
AMU	Arab Maghreb Union
APRM	African Peer Review Mechanism
AU	African Union
AUDA	African Union Development Agency
BRICS	Brazil, Russia, India, China, and South Africa
CAADP	Comprehensive Africa Agriculture Development Program
CFI	Capital Flows Initiative
COMESA	Common Market for Eastern & Southern Africa
DAC	Development Assistance Committee
DBSA	Development Bank of South Africa
DRC	Democratic Republic of Congo
EAC	East African Community
ECCAS	Economic Community of Central African States
ECOWAS	Economic Community of West African States
ESAF	Enhanced Structural Adjustment Facility
FAO	Food and Agriculture Organization
G7	Germany, Canada, United States, France, Italy, Japan, United Kingdom
G8	Germany, Canada, United States, France, Italy, Japan, United Kingdom, Russia G-77 a coalition of developing nations, founded by seventy-seven developing countries and designed to promote its members' collective

	economic interests and create an enhanced joint negotiating capacity in the United Nations
HIPC	Heavily Indebted Poor Countries
HSGIC	Heads of State and Government Implementation Committee
HSGOC	Heads of State and Government Orientation Committee
IBRD	International Bank for Reconstruction and Development
IDA	International Development Association
IFC	International Finance Corporation
IFI	International Financial Institution
IGAD	Intergovernmental Authority on Development
IMF	International Monetary Fund
IO	International Organization
IPPF	Infrastructure Project Preparation Facility
ISAP	Infrastructure Strategic Action Plan
MAI	Market Access Initiative
MAP	Millennium Action Plan
NAFSIP	National Agriculture and Food Security Investment Plan
NAI	New African Initiative
NEPAD	New Partnership for African Development
NICT	New Information and Communications Technology
NPCA	NEPAD Planning and Coordinating Agency
NPoA	National Program of Action
ODA	Official Development Assistance
OECD	Organization for Economic Co-operation and Development
OPEC	Organization of the Petroleum Exporting Countries
OSAA	Office of the Special Adviser on Africa (UN)
PAP	Priority Action Plan
PIDA	Program for Infrastructure Development in Africa
PPP	Public–Private Partnership
PRSP	Poverty Reduction Strategy Paper

REC	Regional Economic Community
SAATM	Single African Air Transport Market
SAP	Structural Adjustment Program
SPD	Spatial Development Program (of NEPAD)
STAP	Short-Term Action Plan (of NEPAD)
UN	United Nations
UN-NADAF	United Nations New Agenda for the Development of Africa
UNDP	United Nations Development Program
UNECA	United Nations Economic Commission for Africa
UNESCO	United Nations Educational, Scientific, and Cultural Organization
UNICEF	United Nations Children' s Fund
WB	World Bank
WTO	World Trade Organization

Introduction

The African Union Development Agency and Africa's Transformation in the Twenty-First Century

The New Partnership for African Development (NEPAD) was adopted by African heads of state and government in October 2001. These leaders defined it as a "pledge by African leaders, based on a common vision and a firm shared conviction, that they have a pressing duty to eradicate poverty and to place their countries, both individually and collectively, on a path of sustainable growth and development and, at the same time, to actively participate in the world economy and body politics" (NEPAD 2001). Thus, NEPAD's formation was rooted in the determination of Africans to extract themselves and their continent from the twin problems of underdevelopment and exclusion from a globalizing planet. On July 1, 2018, NEPAD was officially renamed the African Union Development Agency (AUDA).[*]

There are two levels to the partnership: at the continental level, there is cooperation among African leaders, and internationally, between African and Western leaders.[1] AUDA is highly ambitious, for it aims to strengthen democracy and promote good governance; contribute to economic, social, technological, and human development; and eradicate poverty. In order to reach these goals, AUDA has developed continent-wide strategies and programs to be implemented by its various member countries.

When AUDA, as NEPAD, was created, it claimed to be an "innovative" initiative, although for more than fifty years, the major international financial institutions (IFIs) – mainly the International

---

[*] I use the terms NEPAD and AUDA interchangeably throughout.
[1] The major Western partners are, first, the leaders of the G8 and, more broadly, the member countries of the Organization for Economic Co-operation and Development (OECD). However, NEPAD also counts international organizations among its partners; the most important of these are the World Bank, the International Monetary Fund, the Economic Commission for Africa, and the United Nations Development Program.

1

Monetary Fund (IMF) and the World Bank (WB)[2] – had been working toward these same goals of growth and development. These institutions had encouraged African states to adopt programs[3] intended to bring sustained economic growth and a considerable reduction in poverty, ultimately resulting in long-term development. The similarity of goals between AUDA and IFIs raises three specific questions that guide my research.

1. To what extent does AUDA constitute an innovation or a continuation compared to earlier IMF and WB initiatives? To this end, what are its functions and effects?
2. How and why did AUDA emerge, and how has it changed over time? What does this teach us about the creation and evolution of new continental development institutions and paradigms in Africa?
3. Almost two decades after its adoption, what critical assessment can be made of its institutional development and the implementation of certain key programs, and what changes, if any, have manifested in interstate relations? In other words, why do African states choose to cooperate for development through AUDA when near-anarchy reigns?

In order to answer the first question, I test the following two hypotheses:

1. AUDA represents a change in the behavior and political attitudes of African leaders. In addition, the development of a specific institutional framework for facilitating interstate cooperation and implementing continent-wide development strategies *represents something new*. In other words, AUDA reflects a truly novel

---

[2] The IMF and the WB were born out of a series of multilateral agreements, signed at Bretton Woods (United States) in July 1944, which dealt with international economic relations. While the IMF mainly attends to the equilibrium of the international financial and monetary system, the WB has multiple functions. The WB Group is made up of the International Bank for Reconstruction and Development (IBRD), created in 1946 to finance middle-income and creditworthy low-income countries; the International Finance Corporation (IFC), created in 1956 to promote growth in the private sector; and the International Development Association (IDA), created in 1960 to finance developing countries. For more information, see WB 1998; Cantin 2002, 21–25; Defarges 1996, 37–43.

[3] These structural adjustment programs will be presented and assessed later in the present study.

dynamic on interstate cooperation for economic development and continental integration in Africa.

2. In terms of the development policies and strategies that it promotes, AUDA represents continuity from a paradigmatic or ideational perspective. In other words, its strategies and initiatives are similar to those earlier created or newly developed by international institutions such as the IMF, the WB, the Food and Agriculture Organization (FAO), and the United Nations (UN).

My analysis addresses discourses as well as strategies and programs of various organizations and their leaders. Specifically, since the IMF and the WB have been criticized for limiting the state's intervention in high-priority sectors, I examine whether, with AUDA, African states and regional institutions have, in fact, become key players in producing public policies, particularly in the domains of political, economic, and social development.

In order to answer the second and third questions, I first analyze the context of AUDA's emergence in order to better understand its creation, particularly the institutional environment in which it arose, the ideas it transmits, and the strategies of the actors involved. To better grasp AUDA's evolution and institutional development, I then look at a few specific projects and assess the implementation of certain programs since 2001, exploring the form and degree of interstate cooperation. I focus specifically on projects related to political and economic governance (the African Peer Review Mechanism, APRM), agriculture and food security (the Comprehensive Africa Agriculture Development Program, CAADP), and regional integration and infrastructure (the NEPAD Short-Term Action Plan, which was eventually incorporated into the Program for Infrastructure Development in Africa, PIDA 2010–2040). This analysis helps me to discern AUDA's contributions and limitations and, more broadly, to understand the emergence, development, and efficacy of institutions in Africa and the reasons that African states cooperate for development. Chapter 7 discusses policy options for using AUDA in the future to achieve the Sustainable Development Goals and the Agenda 2063.

NEPAD's creation has prompted a great deal of analysis. For some, the project is no different than earlier ones, as it continues the initiatives already taken by international financial institutions (the IMF and the WB). For others, the project contains alternative solutions and

represents a break with these initiatives. These analyses can be classified into various perspectives according to the frameworks used: the
political-technocratic perspective;[4] the activist or societal perspective
(L'Écuyer 2002; Nkoyokm 2002); and the analytical perspective. Furthermore, the analytical perspective itself contains the following
schools of thought: liberal and neoliberal approaches (Hope 2002,
387–402; de Waal 2002, 475); the neo-Marxist approach (Amuwo
2002, 65–82; Loxley 2003, 119–28); and the historical approach
(Chabal 2002, 447–62). Many of these studies share normative, prescriptive, and prospective aspects, and are weak in terms of their
heuristics and their capacity to explain either change or continuity in
African development strategies. Let us examine these different perspectives, their foundations, and their major limitations.

The political-technocratic perspective is represented by the various
official publications of international institutions working for development in Africa and by experts' discourse on the work of these
institutions. This perspective either presents an official position or
legitimizes the policies and members of these institutions. These analyses focus on the origins and causes of problems, ways to remedy
them, and prescriptions for the future. The publications of the World
Bank (2000a), the G8 (2002), and certain African Union officials, such
as Ahmedou Ould-Abdallah (2002, 97–102) and Vijay S. Makhan
(2002, 5–10), illustrate this perspective.

Ould-Abdallah, a senior UN official, takes a position favorable
to the creation of NEPAD, which he considers "an innovative
program ... which, by its approach and the scope of its intervention
differs significantly from earlier initiatives" (Ould-Abdallah 2002,
98–99). This view is repeated by Makhan, a senior AU official, who
describes NEPAD as an operational program for "self-development,"
whose objective is to offer "an operational vision encompassing social,
political, and economic activities" (Makhan 2002, 9–10). The leaders
of the G8 share a similar view: after the 2002 G8 summit at Kananaskis, they proposed the "G8 Action Plan for Africa," which described
NEPAD as "a bold and clear-sighted vision of Africa's development"
and included measures in partnership with African leaders, whose
project they said offered "a historic opportunity to overcome obstacles

---

[4] See G8 2002. See also the WB's yearly publications, including the *World
Development Report, 2000/2001* (WB 2000a).

to development in Africa" (G8 2002, 1). We may conclude by noting that the purpose of political-technical publications is largely political: to support the institutions and officials that produce development strategies and to guide their future actions. This view, with its normative and political conception of development, is limited in its capacity to explain change or continuity in development strategies heuristically.

The same critique can be made of the activist perspective, which comprises analyses from civil society actors who either condemn or commend various development strategies on the basis of their own values, which they foreground to varying degrees in their analyses. Here, the activist perspective is represented by François L'Écuyer (2002), "The African Civil Society Declaration on NEPAD" (SARPN 2002), and Jacqueline Nkoyokm (2002).

The highly skeptical "African Civil Society Declaration on NEPAD," questioned what it viewed as an initiative pursued by an elite minority, which was not representative of civil society, and which effectively continued the past actions of international financial institutions. In his work, L'Écuyer takes a similar view and also questions AUDA's foundations and the process of its creation. According to him, AUDA's strategies are based on erroneous postulates concerning the causes of underdevelopment, and the program was adopted without serious consultation. Not all of the authors in the activist/societal school share this extremely skeptical view. Nkoyokm, for example, is enthusiastic about AUDA and considers it an innovative initiative, particularly in light of the exceptional willingness of African leaders to participate in it. She also offers prescriptions for AUDA success, notably through increasing the involvement of civil society, which she considers essential to the program's legitimization (Nkoyokm 2002).

It is therefore evident that these partisan analyses take a normative and prescriptive approach, and they are hardly heuristic in their capacity to explain change or continuity with respect to AUDA.

In contrast, authors who take an analytical approach often have heuristic aims, although these are often limited or inadequate. They look for the sources of Africa's underdevelopment in governance and the structure of the international economic system. They criticize the blind spots of development strategies and seek solutions to remedy them. This approach includes liberal, neo-Marxist, developmentalist, self-developmental, and historical perspectives. Many of these schools of thought have a specific understanding about optimal development strategies and how to achieve them. Thus, they are also largely normative, prescriptive, and limited in their ability to explain innovation heuristically. There are, however, a few authors who have attempted to go beyond these limits, particularly within the historical school (see Chabal 2002).

The approaches inspired by liberal theories of development emphasize the stages of growth and the need to follow them (Rostow 1970), good governance (World Bank, quoted in Chang 2002), the free market (Smith 1976), and specialization based on comparative advantage for development to occur.[5]

Kempe Ronald Hope (2002, 387–402) identifies the liberal principles contained in AUDA as preconditions for Africa's renewal. He claims that, in order to become internationally competitive, to reach a high rate of economic growth, and to develop, African countries first must meet certain criteria: good governance, democracy, peace, security, the restoration and maintenance of macroeconomic equilibrium, liberalization, regionalization, productive bilateral and multilateral partnerships, local appropriation of AUDA, and strong leadership (Hope 2002, 396). Hope's analysis is thus normative and implicitly prescriptive. Indeed, rather than analyzing change or continuity, he studies the conditions favorable to the kind of continuity he promotes.

Although Alex de Waal is more critical, his analysis follows the same vein. He considers the partnership to be founded on the principles of good governance, whose main characteristics are good macroeconomic policies and improvement of economic and business governance. In spite of AUDA's excessive ambitions, for him the partnership remains an exceptional and "properly oriented" opportunity for Africa's development (de Waal 2002, 464). According to this perspective, therefore, AUDA represents a true innovation.

Thus, we may observe that analyses inspired by liberal theories have a heuristic value not so different from that of partisan political-technocratic analyses: for the most part, they are normative and prescriptive, which limits their capacity to explain AUDA's elements of innovation or continuity.

The neo-Marxist approach is inspired by theories of unequal exchange (Emmanuel 1972), critiques of imperialism and multinational corporate dominance (Amin 1976; Frank 1966), the core–periphery

---

[5] In particular, Hope 2002 and de Waal 2002.

model (Perroux 1961), and dependency theories (Cardoso 1978). In analyzing African development, Amuwo (2002, 1–2) emphasizes unequal exchange and the economic domination imposed on Africa for centuries by the Western powers. Following his example and starting off from the same premises, Loxley (2003, 119–28) believes that this domination is at the root of the extroversion and vulnerability of African economies within the global capitalist system. For these authors, not only does AUDA fall within this same pattern, it reinforces it by propping up the capitalist system and, thus, risks leaving the continent underdeveloped. This analysis suggests, therefore, that AUDA is not at all new. However, it does not attempt to explain the process of its emergence. Supporters of this perspective implicitly believe that a good development strategy must not be capitalist, and they therefore propose redefining AUDA's strategies. Yet, we may note that some authors in this school have made an effort to keep their analyses heuristic by adopting a historical approach.

Unlike the normative and prescriptive approaches analyzed above, Patrick Chabal's (2002, 447–62) approach is defined by his emphasis on axiological neutrality. He takes a historical approach in order to demonstrate that African leaders' compliance with AUDA's proposed "democratic orthodoxy" plays into the liberal framework and rewards actors who accept the notion of good governance. Thus, these leaders' objective is to increase the transfer of resources toward Africa rather than achieving development. As a result, the instrumental relationship between African leaders and international partners is strengthened (Chabal 2002, 462). It is therefore tempting to conclude that AUDA does not represent a true innovation, but rather a continuation of the kinds of utilitarian partnerships that have always existed between Africa and the donor community.

Although this historical analysis is interesting, it is incomplete. Chabal identifies and explains the reproduction of partnerships,[6] but he does not entirely explain the mechanism of change in development strategies. A greater emphasis on the institutional factors could fill this gap.

---

[6] In fact, Africans adapt to their partners' demands in order to obtain the profits they count on. This adaptation does not imply agreement, but rather strategic imitation.

A review of the literature shows that many authors have exhibited little scientific rigor in establishing their theoretical and methodological frameworks.[7] With this in mind, I adopt a more scientific approach to my own research. First, in Chapter 1, I present the theoretical and methodological approach that allows me to explain the emergence, development, and effects of AUDA. I employ an analytic, neo-institutional, inductive approach in order to explain present phenomena through the lens of the past. Moreover, I complement the institutional analysis by drawing on realist, liberal, and idealist/social constructivist concepts from the field of international relations.

Second, in accordance with the requirements of this approach, I evaluate the fundamental principles and impacts of international financial institutions (Chapter 2). The goal is to observe the context that gave rise to their interventions, the theories and ideologies that underlie these interventions, and their observable results. This helps elucidate the fundamental elements of the comparison of IFIs and AUDA.

Next, I examine the various shifts in IFIs' discourses and strategies and the context that contributed to AUDA's emergence (Chapter 3). The objective here is to test whether there is a connection between the change in these institutions' discourses and the emergence of AUDA and to identify a possible "critical juncture" or institutional "bifurcation."

I then use a strictly comparative process to shed light on the similarities and differences between AUDA and international financial institutions (Chapter 4). First, I take a blanket approach, and by comparing discourses I conclude whether the initiative is endogenous or exogenous. I then take a sector-based approach by observing specific strategies and programs proposed in order to promote democratic governance, economic governance, and the fight against poverty. This analysis makes it possible to conclude whether AUDA's institutional trajectory is different from that of the IMF and the WB in terms of its policies and development strategies for Africa.

Additionally, I analyze the evolution, institutional development, and implementation of certain AUDA programs since its creation in 2001,

---

[7] I should note that the concerns of most of these authors were more empirical than theoretical, and they did not necessarily seek to reach generalizable theoretical conclusions about innovation.

as well as the extent to which it has affected interstate cooperation for development in Africa (Chapter 5). To do this, I pay particular attention to AUDA's organizational transformations, as well as the impact of certain programs on its institutional development. The principal programs analyzed will be those for political and economic governance (the APRM); for agriculture and food security (the CAADP); and for regional integration and infrastructures (the NEPAD Short-Term Action Plan, eventually incorporated into the PIDA 2010–2040). I also explore African countries' levels of involvement, ownership, and degree of implementation of such programs. All of this contributes to a better understanding of the key actors, their motivations, and the determinants of interstate cooperation for development in Africa.

I also assess AUDA's resource mobilization strategy (Chapter 6). The AUDA resource mobilization strategy is constituted by the Capital Flows Initiative and Market Access Initiative. The Capital Flows Initiative focuses on increasing domestic resource mobilization, overseas development assistance, and private capital flows while seeking "the extension of debt relief beyond its current levels." While the Market Access Initiative focuses on the removal of nontariff barriers, the diversification of production, and the promotion of the private sector, African exports, and specific sectorial activities. Chapter 7 discusses policy options to achieve the Sustainable Development Goals and the African Union Agenda 2063, and explore the newly created African Continental Free Trade Area (AfCFTA) and Single African Air Transport Market (SAATM).

To conclude, this book will allow us to better understand, both theoretically and practically, the emergence and development of continental institutions, the implementation of regional programs for Africa's integration and development, and interstate cooperation through continental institutions.

1 | An Analytical Framework to Explain the Origin, Development, and Effects of AUDA

As stated earlier, the aim of this book is to understand the emergence, development, and effects of a continental institution (the African Union Development Agency, or AUDA, and formerly known as NEPAD) on Africa's development and interstate cooperation. Questions related to the origins and effects of international institutions are important in theories both of international relations (realism, liberalism, constructivism, and critical theories) and comparative politics (neo-institutionalism).

Neo-institutionalism is an increasingly prominent theoretical and analytical approach in political science research (Hall and Taylor 1996), especially in the United States.[1] As André Lecours (2002) notes, this school has two dominant lines of analysis:

The first concerns the influence of institutions on action. It encourages exploration of the impact of institutions on the behavior of actors, their strategies, their preferences, their identities, their nature, and even their existence. The second concerns the question of institutional development. It leads the researcher to investigate the origins and nature of institutions by examining how their production and reproduction belong to a process in which the institutional landscape at a certain moment in time and space conditions the possibility and trajectory of institutional change. (3–4)

These two central paradigms correspond well to the goals of my study: to explain the influence of international financial institutions on the behavior of the African leaders who initiated AUDA to explain whether AUDA represents change or continuity in relation to international financial institutions, and to explain the origin, development, and impact of

---

[1] The neo-institutional approach was developed in the United States, and developed differently in Canada, England, and France, where it is increasingly used. On this subject see the following authors: for French Canada, Montpetit 2002a and 2002b; for English Canada, Smith 2002; for France, Palier and Bonoli 1999.

AUDA. These central questions are also well understood through a number of approaches in the field of international relations.

For this reason, my study makes the case for "eclectic theorizing" (Katzenstein and Sil 2008), an "eclectic perspective" (Signé 2017), or an "assemblage approach" (Abrahamsen 2017) that I believe to be an appropriate method for explaining and presenting the contributions of Africa as unique and global. Although using a predominantly neo-institutional approach, the theoretical perspective is enriched by realist, liberal, and idealist/social constructivism in international relations. What does each of these perspectives contribute?

In this chapter, before elaborating on the neo-institutional approach, I highlight the contribution of international relations and development theories to an analysis of AUDA and interstate cooperation in Africa. Then, I consider central theoretical questions through the lens of international relations, from various theoretical perspectives – realism, liberalism, constructivism, and Marxism/critical theories – providing a summary of each and applying the findings to the topic of AUDA. Next, I present the neo-institutional approach in greater detail, presenting three variants: historical, rational choice, and sociological neo-institutionalism. I conclude with an exposition of the analytical procedures I use to explain AUDA.

I THEORIES OF INTERNATIONAL RELATIONS AND THE AFRICAN UNION DEVELOPMENT AGENCY

In this section, I consider how theories of international relations (realism, liberalism, constructivism, and critical theories) would explain the origin, development, and effects of a continental organization such as the AU Development Agency.

Realism/Rationalism and International Organizations

In realist theories of international relations,[2] AUDA is be viewed as an attempt by African powers to shape and dominate interstate

---

[2] The assumptions of realism include groupism for safety and survival; an egoistic and self-interested human nature; power-centrism and state-centrism, with the

cooperation on the continent. AUDA was created out of the merger of two competing programs, the Millennium Action Plan (MAP) – initiated by South Africa and supported by Nigeria, Algeria, and Egypt, some of the largest African economies – and the Omega plan. After MAP was proposed, President Abdoulaye Wade of Senegal proposed the Omega Plan as an alternative that addressed some limitations of the previous plan but also attempted to counter the domination of the development agenda by the large economies, which endangered the interests of smaller countries. The two plans were ultimately merged to form the New African Initiative, later called NEPAD and now called the AUD Development Agency, or AUDA. These five founding countries of NEPAD (AUDA) are also permanent members of the AUDA Heads of State and Government Orientation Committee (HSGOC), a twenty-member committee, of which the

state as a primary focus of international relations; the unitary, autonomous, and rational nature of the state; the conflictive nature of international relations; and an anarchic or quasi-anarchic structure of the international system (absence of efficient central authority), in which each state is responsible for its own security, survival, and prosperity. Theoretical schools include classical realism, neorealism, defensive realism, offensive realism, and neoclassical realism, with specific theories such as the balance of power, the balance of threat, hegemonic stability, and power transition theories. Thucydides, Machiavelli, Hobbes, Grotius, von Clausewitz, and Hamilton were precursors of realism. Carr (1964) and Morgenthau (1993) are among the most prominent classical realists, and Gilpin (1981), Griesco (1988), Kennedy (1987), Mearsheimer (2001), Waltz (1979), and Kindleberger (1976) are among the most notable neorealists. For realists, international organizations are of limited help in addressing international challenges, as these organizations cannot change the anarchic structure of the international system. The creation and success of an international organization (IO) depends on the existence of a hegemonic state, which structures that IO according to its interests. In the case of cooperation in IOs, relative gain is extremely important, and states should ensure that the gain of others is limited, as today's friends can become tomorrow's enemies. For the realist state, cooperation through IOs is only possible when there is an asymmetric power relation, which allows for marginal relative gain by other states while the dominant realist state pursues its own absolute gain. Related to AUDA, realism/rationalism would also try to answer a different set of questions: Does AUDA serve as a tool of the major African powers (its initial promoters) to dominate interstate cooperation on the continent? Is AUDA an instrument for these countries to leverage regional power in order to weigh in on development questions in global politics? Is AUDA a useless and powerless organization unable to truly effect development change?

"other 15 member states rotate every two years, or following regional consultations with the AU."[3]

Given the initial dynamics surrounding its creation, realist theories in international relations or strategic perspectives in comparative politics would also consider AUDA a tool for the major African powers to better concentrate and leverage regional/continental power in the context of a quasi-anarchic international society (Waltz 1979) and to become stronger players in the globalized economy. AUDA could therefore be understood as a state-centric, utilitarian initiative by African leaders hoping to better dominate the continent and influence global politics. Founded during the promotion of the "African renaissance" and the renewed role of South Africa and the continent in global affairs, AUDA could be considered a tool for redefining the rules of the game structuring cooperation among African countries as well as between African countries and the rest of the world, with South Africa in a leadership position. This perspective is even clearer given that, for realists, international organizations represent social arrangements in which the interests of the most powerful are institutionalized. Two of NEPAD's cofounders, South Africa and Nigeria, are also among its largest financial contributors. But the initial project was substantially diluted on the basis of both the alternative Omega plan proposed by Senegal and African leaders' interactions with Western powers.

Indeed, some realists may consider the dilution of the agenda of the major powers, which have now accepted compromises under pressure from smaller states and Western institutions, the root cause of AUDA's difficulties. If major African powers do not have an interest in advancing their agenda through AUDA, they will be less likely to support the continental institution. Its limited power at inception as an independent organization would partly explain its transformation into a specialized agency of the African Union. Given that the founders faced difficulty in advancing their own interests via AUDA, realists might conclude that AUDA was unable to change the structure of intra-African relations or to independently shift the balance of power in Africa's favor. In terms of international organizations more generally, realists would likely be pessimistic about the creation of AUDA, expecting it to fail to solve Africa's development challenges.

---

[3] NEPAD. "About NEPAD: Governance." NEPAD.org. www.nepad.org/content/about-nepad#gov (accessed April 27, 2018).

Liberalism/Institutionalism in International Organizations

According to liberal/institutionalist theories,[4] and given the marginalization of Africa in global affairs and trade,[5] African countries need to cooperate through regional institutions in order to reverse collective marginalization, achieve collective gain (Keohane 1984), mobilize financial resources, generate growth, and extricate countries from underdevelopment and extreme poverty. Structural interactions through regional institutions such as AUDA thus facilitate cooperation by reducing transaction costs and increasing access to information in a context where no single country can manage all of the region's complex problems alone. According to the framework of Keohane and Nye (2001), even the most powerful states such as South Africa or Nigeria must cooperate given their mutual interdependency and vulnerability. Therefore, multilateral institutions such as AUDA and the African Union contribute to regional problem-solving. Moreover, AUDA is theoretically guided by liberal principles (e.g., the promotion of good governance, human rights, democracy, capitalism, free markets, trust

---

[4] Liberalism assumes that the structure of the international system is anarchic or quasi-anarchic; that states are the main but not the only significant actors; that states are rational; that human nature is good; that reciprocity is good; that cooperation is crucial; that international institutions and interdependency are necessary for prosperity; that the state, though naturally selfish, has a propensity to cooperate rather than seek conflicts; that democracy and market capitalism are fundamental; that conflicts can be explained as the result of mutual misunderstanding; and that multilateralism is preferred in international relationships and actions. Theoretical schools of liberalism include institutionalism (Keohane and Nye 2001), functionalism (Jean Monnet), international regime theories, and collective-good theories (Hardin 1968; Olson 1965). Precursors of liberalism include Hugo Grotius, John Locke, Adam Smith, Immanuel Kant, and David Ricardo. Works by contemporary scholars of liberalism include Keohane and Nye (2001); Keohane (1984, 1989, 1990); Moravcsik (1997); Russett (1993); Ikenberry (2000); Krasner (1982), and Katzenstein et al. (1998). According to this school, international organizations are created to solve specific problems in situations where interests are shared and universal gain is preferred to the rat race. Liberalism/institutionalism offers other interesting research questions for AUDA: Do African countries, whether big or small, take a mutual interest in achieving collective gains and avoiding collective losses in global affairs, and could they achieve these ends through interstate cooperation within AUDA?

[5] Of which they represent less than 2%.

and protection of the liberal community, continental economic integration, etc.), even if those ideals do not systematically reflect reality. NEPAD, now AUDA, was created to avoid worst-case outcomes and to realize the potential gains from cooperation, especially those related to the continent's shared goals and common interests (Hasenclever et al. 1997).

Marxism and Critical Theory in International Organizations

According to Marxist and critical theories of international relations,[6] AUDA reflects the triumph of global capitalism and the neoliberal order in Africa, as African leaders, while critical of past domination, have adopted an institution that can only serve to crystalize Africa's exploitation and marginalization. In fact, being integrated in the globalized system exposes African leaders to further exploitation, since the exchange is always fundamentally unequal. Moreover, AUDA could be interpreted as an attempt by African leaders to partner with global actors in order to better exploit their own citizens – i.e., collusion between the elites of the core and those of the periphery.

---

[6] The assumptions of Marxism and various critical theories are very diverse. Wallerstein (1983) speaks of the relation between the core (the industrialized countries) and the periphery (the least developed countries). The core keeps the periphery underdeveloped because its wealth depends on the exploitation of the periphery. Gramsci (Gill 1993) highlights the cultural hegemony of dominant groups in the West: Citizens accept their conditions. Emmanuel (1972) presents his theory of "unequal exchange," in which international trade is a tool of exploitation (lower compensation and an unequal rate of labor costs). Frank (1979) examines the "development of underdevelopment," using a metropolis (core)-satellite (periphery) structure. Cox (1987), one of the best-known scholars in critical theory, argues that theories are tools used to benefit elites' interests. These theories usually follow in the tradition of scholars such as Marx and Engels (1975). Marxists consider IOs to be capitalist initiatives created by a hegemon to exploit and dominate, as tools for the development of modern capitalism, which they not only reflect but also reinforce. Marxism and critical theory would raise other specific questions about AUDA. Does AUDA reflect the triumph of capitalism and the neoliberal economic order that is likely to perpetuate the exploitation and domination of Africa? Is AUDA a tool from the core to dominate and exploit the periphery, at the national level (rulers versus citizens), the continental level (powerful countries versus small states), and the international level (greatest world powers and institutions versus African countries)?

Idealism/Social Constructivism and International Organizations

An analysis of the AU Development Agency through the lens of social constructivism[7] shows that ideas and values affect interstate cooperation in Africa. AUDA is an organization not only serving member states and reflecting their interests, but also acting as its own source of ideas and generator of new norms. To AUDA's promoters, the organization represents a new Africa, delivered from Western domination and exploitation and recognized as a respectable contributor to and beneficiary of globalization. The idea of an African renaissance reflects South African foreign policy of the late 1990s. AUDA's idealist goals transcend sectoral policy issues and aspire to realize Africa's destiny as a global leader.

From an endogenous perspective, AUDA's goal is to represent the new Africa, a proud continent determined to shape its own destiny and willing to engage with the world on equal terms and with mutual respect. AUDA was founded on the basis of the shared values and norms of participating countries, which had reached agreement on

[7] Characteristics of constructivism include the social construction of reality (Berger and Luckmann 1966; Wendt 2001); the importance of ideational factors and norms (intersubjectivity and shared knowledge shape the interpretation of the world); the key roles of identity, culture, and values; the "logic of appropriateness," and the mutually constitutive nature of the relationship between ideas and interests. As noted by Wendt (1992), "Anarchy is what states make of it": This means that the structure of the international system is not automatic or made from a template but depends on the role and character of identities that may generate collective interests or conflicts. Works by key ideational and constructivist scholars include Berger and Luckmann (1966); Adler and Haas (1992); Risse (2000); Wendt (1992, 1999); and Finnemore and Sikking (1998). In the constructivist school, international organizations represent values and identities and are created when a consensus on norms and values or a shared identity exists, particularly the same perception of the problems to be solved and of the solution. These norms also structure the behavior of actors. Idealism/social constructivism explores specific questions for AUDA such as the following: Is there an African idea/paradigm of development, and how strong is it? Is AUDA a regional organization that emerged to initiate, represent, stabilize, or diffuse shared ideas and paradigms that shape interstate cooperation and development policies and outcomes? How could its emergence and effect be explained through ideational variables? To what extent does it shape preferences for African development? Why do African states cooperate through AUDA, and what does this tell us about collective values, identities, norms, and interstate cooperation in Africa at a continental level?

the nature of the problems to be solved. On the other hand, this perspective faces the reality that, in terms of concrete development policies and solutions, AUDA has taken its inspiration and methods from the paradigm of international institutions such as the United Nations, the International Monetary Fund, and the World Bank.

From an exogenous perspective, the AU Development Agency was created to show the international community, especially IFIs, that Africa can take ownership of its development and develop homegrown initiatives to fulfill its goals, instead of being wholly dependent on the international community. AUDA's creation demonstrates that Africa shares its principles with the world at large, as the values promoted in AUDA are largely similar to those dominant in the global community. AUDA also results from the influence of the global system on African values, in particular through the classical economic theories of development that have been implemented by IFIs.

In explaining AUDA, the various international relations perspectives can be understood as complementary rather than competing. What is the role of actors' preferences, and where do they come from? Constructivism and idealism perhaps best explain the formation and evolution of preferences, identities, and norms, capturing the ideational dimensions that bring African countries together or keep them apart. It is thus important to explore the origins of actors' preferences and understand their fundamentals, instead of taking them as given, as realists do. Why would actors favor collective action through an international institution instead of trying to achieve their preference individually? Liberalism and institutionalism perhaps better identify the mechanism through which international institutions allow states to achieve collective gains or prevent collective loss. Why do certain cultural norms persist despite attempts to change them? Some critical perspective would help explain the nature/role of cultural hegemony, and the difficulty of overcoming it and creating new norms/ideologies. When and why are international institutions efficient and effective, or not? Realism might help explain the effect, impact, and effectiveness of international organizations by linking preferences with material interests; it also sheds light on the ways in which some preferences, especially those of the most powerful countries, matter more than others. In sum, I use constructivism to understand the origin and evolution of the preference and ideational components of AUDA, liberalism to understand why African countries have decided to cooperate through AUDA instead of through bilateral cooperation, and realism to understand the level of effectiveness of AUDA and its evolution since its creation.

In conclusion, by interpreting the AU Development Agency from the perspectives of various theories of international relations, my goal is not to definitively answer the questions raised but to show the ways in which each perspective complements the others, with the potential for mutual reinforcement.

II NEO-INSTITUTIONALISM: A PLURAL THEORETICAL AND METHODOLOGICAL APPROACH

Neo-institutionalism does not represent a single theoretical and methodological approach. Peter Hall and Rosemary Taylor (1996, 468–96) distinguish three branches of this school of thought: historical institutionalism, rational choice institutionalism, and sociological institutionalism. These different approaches are discussed here with an emphasis on their origins, the ways in which they define institutions, their main foci of analysis, and the conclusions they draw about both the influence of institutions on the behavior of actors and the origins and modification of institutions. This presentation makes it possible to identify the theoretical and methodological tools that contribute to shaping my own approach.

Historical Institutionalism: Origin and Definition

Explanations of the origin of historical institutionalism vary slightly according to the author. For Hall and Taylor (1996, 470) as well as for Lecours (2002, 8), this approach arose in response to structural functionalism and behaviorism. Denis Saint-Martin (2002, 21) sees it as a reaction by institutionalists to the dominance of rational choice theory during the 1980s, while Daniel Béland (2002, 22) emphasizes it as a response to the limits of the socioeconomic approach that was widely used during the same period. In fact, neo-institutionalism borrowed parts of its explanatory capacity from each of these methods.

Historical institutionalists define institutions as

the formal or informal procedures, routines, norms, and conventions embedded in the organizational structure of the polity or political economy. They can range from the rules of a constitutional order or the standard operating procedures of a bureaucracy to the conventions governing trade union behavior or bank-firm relations. (Hall and Taylor 1996, 938)

Hall and Taylor (1996, 472–74) observe four characteristics specific to the historical institutionalist approach. The first is an overly general understanding of the relationship between institutions and the behavior of actors. Next is a consideration of the asymmetry of power that determines institutional behavior. Third, this approach tends to be better at explaining continuity than change. Finally, the approach is eclectic as it incorporates variables such as ideas, processes, and culture.

Two remarks should be made before I investigate historical institutionalism's capacity to explain the behavior of actors and institutional development. On the one side, Hall and Taylor (472) distinguish between the "calculus approach," which focuses on the strategic calculations that serve to defend actors' interests, and the "cultural approach," which emphasizes the influence of institutions on actors' preferences. On the other side, Yves Surel (1998, 161–68) insists on the importance of the "three *i*'s"[8] – institutions, ideas, and interests – in analyzing public policies. Looking at institutions is more useful for explaining change than for explaining continuity; the phenomenon of path dependence reveals the impact of old institutions on new ones. The role of interests lies in the strategic interactions by which actors seek to maximize their gains; such strategic interests explain the institutional stability that may sometimes be observed. Ideas are better at explaining the spread of new models.

Thus, the two sides can be harmonized by considering that the "calculus approach" and the focus on interests are part of the same category. The same goes for the "cultural approach" and ideas.

How do the specific characteristics of historical institutionalism explain the influence of institutions on the behavior of actors? From the calculus, or interest-based, perspective, actors' behavior is explained in terms of instrumentality and strategic calculation. Actors on the political stage examine the field of possibilities and anticipate competitors' reactions before making decisions to maximize their own

[8] I note that in 1986, Peter Hall was already examining the interaction among interests, institutions, and ideas to explain the different paths followed by British and French interventionist policies (Hall 1986, 5).

interests. Preferences explain behavior, and actors choose the most profitable option offered by the institutional configuration in which they find themselves. Thus, the role of institutions is to

provide information relevant to the behavior of others, enforcement mechanisms for agreements, penalties for defections, and the like. The key point is that they affect individual action by altering the expectations an actor has about the actions others are likely to take in response to or simultaneously with his own action. (Hall and Taylor 1996, 939)

According to the "cultural approach," which accounts for the role of ideas, actors' behavior is connected to their understanding of the world and relation to others. Thus, social references determine preferences, and individuals seek to conform to certain social norms rather than to maximize profits (Hall 1989;[9] Saint-Martin 2002, 41–68). Within this perspective, the main role of institutions is to provide the cognitive schema and the social and moral references that guide actors in their actions and in their relations with others.

It is now important to consider the ways in which historical institutionalism explains the origin and development of institutions. The phenomenon of path dependence[10] is a key concept used to explain the origin and trajectory of an institution at a given moment in time. Through this lens, the institutions of the past influence the trajectory of the institutions of the present, which in turn determine those of the future. According to Lecours, path dependence is "the idea that socio-political phenomena are strongly conditioned by contextual factors, exogenous to actors, many of which are institutional in nature" (2002, 8).

From here, two additional key concepts explain institutional trajectories: "critical junctures" and "bifurcations." The first consists of favorable contexts that can be translated into significant institutional changes at specific moments in history. The second comprises new trajectories that owe their origins to the critical junctures that orient institutional development.

Historical institutionalists would explain AUDA by looking at the critical juncture that has led to its creation, within the context of the

---

[9] See the chapter entitled "Conclusion: The Politics of Keynesian Ideas" in Hall 1989, 361–91.

[10] This concept is at the heart of many research projects that present its advantages or limits: Berman 1998; Palier and Bonoli 1999; Pierson 2000; Surel 2000.

African renaissance and the end of the debt crises. They would also consider AUDA path-dependent from previous development trajectories, as change is viewed as a complex adventure in an overly structuring context. In other words, scholars in this school usually identify more continuity than change, which is itself generally viewed as incremental rather than radical.

These explanations are further developed in the next chapters. I have just presented the first of the three branches of neo-institutionalism: historical institutionalism. Let us now turn to rational choice and sociological institutionalism.

Rational Choice Institutionalism: Origin and Definition

Rational choice institutionalism began with analysts seeking to understand political behavior within the US Congress. Rational choice theorists found it difficult to explain the stable majority for passing legislation that they observed in Congress. They were thus obliged to incorporate contextual institutional variables such as rules, procedures, and committees into their analyses (Shepsle 1986). These institutional variables structure the choices that members of Congress make and the information they have available. The rules of Congress divide responsibilities among various actors – committees and lawmakers – and the stability of decisions can be explained by members' ability to anticipate other actors' behavior and to negotiate agreements that reduce transaction costs.

Rational choice institutionalists "model institutions as 'humanly devised constraints on action' (North 1990). Methodologically, this definition translates into studying how institutions constrain the sequence of interaction among the actors, the choices available to particular actors, and the payoffs to individuals and groups" (Weingast 2002, 661).

Rational choice institutionalism focuses on many objects of study. It endeavors to explain, among other things, the functioning of institutions such as Congress and Parliament, political coalitions, institutional development, ethnic conflicts, the rise and fall of international regimes, the responsibilities that states delegate to international organizations, and various forms of organization (Gazibo and Jenson 2004, 189–216).

Hall and Taylor (1996) present several specific characteristics that sum up this approach. First, its analysis of actors' behavior is based on "behavioral assumptions," which stipulate that individuals have a fixed set of preferences that they try to maximize in a highly strategic manner via their methods and calculations. The second tenet of this school is that it sees politics as "a series of collective action dilemmas" (Hall and Taylor 1996, 945): instances in which individuals seeking to maximize their personal interests in a given institutional configuration cause a collectively suboptimal output. One example is the well-known "prisoner's dilemma." Third, within rational choice analysis there is a strong emphasis on the strategic calculations that allow actors to anticipate other actors' behavior.

Rational choice institutionalism uses a deductive approach to explain the origin and development of institutions. Its deductions lead to specifying the norms and functions of an institution, whose birth and importance are explained by the functions and values these institutions have for the relevant actors. Theorists consider the creation of a new institution to be explained more by the will of actors than by the structures that constrain them, and they believe that certain institutions survive because they provide greater benefits to the actors involved than competing institutions do (Hall and Taylor 1996, 945). Barry Weingast, for example, argues that institutional survival results from the strengthened preferences of dominant actors (2002).

Rational choice institutionalists would explain the origin and development of AUDA by looking at its ability to maximize the interests of dominant actors and strengthen their preferences. From this perspective, AUDA will survive as long as it continues to provide a platform where the most powerful actors optimize their gains.

Now that I have discussed historical and rational choice institutionalism, I finally turn to sociological institutionalism.

Sociological Institutionalism: Origin and Definition

Sociological institutionalism developed within sociology (Koelbe 1994, 231) before spreading to political science at the same time as the other institutionalist currents. Sociological institutionalism arose in response to the failure of existing institutionalist approaches to take cultural factors into account (Hall and Taylor 1996, 946). Sociologists observed that efficiency is not the only factor that determines institutional procedures, since cultural norms and moral references also influence forms of organization. The goal is not necessarily efficiency but, rather, the more or less voluntary reproduction of a culture, following a process specific to that culture.

The sociological institutionalist definition of institutions differs from that of the other institutionalisms. Lecours (2002, 11) defines institutions as a collection of norms, symbols, and cultural and cognitive parameters. Hall and Taylor maintain that "sociological institutionalists tend to define institutions much more broadly than political scientists do to include not just formal rules, procedures, or norms, but the symbol systems, cognitive scripts, and moral templates that provide the 'frames of meaning' guiding human action" (1996, 947).

To understand this approach's explanation of political phenomena, we must examine its specific characteristics. The principal problematic that sociological neo-institutionalists often focus on studying the forms, procedures, and symbols adopted by institutions, as well as they ways in which these are transmitted to actors (and shaping their behaviors).[11] Hall and Taylor (1996, 947–50) distinguish the main characteristics of this approach. The first, as stated, is that it considers culture an institution.

The second characteristic relates to explanations of institutions' influence on the behavior of actors. While the "normative dimension"[12] of institutions is still used to explain actors' behavior, the "cognitive dimension" is dominant in the sociological perspective. It is this latter dimension that makes it possible for actors to interpret the world and the behavior of other actors (Di Maggio and Powell 1991). In addition to influencing strategic calculations, as rational choice institutionalists maintain, institutions themselves influence the preferences of actors. An individual constructs and identifies him- or herself in relation to others and, as such, reasoning and "interests are institutionally constructed" (Di Maggio and Powell 1991, 28). Thus, in acting, the individual will seek to respect social conventions. In addition, to gain or maintain power at the organizational level, dominant actors adopt a strategy of control, either to socialize new arrivals or to utilize existing state and legal institutions (30–31). This is how theorists

---

[11] See, for example, Loriaux 2003. The author presents the influence of French culture on the organization of a kind of capitalism specific to the French. This culture is transmitted, in particular, by the *"grandes écoles"* system, which guarantees social reproduction.

[12] By the normative dimension I mean the norms to which behavioral prescriptions are attached.

of sociological institutionalism explain the influence of institutions on the behavior of actors. As for the origin and development of institutions,

sociological institutionalists argue that organizations often adopt a new institutional practice not because it advances the means-end efficiency of the organization but because it enhances the social legitimacy of the organization or its participants. In other words, organizations embrace specific institutional forms or practices because the latter are widely valued within a broader cultural environment. (Hall and Taylor 1996, 949)

We must explain the origin of this legitimacy, which is born out of social and cultural references. Cultural references are created through the exchange of ideas within networks and through the forums and debates that serve to institutionalize new practices.[13] The reproduction of institutions may also be associated with the demands of central actors and dominant agents within an organization (Di Maggio and Powell 1991, 28).

Sociological institutionalists would explain the emergence of AUDA as the reflection of dominant cultural practices among African leaders, but also as an attempt to institutionalize such values and interests by socializing other members. The next section provides a more detailed perspective on the analytical framework.

III FINAL PERSPECTIVE: HISTORICAL NEO-INSTITUTIONALISM AND THE STRATEGIC/REALIST AND IDEATIONAL/ CONSTRUCTIVIST PERSPECTIVES

I have presented the three branches of the neo-institutional approach, which comprise the theoretical and methodological framework used in this book. It is now important to present in greater detail the specific approach I employ in order to test whether AUDA, as an institution, constitutes change or continuity and to explain AUDA's institutional development almost two decades after its creation.

Hall and Taylor (1996, 955) conclude their analysis of neo-institutionalism by asserting that it is absolutely necessary to deepen the exchanges among the three branches – historical, rational choice,

---

[13] See Montpetit 2003, who demonstrates the importance of the exchange of ideas between various actors in constructing references, which guide policy development. See also Gaye 2002, 181–231.

and sociological – to best account for political phenomena. Since each of these schools only partially explains reality, it is important to use them complementarily in order to arrive at a more meaningful, comprehensive explanation. My eclectic approach serves this goal. My objective here is not to achieve a "crude" synthesis of the three institutionalisms or of international relations theories but, rather, to highlight the best and most appropriate in each one, relying on the historical approach as a starting point. Such eclecticism is all the more imperative given the high complexity of the phenomena I am trying to explain.

Historical Neo-Institutionalism Supplemented by the Strategic and Ideational Perspectives

The choice of historical neo-institutionalism as my main approach is based on its broader understanding of the relationship between institutions and the behavior of actors. As we have already seen, this understanding incorporates institutions, interests, and ideas, thereby integrating the calculus approach and the cultural approach in order to analyze phenomena. Of the three branches, it is therefore the most eclectic (Hall and Taylor 1996, 940; Gazibo and Jenson 2004). In analyzing the emergence of AUDA, a major strength of this approach lies in its ability to explain the birth and evolution of institutions through the lens of "path dependence," "critical juncture," and "bifurcation." A second advantage is that it highlights asymmetrical power relations, in which certain actors have more influence over the creation of a new institution than do others. The inductive dimension of historical neo-institutionalism is also a considerable advantage. Analysts who use this method seek to explain the behavior of actors or the evolution of institutions at a particular moment by starting from the historical events that occurred before the behavior or evolution in question. However, its overly broad and macro-sociological conception of political phenomena turns out to be a handicap in explaining the ways in which institutions influence the behavior of actors.

This is where the strategic perspective, drawn from rational choice institutionalism, becomes important, specifically in helping to clarify African leaders' mutual interests at AUDA's origin in achieving collective gains, avoiding collective losses, and fostering interstate cooperation through the creation of a new organization, (Keohane and Nye 2001). Rational choice institutionalism thus offers a more precise understanding of the relationship between institutions and actors' behavior, and explains this dynamic better than historical institutionalism's calculus approach can alone. Its main strength is its emphasis on strategic interactions for determining political phenomena and explaining the evolution of institutions. This perspective is complemented by realist assumptions such as the egoistic and self-interested human nature; the focus on power to explain the relation between actors; on states - who are [also] unitary, autonomous, and rational – as primary actors in international relations; and the conflictive nature of international relations under conditions of near-anarchy (Gilpin 1981; Kennedy 1987; Mearsheimer 2001; Waltz 1979). This will be important for explaining the foundation of AUDA's strategy and the balance of power among its principal leaders. The main goal of incorporating these approaches is to strengthen the historical perspective. However, the main weakness of rational choice institutionalism and realist theories of international relations is their simplification of human motivations, which they reduce to the logic of material interest and the maximization of profit. For this reason, it is also important to include the ideational perspectives from sociological institutionalism and social constructivism.

Sociological institutionalism accounts for the origin of preferences by insisting on social references, cognitive schemas, and the diffusion of ideas. This approach is completed by constructivist characteristics, including the importance of ideational factors and norms in shaping interstate cooperation; the key roles of shared identity, culture, and values with the "logic of appropriateness"; the mutually constitutive nature of the relationship between ideas and interests, and the constructed nature of the continental system (Wendt 1992; 1999). These approaches will allow us to better understand AUDA's ideological foundation by revealing the influence of the WB's and IMF's discourse on change or continuity in African leaders' ideological and social references.

Ultimately, I specify my eclectic approach as the use of historical institutionalism strengthened by rational choice/realism and sociological institutionalisms/constructivism, in light of their contribution of the variables of interest/power and ideas/norms/identities. This strengthens the explanatory capacity of the institutional approach and makes it possible to better understand reality by compensating for the individual shortcomings of each sub-branch.

The empirical justification of the approach I am using here is as follows: AUDA is a newly created institution whose objective is development in Africa, in other words, to effect change on the continent from a state of underdevelopment to that of development. AUDA considers its role to be different from that of other institutions previously working toward this goal. However, the existing institutions remain privileged partners of AUDA, and we therefore may wonder about the influence that a "new" institution has on the behavior of leaders and the policies that leaders adopt. This so-called "new" institution is made up of the same actors as the earlier institutions, and it shares the same financial partners who had previously imposed programs in exchange for funding. For these reasons, the neo-institutionalist framework discussed earlier is best suited for explaining AUDA and analyzing change or continuity within it.

How Do I Proceed in the Next Sections?

The dependent variable in my study is the degree of change or continuity across two categories of institutions: the African Union Development Agency (AUDA) and the IFIs. To test this, three independent variables are examined: discourses, strategies, and programs. These choices seem the most relevant for obtaining a valid and comprehensive answer to the question of change or continuity. The comparison of discourses helps to situate the institutions and their leaders in relation to the ideas and ideologies of other actors. In this context, a change in ideas implies a real change of discourse. Meanwhile, strategies serve as guidelines for reaching the objectives set in discourse. A change in ideas must therefore imply a change in strategy – if the strategy remains the same, any ideational change is not a true change. Finally, programs allow strategies to be implemented and objectives to be reached. If there is a change of ideas and strategy, implementation takes place through the adoption of a new program. A change has occurred if the new program differs from earlier programs adopted by other institutions.

My methodological procedure is qualitative, and the analysis will be inductive[14] and comparative. It begins with an examination of past

---

[14] This is a fundamental characteristic of the kind of mixed institutionalism with a historical emphasis that I have developed previously.

events – the actions of international organizations – in order to explain the events of the present: the origin of AUDA and its relation of change or continuity with respect to the WB and the IMF discourses. To do this, the explanatory model developed earlier, based on neo-institutional theory, represents an opportunity to make advances in knowledge.

I draw heavily on data from official and academic sources, including administrative data and official international publications such as those of AUDA, the WB, and the IMF. Content analyses provide the empirical data needed to compare discourses, strategies, and pro-grams – the variables that characterize the policies and development strategies prescribed by the IFIs to African countries. Particular atten-tion is paid to AUDA's founding documents in relation to discourses, strategies, and programs, making it possible to compare these variables with those of IFIs. This comparison helps to identify similarities and differences and to determine whether and how AUDA represents an innovation in contrast to the IFIs.

Academic publications are also employed in order to develop the theoretical basis of the explanatory model and to present critical analyses of each of the variables. The goal is to guarantee that my results are reproducible and reliable for comparing phenomena of change or continuity between AUDA and the WB and the IMF.

2 | The Foundations and First Generations of Structural Adjustment Programs

Favorable Context: A Series of Crises

After gaining independence in the 1960s, African countries experienced growth rates that were comparable and sometimes superior to those of other developing countries around the world.[1] However, just one decade later, the neocolonial model of growth rapidly began to fail.[2] At the beginning of the 1970s, some common themes of the crisis in this model in many countries were

a loss of momentum in agricultural growth; an increase in imports due to "modernization" and urbanization at rates higher than the rate of growth of exports; blockage of the import-substitution process; and finally, growth in state expenses at a rate that outstripped the rate of growth of the economy, leading to increased taxation on agriculture (which disrupted it) and to increased appeals for outside funding. (Duruflé 1988, 8)

The exhaustion of the neocolonial model of growth manifested itself in great macroeconomic upheavals, with the state increasingly required to improve the deteriorating internal situation. To these endogenous factors were added exogenous crises, the harmful consequences of which made outside interventions by international financial institutions necessary.

---

[1] For example, Cameroon experienced 13% growth between 1965 and 1970 (see Gankou 1985). More generally, whereas average growth in sub-Saharan Africa was 5.9% between 1965 and 1973, it was 3.7% for South Asian countries. See WB 1989.

[2] The neocolonial model of growth has many characteristics; the major two are a trade economy with exportation of primary products and the development of import substitution industrialization. These are both dominated by foreign companies. However, the state has an important place in the economy, with a highly centralized administration that is in charge of many development functions: education, health, infrastructure, and, gradually, the control of many industries. For more information, see Duruflé 1988.

According to Giovanni Cornia (1987, 11–47), these crises began in industrialized countries before spreading to developing countries, caused by significant gaps in labor productivity growth rates in manufacturing sectors.[3] There was also an increase in oil prices, resulting in oil shocks in 1973, 1974, and 1979. The consequence was deflation and balance of payments deficits in the West. At the same time, the budget austerity policies put into place by Ronald Reagan in the United States and Margaret Thatcher in the United Kingdom – that were characterized by strict monetary policies, reductions in public spending and public aid for development, and higher interest rates – were at the root of a new way of managing public affairs referred to as "new public management" (Felts and Jos 2000; Ventris 2000).

These crises in industrialized countries soon extended to the developing world, resulting first in stagnation and later in declining export trade volumes, especially of products destined for Europe due to the lack of international demand. There was also a depression in the prices of basic products as a result of competition with imports. In addition, limited change occurred in the levels of development aid, which failed to compensate for the revenue shortfall caused by the trade deficit – not to mention the debt crisis. The combination of all these factors had many consequences: serious monetary, fiscal, and balance of payment deficits; rampant inflation; the deterioration of trade terms; the inability to access private capital markets; a drop in per capita gross domestic product (GDP); and social disasters, particularly in health, nutrition, and education (Jespersen 1992).

It became crucial to find solutions, the first of which – called the "Washington Consensus" – proposed expanding adjustment reforms conditional on aid flows. I call this an expansion of structural adjustment rather than its creation because adjustment had already been sporadically and quietly applied in certain countries in Europe.[4] According to John Toye (1994, 18–34), the WB adopted this strategy because of the slow pace of traditional disbursements, the need for funding, the difficulty in planning viable projects, the deterioration of the payments situation, and finally a lack of effectiveness of its anti-poverty program. The quest for growth in developing countries was

---

[3] For example, between 1971 and 1980, it was 7.4% in Japan, 4.5% in Western Europe, and 2.5% in the United States.

[4] See Toye 1994, 18–34. The author cites the example of India, where the WB applied adjustment measures after secret negotiations.

subsequently carried out in accordance with macroeconomic considerations. But what are the fundamental principles of structural adjustment programs (SAPs)?

The Washington Consensus and the Fundamental Principles of SAPs

The WB has pointed to many factors that were hindering growth
and that made structural adjustment necessary in Africa (WB 1994,
19–47), which can be classified as either endogenous or exogenous.
Among the endogenous factors were poor macroeconomic policies,
characterized by an overvaluation of currencies, massive public spending, inwardly focused commercial policies, political instability, and
Africa's lagging social indicators, especially human capital. Among
the exogenous factors the WB strove to mitigate was a drop in terms
of trade and the increase of foreign transfers. To resolve these problems
various actors within international development came to what came to
be known as the "Washington Consensus."

The Washington Consensus reflected a vision shared by the IMF and
the WB, both of which are headquartered in Washington, DC, as well
as organizations such as the G7, the World Trade Organization
(WTO), and the Organization for Economic Co-operation and Development (OECD). The term was used for the first time by John
Williamson[5] in a 1990 report that examined its ten priorities:

(1) Fiscal deficits must not exceed 1 or 2 percent of GDP.
(2) Public expenditures:
   (a) subsidies must be eliminated on principle because they stack
       the deck when it comes to allocating resources;
   (b) education and health are to be considered investments in
       human capital and should be publicly funded to the extent
       that they correspond to the goal of equality (support for the
       underprivileged);
   (c) investment in economic infrastructure is to be promoted.
(3) The tax system must strive to have the largest possible base and
    be based on a model of moderate marginal tax rates.

---

[5] Williamson 1990, 7–20.

(4) Interest rates must be set by the market, and, if they are regulated, real interest rates must be positive so as to discourage capital flight and to encourage saving.

(5) Exchange rates: As with interest rates, although the ideal system would be a flexible rate determined by the market, the preferred regulated system is one that encourages competitiveness and makes it possible to maintain a sustainable current account deficit.

(6) Trade policy: openness to trade, with import liberalization. Quantitative restrictions must be abolished, and tariffs must be relatively uniform and moderate (between 10 and 20 percent).

(7) Direct foreign investment must not be restricted.

(8) Privatization is justified by its positive fiscal effects in the short term and in the name of more efficient management.

(9) Deregulation: Various regulations on investment, prices, credit, etc. are sources of corruption and must be ended.

(10) Property rights must be clearly defined and defended.

The Washington Consensus served as the *sine qua non* of structural adjustment plans. Within it, the state is relegated to a mere administrator. It is expected to withdraw from economic activities and be replaced by private investors. Finally, the state is not to intervene in the market except to secure its proper functioning. Thus, under this plan, financial liberalization, privatization, competitive exchange rates, and openness to the global market are all required reforms for countries wishing to obtain loans from international financial institutions.

The fundamental principles of SAPs are ideologically neoliberal in nature and were adopted in the context of the Cold War, which pitted neoliberals against communists. More important than the ideological framework of these programs, however, is their relative effectiveness (or ineffectiveness). Thus, I will evaluate whether SAPs were able to reach the goals they set for themselves: to restore macroeconomic equilibrium and generate sustainable growth.

Structural Adjustment Programs: Weak Results

SAPs have been the focus of numerous assessments, which can generally be categorized either as orthodox (WB and UNDP 1989; WB 1994) or heterodox (Cornia et al. 1987, 1992). I will show that political concerns have influenced the methodological choices and results of these assessments, but first I will present their main findings.

The results of the orthodox assessments converge with one another. The study done by the WB and UNDP on the impact of adjustments between 1980 and 1987 found that adjustment had a positive effect on nearly all of the aspects addressed by the reforms (WB and UNDP 1989). The following is a summary of their analysis:

Export earnings fell, but most of the decline came from falling oil prices, which helped oil importers. Africa's terms of trade, despite recent declines, are still 15% higher than in the early 1970s, as export prices in Africa have fallen less than elsewhere. Sub-Sahara's share of global official development assistance (ODA) has also doubled, but exports haven't grown, while debt continues to mount. And Africa's debt service ratio is almost twice what it might be. Net nonconcessional capital dried up between 1981 and 1985, but has begun to flow again. Net ODA disbursements have continued to climb. Policy improvements are evident in declining exchange rates. Agriculture is growing faster than the population for the first time since 1970. And GDP growth, though still lagging behind that of other developing countries, has started to pick up. (WB and UNDP 1989, 1–3; quotes refer to the graph headings that appear on these pages)

Although the social effects of SAPs are not discussed, the findings of the self-evaluation are generally positive in economic terms.

The second orthodox study was conducted by the WB in 1994, evaluating the impacts of SAPs between 1987 and 1991 (WB 1994). Its conclusions were also positive. Adjustment seems to have been profitable for the countries that undertook and sustained macroeconomic policy reforms in this period. In turn, this translated into a positive impact on annual GDP and industrial growth, outside revenues, exports, gross domestic savings, and investment rates. The study finds that "adjustment-led growth has probably helped the poor" (WB 1994, 165). However, the report states that certain countries must improve their reforms by applying good macroeconomic policies in order to benefit from the positive effects of adjustment.

Thus, we may say that, according to orthodox evaluations, the results of adjustment were generally positive. Notably, for the most part, these evaluations take only economic indicators into account, while social indicators are relegated to the background.

As an example of the heterodox authors, who analyze both the economic and the social impact of SAPs, Cornia (1987, 11–47; 48–72) evaluated the impact of adjustment on the protection of childhood in the period between 1980 and 1985. I focus on his evaluation in particular since the well-being of children is understood as part of a long-term development strategy (Stewart 1992). Cornia notes that children's quality of life generally reflects that of the household. His study shows that, contrary to the statements of the WB, adjustment had contributed to poverty and worsened the situation of children and, ultimately, its effects would not allow for sustainable growth. Cornia observes the following negative impacts of adjustment: a drop in real household revenues, fewer resources for the poor, an increase in the number of people living below the poverty threshold, a reduction in real social spending per capita, a reduction in spending on food subsidies, a reduction of food rations, a reduction in the time parents dedicate to their children, a reduction in vaccine coverage, increased hospital closures, increased health costs, fewer health and education workers, higher school dropout rates, and a rise in infant mortality and malnutrition rates. In short, conditions for the most vulnerable had worsened under SAPs.

A second heterodox author, Eva Jespersen (1992), evaluated the social and economic impacts of adjustment and the process of adjustment itself. Her results show that not only was there social and economic decline but that the attempt at structural adjustment failed. This failure of adjustment meant that the process of implementing reforms was not operationalized in conformity with objectives. But, Jespersen suggests, it would be possible to remedy this by redirecting SAPs toward a coherent vision that incorporated the development of human resources as part of a growth strategy.

The elements supporting the assertion are as follows: negative per capita GDP growth, lower production within industries affected by increased competition from imported products, higher unemployment, a drop in average and minimum real wages, a brain drain, increases in urban populations, an expansion of the informal sector, a reduction or stagnation of public revenue, and a disproportionate reduction in spending on education, health, nutrition, economic services, and basic infrastructure. These reductions outcomes then resulted in worsened living conditions for the poor.

Our final heterodox author, Frances Stewart (1992), argues that there is a contradiction between SAPs, which she considers short-term policies, and the long-term development of the countries that implement them. Not only are SAPs viewed as failing to reestablish growth, some of the reforms actually contribute to economic deterioration.

After comparing two types of evaluation of the SAPs – the first coherent development strategy implemented by foreign lenders in post-independence Africa – we may conclude that their success should be put into perspective.[6] Almost no African country reached the high growth levels promised by the IFIs, which would have been comparable to those of the Asian tigers, and the social consequences were largely negative[7] in almost every domain evaluated. It is important to specify that this failure was connected to a complex set of causes, for which some African leaders bear partial responsibility, and thus cannot be attributed to international financial institutions alone. However, this does not change the fact that SAPs ultimately overlooked the goals of improving living conditions and sustainable development, focusing instead on the urgent need to reorient policies. These evaluations represent a form of social learning, which contributed to a perceptible change in the discourse of international financial institutions.

The next chapter of this book examines this new policy orientation and its effects on the context of NEPAD's (now AUDA) emergence.

---

[6] Joseph Stiglitz is more radical in his assessment: According to him, "Half a century after its foundation, it is clear that the IMF has failed in its mission." See Stiglitz 2002, 40.

[7] Macleans A. Geo-Jaja and Garth Mangum demonstrate that adjustment accelerated the deterioration of living conditions – and in this way became an enemy of human development in Africa. See Geo-Jaja and Mangum 2001, 30–49.

3 | Partial Reorientation of the International Monetary Fund and World Bank Discourse and the Creation of AUDA

As we have seen, the overall result of the first phase of adjustments was negative. As a result, international civil society and certain organizations within the United Nations – particularly the United Nations Children's Fund (UNICEF) – increasingly sought a reorientation of adjustment policies.

From *Adjustment with a Human Face* to the Strategic Framework for the Fight against Poverty: A Change in Discourse

In the first volume of its 1987 publication *Adjustment with a Human Face* (Cornia et al. 1987), UNICEF proposed an "alternative approach"[1] that would take human and social factors into account in adjustment policy. The factors emphasized in this report are important, since they later inspired the discourse of the World Bank. In this approach, while growth is still considered necessary, it is vital to "incorporate the well-being of vulnerable groups into the objectives of adjustment policy" (Cornia et al. 1987, 132). The six principal measures UNICEF proposed were:

(1) more expansionary macroeconomic policies in order to transition from growth to development,

(2) mesoeconomic policies that respect priorities by responding to the needs of the most vulnerable,

(3) sectoral policies to provide for restructuring the manufacturing sector,

(4) measures to increase equality and efficiency in the social sector,

---

[1] For a brief description, see "An Overview of the Alternative Approach" in Cornia et al. 1987, 131–46. This is the first chapter of part II of volume I of the work; the rest of the articles in the section ("An Alternative Approach: Growth-Oriented Adjustment with a Human Face," 131–297) expand on this approach.

(5) compensatory programs to protect the essential norms of life, health, and nutrition among low-income groups during adjustment, and

(6) monitoring of the standards of living, health, and nutrition of vulnerable groups during adjustment

(Cornia et al. 1987, 134–35).

The importance of this discourse lies in its political implications. Indeed, one could consider UNICEF here to be the spokesperson for African leaders who feared that if they publicly criticized the drawbacks of adjustment, IFIs would cut off funding. Combined with poor SAP results, criticism from UNICEF and African leaders created enough pressure to convince the WB to adopt a new discourse. In addition, with the end of the Cold War, it became possible not only to pay more attention to democratic exigencies, but also to better account for human rights. A series of publications increasingly critical of the SAPs followed.

In 1990, the subtitle of the WB's World Development Report was *Poverty* (WB 1990), which is indicative of its content: the WB addressed UNICEF's criticism by incorporating into SAPs measures to fight poverty by addressing fundamental needs. The specific measures mainly concerned education, health, and nutrition. The report examined the capacity of and necessity for the public sector to respond to the needs of the poorest during the process of structural adjustment, considering that, in comparison with the wealth of developed nations, poverty in developing nations was "staggering and shameful" (WB 1990, 1).

This was the first time the WB so clearly brought the fight against poverty into SAPs, although it is important to note that these measures, especially in sub-Saharan Africa, largely aimed at attenuating the negative effects of SAPs on the poor. As Venkatesh Seshamani notes, "it is interesting that PAPs [poverty alleviation programs] are often created as a follow-up to SAPs which themselves produce the consequences which PAPs are expected to mitigate" (1994, 115). However, in spite of some innovation, the discourse of the WB still remained limited, as liberal social measures targeted only the poorest of the poor with "social safety nets" (Valier 2000). The monetary aspect of poverty was still very much present, and the market was thus intended to be put in the service of the poor.

In 1993, the WB's report was dedicated to "investing in health" (WB 1993). This report further indicates that the WB, which was initially occupied with macroeconomic problems, had become increasingly interested in social issues. It had began to view health as an essential aspect of development, and argued that investment in health should be promoted by improving the economic environment. The key message of the report was the need to "foster an environment that enables households to improve health ... improve government spending on health ... and promote diversity and competition" (WB 1993, 6). Including the dimension of health in its discourse was framed as improving growth prospects and, specifically, encouraging better competition between public and private services – thereby providing citizens with a better price–quality ratio. Moreover, incorporating social concerns served to better legitimize economic actions already underway.

The two publications discussed here show the evolution of the WB's discourse from an overwhelming focus on the economics of adjustment in the 1980s towards an increasingly social and human perspective in the 1990s. Although this evolution remained limited, there were non-negligible changes that help us to better understand the genesis of AUDA. Two of the WB's more recent publications make this relationship even clearer.

First, in its *Report on Development in the World 1999–2000* (WB 1999), the WB discussed the challenges of development at the opening of the twenty-first century. The Report reviewed various trends in development over the past fifty years and concluded with prescriptions. It found that:

First, macroeconomic stability is an essential prerequisite for achieving the growth needed for development. Second, growth does not trickle down; development must address human needs directly. Third, no one policy will trigger development; a comprehensive approach is needed. Fourth, institutions matter; sustained development should be rooted in processes that are socially inclusive and responsive to changing circumstances. (WB 1999, 1)

We may observe that the discourse here is innovative in several respects: The essential needs of populations are taken into account, adequate institutional structures are to be implemented, and an overall strategy of development is adopted. However, for the WB, economic growth remained the essential prerequisite to development, and to achieve this growth, macroeconomic stability was considered indispensable. For the countries of sub-Saharan Africa, the tool for macroeconomic stability remained the implementation of structural adjustment programs. Although the WB innovated by gradually shifting from its narrow focus on growth to a broader understanding of development, we see that the justification of SAPs and the use of growth remained constant. Other measures for development in the twenty-first century included taking supranational and subnational aspects into account, which requires working both with local partners to find solutions to domestic problems and with international partners to limit the negative influence of external factors.

The WB had also already sufficiently delineated the roles of the state and the market in previous reports. Institutional mechanisms and the creation of partnerships remained key elements of a general strategy in which the state's main role is viewed as formulating public development policies. The liberalization of commerce under the guidance of the WTO, competition with foreign companies, international financial flows, globalization, political pluralism, and decentralization were all seen as capable of yielding significant economic benefits. From this perspective, what the WB considered obstacles to development – poverty, hunger, illness, lack of housing, and illiteracy – were, in fact, obstacles to the market. However, even if economic concerns dominated these proposals, at least the WB began to acknowledge these social factors in its discourse. Eventually, in 2000, it specified that these factors would guide its own interventions as an international development institution. In other words, improving *human* development represented a new, different type of aid conditionality.

Following the 1999 report, which states that reducing the absolute number of poor people by harnessing the forces of globalization is "to the benefit of the world's people" (WB 1999, 11), the WB next published a "revolutionary" 2000–2001 report, the theme of which was *Attacking Poverty: Opportunity, Empowerment, and Security* (WB 2000a). At the time, it represented the WB's most ambitious publication on the fight against poverty. Adjustment instruments from earlier years – the Policy Framework Papers, the Structural Adjustment Credit, and the Enhanced Structural Development Facility – became, respectively, the Poverty Reduction Strategy Papers, the Poverty Reduction Support Credit, and the Poverty Reduction and Growth Facility, all placed within the context of the fight against poverty.[2] The definition of poverty was also extended beyond simply monetary, health, and

[2] For a critical presentation of the Poverty Reduction Strategy Papers, see Cling et al. 2006, 180–202.

educational aspects. Indeed, according to the report, "poverty is more than inadequate income or human development – it is also vulnerability and a lack of voice, power, and representation" (WB 2000a, 12). Thus, freedom and agency became elements of the WB's definition of poverty.

In addition, the WB put forth a strategy to change the fact that half of the planet's inhabitants live in a state of poverty, a plan which comprised three areas of action: opportunity, empowerment, and security (8–11). The first area, creating opportunities, specifically entailed encouraging profitable private investments (a motor for growth, employment, and income), ensuring expansion in international markets (growth, employment, and income), developing the assets of the poor (human, physical, natural, and financial), remedying unequal resource distribution between the sexes, ethnic groups, races, and social categories (fighting against social inequalities), and providing infrastructure and knowledge to rural and urban poor areas. At the international level, Western countries were encouraged to open their markets by ending subsidies, and lenders were encouraged to increase funding to countries with good policies.

The second area of action was empowerment, which comprised laying political and legal foundations, instituting public administrations to encourage growth and equality, promoting decentralization and community development, improving gender equality, and lowering social barriers. On the international level, the active participation of civil society and that of the private sector were viewed as essential – including favorable actions by multinational corporations to end the marginalization of the poor – and the strategies of international financial institutions were to be more transparent.

Security, the third area of action, consisted of helping the poor manage risks through a modular approach: developing national programs to prevent, prepare for, and react to financial and other macroeconomic shocks; formulating systems to manage social risks and encourage growth, including ending civil conflict; and, finally, fighting the HIV/AIDS epidemic. Here, action at the international level consisted of limiting economic volatility for financial institutions and producing more global public goods, such as vaccines against epidemics and pandemics.

After the publication of this report, several development analysts began to call into question the Washington Consensus. One such author was Jean-Pierre Cling, who stated that the 2000 report "challenges the model of economic openness that was the basis of the strategies recommended in the 1990 report, although its position was very much watered down between the draft version and the final version of the Report" (2006, 32). According to Cling, even if there was no open, explicit criticism of liberalism, criticism of the reform implementation process called liberal reforms into question. On the other hand, he said, the critiques and recommendations largely remained superficial and were insufficient to generate an effective solution to the problems posed.

Since the WB's strategy to fight poverty referred to international development objectives, I now provide a critical overview of those objectives. This allows us to better understand the context of AUDA's genesis and whether a relation of change or continuity existed between AUDA and the strategies of the WB and the IMF.

Millennium Development Goals

The Millennium Development Goals were adopted by the United Nations General Assembly in a document entitled the *Millennium Declaration*.[3] It represented a commitment on the part of the leaders and governments of the UN member states. The declaration was divided into eight main points: (1) values and principles; (2) peace, security, and disarmament; (3) development and poverty eradication; (4) protecting our common environment; (5) human rights, democracy, and good governance; (6) protecting the vulnerable; (7) meeting the special needs of Africa, and (8) strengthening the UN.

To make "the right to development a reality for everyone and to [free] the human race from want" (UN 2000, III.11), eight goals were specified and various targets set for them (see Table 3.1). The majority of these objectives were intended to be reached between 1990 and 2015, although Cling (2006, 21–50) contends that this was unrealistic. In addition, even if poverty declined at the global level, the real changes would primarily occur in India and China, while the situation in Africa would remain catastrophic or, at best, improve only slightly.

---

[3] This was adopted during the fifty-fifth session of the United Nations General Assembly (point 60b of the agenda). The *Millennium Declaration* is Resolution A/55/L.2. For more information, see UN 2000.

Table 3.1 *Millennium development goals and targets*

Goal	Targets
1. Eradicate extreme poverty and hunger	1. Halve, between 1990 and 2015, the proportion of people whose income is less than $1 a day 2. Halve, between 1990 and 2015, the proportion of people who suffer from hunger
2. Achieve universal primary education	3. Ensure that, by 2015, children everywhere, boys and girls alike, will be able to complete a full course of primary schooling
3. Promote gender equality and empower women	4. Eliminate gender disparity in primary and secondary education, preferably by 2005 and in all levels of education no later than 2015
4. Reduce child mortality	5. Reduce by two-thirds, between 1990 and 2015, the under-five mortality rate
5. Improve maternal health	6. Reduce by three-quarters, between 1990 and 2015, the maternal mortality ratio
6. Combat HIV/AIDS, malaria, and other diseases	7. Have halted by 2015 and begun to reverse the spread of HIV/AIDS 8. Have halted by 2015 and begun to reverse the incidence of malaria and other major diseases
7. Ensure environmental sustainability	9. Integrate the principles of sustainable development into country policies and reverse the loss of environmental resources 10. Halve by 2015 the proportion of people without sustainable access to safe drinking water 11. Have achieved by 2020 a significant improvement in the lives of at least 100 million slum dwellers
8. Develop a global partnership for development	12. Develop further an open, rule-based, predictable, nondiscriminatory trading and financial system (includes a commitment to good governance, development, and poverty reduction – both nationally and internationally)

Table 3.1 (*cont.*)

Goal	Targets
	13. Address the special needs of the least developed countries (includes tariff- and quota-free access for exports, enhanced programs of debt relief for and cancellation of official bilateral debt, and more generous official development assistance for countries committed to poverty reduction)
	14. Address the special needs of landlocked countries and small island developing states (through the Program of Action for the Sustainable Development of Small Island Developing States and 22nd General Assembly provisions)
	15. Deal comprehensively with the debt problems of developing countries through national and international measures in order to make debt sustainable in the long term
	16. In cooperation with developing countries, develop and implement strategies for decent and productive work for youth
	17. In cooperation with pharmaceutical companies, provide access to affordable essential drugs in developing countries
	18. In cooperation with the private sector, make available the benefits of new technologies, especially information and communication technologies

Source: UNDP, *Human Development Report*, 2003, 1–3.

The WB itself acknowledged that it would be difficult to reach the goals set and that doing so would require creating international partnerships to effectively foster strong economic growth. The idea raised here of a worldwide partnership for development, put forth by the UN and the WB in 2000 and 2001, leads us to the creation of NEPAD, the New Partnership for African Development.

The Creation and Fundamental Principles of NEPAD

As previously discussed, the actions taken by IFIs in the 1980s to promote development in Africa largely failed. Subsequently, a gradual reorientation of the discourses of major development organizations and bilateral and multilateral lenders occurred – mainly the WB, IMF, UNDP, and UN. These changes took place during the 1990s and at the beginning of the twenty-first century, and focused on promoting new partnerships and redefining development practices by integrating them into a single comprehensive strategy. It is in this context that NEPAD, now the African Union Development Agency, was born. Scholars within the neo-institutional school describe such a favorable context as a "critical juncture," or a set of events that might lead to an institutional "bifurcation," whereby a new institutional trajectory is taken. This trajectory is also determined/shaped by the past, a dynamic that the concept of "path dependence" seeks to describe and explain. In addition, as NEPAD was being created, a race for leadership among prominent African political players occurred, demonstrating the complementary dynamics of strategic interests and ideological referents.

NEPAD emerged out of two initiatives: the Millennium Action Plan (MAP),[4] whose principal advocate was President Thabo Mbeki of South Africa, and the Omega Plan, spearheaded by President Abdoulaye Wade of Senegal. I briefly present these two plans, the dynamics that engendered them, and their ultimate merger into a single project.

The Millennium Action Plan

In January 2001, President Mbeki presented his MAP[5] to the World Economic Forum at Davos. The project was initiated by South Africa[6] and inspired by its foreign policy, which was based on the concept of

---

[4] The Millennium Action Plan is also called the Millennium Partnership for the African Recovery Programme (MAP).

[5] According to Ian Taylor and Philip Nel, the MAP recalls the concept of African renaissance, which has guided South African politics in the post-apartheid era and especially the policies of President Mbeki. See Taylor and Nel 2002.

[6] According to Taylor, NEPAD would never have been created without South Africa. See Taylor 2003, 121.

an African renaissance.[7] Its main African proponents were Mbeki, Nigerian President Olusegun Obasanjo, Algerian President Abdelaziz Bouteflika, and Egyptian President Hosni Mubarak.

The MAP dealt primarily with political and economic governance (Millennium Partnership for the African Recovery Programme 2001), while emphasizing Africa's place in the global community and calling "for a new relationship of partnership between Africa and the international community, especially the highly industrialized countries, to overcome the development chasm that has widened over centuries of unequal relations" (Millennium Partnership for the African Recovery Programme 2001, 2). Similar references to "partnership" were also found in the discourse of leaders such as Bill Clinton of the United States, Gerhard Schroeder of Germany, Tony Blair of England, and Kofi Annan of the United Nations (Taylor and Nel 2002, 165). Given the emphasis on partnership by major donors, the MAP's supporters had an extra incentive to espouse a similar position. The plan was ultimately adopted due to the strategic calculation made by African leaders, who had acted to maximize their gains. As the MAP was being promoted, a second plan emerged: the Omega Plan.

The Omega Plan

The initiator of the Omega Plan was Senegalese President Abdoulaye Wade, who presented his project at the Africa–France summit in Yaoundé, Cameroon in January 2001. Wade viewed the MAP as flawed, and in his speech, he emphasized the importance of development aid, infrastructure, agriculture, health, and education.

The existence of two simultaneous plans reflected the competition over leadership roles. Whereas the leader of Libya, Muammar Gaddafi, claimed fathership of the AU, Mbeki was looking to lead a renewal of African development. Thus, he looked for associates among the leaders of countries with significant economies. The initiative of the

---

[7] The African renaissance can be seen as a catchall concept that served as the basis for post-apartheid South African foreign policy and became increasingly utilized when Thabo Mbeki came to power. This concept seeks to restore Africa in its own eyes and in the eyes of the world through a Pan-Africanist ideology and a recovery plan connected to liberal notions of governance and market economy. For more on this, see Taylor and Williams 2001.

Senegalese president can be explained by his desire to be part of the driving force of African development and to represent the interests of the franc zone countries, which until then had been excluded from the process.[8] According to Ian Taylor and Philip Nel (2002, 172), these new elites represented hope for their people, either because they were guided by plans for liberal democracy (Wade) or because they were considered liberators from the past (Obasanjo). However, there was a great deal of convergence between the visions behind the two plans, and they eventually merged into a single initiative.

The Fusion of Two Plans: The Emergence and Fundamental Principles of NEPAD/AUDA

It is important to note that NEPAD (now AUDA) was born out of a group of individual initiatives and not from within the normal institutional framework of the AU. After numerous negotiations, the MAP and Omega plans merged to become the New African Initiative (NAI) on July 3, 2001. Subsequently, at the Organization of African Unity (now the AU) summit in Abuja on October 23, 2001, the NAI became NEPAD. This program was integrated into the AU action plan. Vijay S. Makhan claims, "NEPAD is thus not a new institution, let alone an institution entirely autonomous from the AU. Far from it: the African Union is the framework within which NEPAD's implementation must be situated" (2002, 5). In July 2018, the African Union transformed NEPAD into the African Union Development Agency, or AUDA. We must now examine AUDA's main priorities and the theoretical framework in which it is situated.

AUDA identifies itself as an attempt to address the following problems in Africa: poverty, underdevelopment, and marginalization and exclusion from globalization. To this end, it highlights three fundamental reform goals: good governance, regionalization, and the use of private capital (Wade 2002).

To reach its goals, NEPAD (2001) has defined various priority areas: good political governance, good economic governance, the flow of private capital, infrastructure, education, health, new information and communication technologies (NICT), agriculture, energy, access to the markets of developed countries, and the environment. Table 3.2

---

[8] The franc zone is made up of former French colonies in sub-Saharan Africa.

Table 3.2 *Summary of the ten priority areas of AUDA*

Priority Area	Goals	Means
1. Good political governance	• Promote the conditions for peace and security • Promote and strengthen democracy and public policy	• Prevent, manage, and resolve conflicts • Reform and reinforce democratic institutions (legal systems, parliaments, etc.)
2. Good economic governance	• Improve economic management and public finances • Improve corporate governance	• Define concrete programs favorable to good governance and match them with timetables • Take into consideration proposals from a special team from finance ministries and central banks
3. Infrastructure	• Improve access to infrastructure, cooperation, and regional trade • Develop the expertise necessary to utilize networks and reduce the risks to foreign investments	• Encourage competition and standardize legislation to facilitate transborder commerce • Increase investments in infrastructure renovation and maintenance • Develop training institutions
4. Education	• Collaborate with donors to reach the international development goal for education • Reform curricula and form networks for higher education and research	• Examine current joint initiatives with the UN, UNESCO, and main donors • Accelerate the introduction of NICT in schools • Examine spending for education and the research capacities the continent needs

Table 3.2 (*cont.*)

Priority Area	Goals	Means
5. Health	• Strengthen programs that fight transmissible diseases and establish a solid system of care • Ensure education	• Obtain medications at affordable prices, fight HIV/AIDS • Ensure collaboration and the mobilization of resources
6. NICT	• Participate in growth and training • Double the density of telephone lines • Reduce costs and improve the reliability of services	• Collaborate with regional institutions to implement laws and with training institutions • Collaborate with financing institutions
7. Agriculture	• Improve agricultural performance (a prerequisite for development) • Achieve food security	• Eliminate structural constraints • Provide institutional support • Attract the attention of donors
8. Energy	• Increase energy production as a domestic necessity and a factor in the production of goods and services • Reduce costs and develop new sources of energy	• Establish an African regulation forum • Establish special teams for large regional projects and for the acceleration of developing supply
9. Market access and capital flows	• Encourage access to foreign markets by African products • Obtain the necessary capital for annual growth of 7%, US$64 billion	• Diversify production • Improve agricultural productivity • Develop mining industries • Develop tourism • Promote the private sector and exports • Eliminate nontariff barriers • Mobilize internal resources

Table 3.2 (*cont.*)

Priority Area	Goals	Means
		• Reduce debt • Increase official development assistance • Attract direct foreign investments
10. Environment	• Fight against poverty and contribute to the socioeconomic development of the continent through a healthy environment	• Fight against desertification and global warming • Protect wetlands • Manage coastlines • Govern in an ecological manner

Source: NEPAD, *The New Partnership for Africa's Development*, 2001.

summarizes these goals and the means associated with each of the ten priority areas.

Ultimately, NEPAD's founding document (2001) heavily emphasizes economic growth, industrialization, diversification, export promotion, market liberalization, reduction in the role of the state in the economy, protection of private interests, and increased enhanced regionalism the main vectors of development in Africa.

Now that we have seen NEPAD's (AUDA's) fundamental principles, let us test whether it constitutes a change from or continuation of the previous development initiatives of IFIs.

4 | AUDA and International Financial Institutions

Change or Continuity?

In order to determine whether AUDA constitutes change or continuity in relation to the previous development strategies of IFIs, I rely on the theories of historical neo-institutionalism supplemented by the strategic and ideational approaches presented in the previous chapters. A comparison of the theoretical framework of the discourse, strategy, and programs between AUDA and the WB will help demonstrate change or continuity.

In making this comparison, I employ the various WB publications already cited and its 2000 publication, *Can Africa Claim the 21st Century?* (WB 2000a). This highly revealing document advocates the development policies the WB views as indispensable if Africa is to claim its place in the twenty-first century. It is even more significant in that it was released one year before AUDA's creation, at a time when development policies and strategies were being redefined.

The Discourse: An Endogenous or Exogenous Initiative?

A Comparison of Key Discursive Elements

In order to test whether the initiative behind AUDA's creation was exogenous or endogenous, I compare AUDA's and the WB's discourses on the initiative and consider authors who have discussed the matter. In light of their preeminent place in the discourses of these institutions, I focus my examination on the following key elements: the vision shared among African leaders, the opportune historical context for the birth of a partnership, the leadership required for development, the need to accelerate the gains of the past, the ownership of the program, the investment and infrastructure, and the Internet. This comparison will shed light on whether institutional imitation occurred or whether AUDA represents a clean break with the past.

The WB and AUDA have both supported a shared vision among African leaders. In its 2000 publication the WB recommended a strategy for them to succeed in development: "African countries need to work together" (WB 2000a, 4); "to succeed in the 21st century, Africa has to become a full partner in the global economy" (208); "the issue is not whether Africa should be quickly integrated, both regionally and with the global economy. The question is how" (209). In 2001, the founders of AUDA presented the partnership as being "based on a common vision and a firm and shared conviction" (NEPAD 2001, 1).

There is a strong similarity between the vision outlined by the WB in its 2000 publication and the one adopted by the leaders of AUDA in 2001, which seems almost like a response to the call of the former. However, it is difficult to reach any definitive conclusions about this, for in fact, Pan-African discourse has always encouraged African unity. In this case, the WB proposed the concept of unity to African leaders in the framing of a formal partnership. NEPAD (AUDA) then sought to reflect this same form of unity, although the role of Mbeki, the principal proponent of African unity and solidarity through NEPAD, was in this respect antithetical. While preaching this message to his African counterparts, he was the first to undermine the potential for true unity (Taylor 2003, 120–38).

The second dimension of comparison is the discourses of both institutions concerning the favorability of the timing for creating a new initiative, such as AUDA. The WB seemed to suggest to African leaders that they initiate a project when it asked, "Will Africa be able to take advantage of the window [of opportunity]?" (WB 2000a, 47). AUDA, in turn, seemed to respond to this question when its leaders stated, "We are convinced that an historic opportunity presents itself to end the scourge of underdevelopment that afflicts Africa" (NEPAD 2001, 1). Once again, AUDA's discourse appears like a response to that of the WB, this time regarding the opportunity presented by a favorable context. It is also true that the international context lent itself to the birth of such an initiative, given the reorientation of the WB's discourse and the UN's adoption of the MDGs, as discussed in Chapter 3.

The third fundamental element of the two discourses concerns leadership. The WB specified that Africa had a chance to claim its place in the twenty-first century only under strong leadership: "Africa can claim the century – with determined leadership" (WB 2000a, 11). In the NEPAD document, African leaders confirmed the sentiment that in order for the continent to emerge from underdevelopment, "what is required ... is bold and imaginative leadership that is genuinely committed" (NEPAD 2001, 1). In this third comparative element, again, the language of the two institutions is strikingly similar. The adoption of such discourse related to leadership by the African Union Development Agency (AUDA, prior NEPAD) is not just rhetorical. Prior to the publication of such reports, African leaders were already competing for continental and global leaderships. The rivalries in the late 1990's early and 2000's explain the multiplication of initiatives by leaders as discussed earlier, such as Mbeki's MAP and Wade's OMEGA Plan later merged to form the NEPAD[1], but also Gaddafi idea of transforming the then Organization of African Unity into a United States of Africa, which was instead transformed into the African Union.[2]" Although this rivalry for leadership was quite real, AUDA's founding document seems to focus more on external perceptions of Africa – especially how it is perceived by its primary international partners – than on internal dynamics. In fact, the second section of the NEPAD's framewok discusses Africa's place in the global community (page 3 to 8), and conclude: "we hold that it is within the capacity of the international community to create fair and just conditions in which Africa can participate effectively in the global economy and body politics" (page 8). The following section therefore discusses "the new political will of African leaders" (pages 9 to 11), considering that "there is today a new set of circumstances" favorable to Africa's success.

I turn now to key elements of the discourse of the WB and NEPAD to verify whether the pattern of convergence I have postulated is, in fact, spurious.

For the fourth element of comparison, I analyze the discourse about increasing the benefits from reforms that had already been implemented. Once again, the WB was very clear: It specified that African development "will require more than simply 'staying the course' and deepening current reforms" (WB 2000a, 47). The process of reform

[1] See Igué 2002, 103–6. The author gives a brief overview of the rivalry between Libyan and South African leaders.

[2] For more detailed information on the rivalry that preceded the birth of the AU, see Amaïzo 2001.

and development already existed and now the WB viewed it as "in the interests of Africa's people to accelerate" (82) the process.

One year after the WB's publication, African leaders echoed that "the New Partnership for Africa's Development is about consolidating and accelerating these gains. It is a call for a new relationship of partnership between Africa and the international community" (NEPAD 2001, 2). Once again, AUDA appears to have been a direct response to the WB's call. On the other hand, it is possible that the repetition of discourses, combined with financial incentives, led many African leaders and analysts to appropriate liberal ideals, resulting in an internalization of the idea of the microeconomic efficiency of the free market (Coussy 2004, 7).

The ownership of the development program is the fifth element of comparison, and African leaders insisted greatly on its importance for successful implementation of AUDA. Taking a positive perspective, the WB asserted that "making these benefits materialize will require a 'business plan' conceived and owned by Africans, and supported by donors through coordinated, long-term partnerships" (WB 2000a, 3).

Similarly, African leaders specified on several occasions throughout the NEPAD document that they have ownership of the program: "The New Partnership for Africa's Development is envisaged as a long-term vision of an African-owned and African-led development program" (NEPAD 2001, 13). Indeed, as one analyst[3] holds, of all the initiatives undertaken to date, only NEPAD constitutes an African solution to African problems. Once again, the convergence between the discourse of the WB, which proposed to Africans that they own their own initiatives and partnerships, and African leaders, who themselves claimed to have ownership of the initiative, is striking.

When it comes to infrastructure, the WB stated that "there is no doubt that Africa's weak and often worsening infrastructure performance is linked to low spending on investment and maintenance" (WB 2000a, 143). The response of African leaders one year later was very similar: it is necessary to "increase investment in infrastructure ... and improve system maintenance practices that will sustain infrastructure" (NEPAD 2001, 23). In this case, again, it seems as though the WB analyzed the problem and proposed the solution and African leaders

---

[3] Tayeb Chenntouf of the University of Oran Es-Senia in Algeria. See Chenntouf, 2005.

appropriated the solution in their discourse, claiming it as their own. I should note, however, that for several decades now the infrastructure sector has been widely recognized to be crucial for African development, although this does not rule out the possibility of imitation between the two institutions.

The discourse regarding the relationship between the Internet and development strikes me as one of the most interesting points of imitation between the WB and AUDA. The WB believed that "the greatest challenge for Africa's Internet connectivity is not access but content" (WB 2000a, 156). In what was perhaps an ideal example of imitation, African leaders in 2001 proposed that the goal should be "to develop local-content software, based especially on Africa's cultural legacy" (NEPAD 2001, 25). Peculiarly, this was the solution proposed despite the fact that over half of Africa's population living below the poverty line and only a very small proportion of elites on the continent with access to the Internet.

This comparison of the two institutions' key discursive elements in 2000–2001 reveals a general pattern. AUDA's discourse on its objectives does, indeed, seem rooted in Pan-Africanism – it seeks to defend the continent's cause through a homegrown initiative and promote real local leadership.[4] However, in-depth analysis of discursive elements related to AUDA's genesis shows that these were borrowed from the language of the IFIs of the day, particularly the WB.

In conclusion, and in accordance with the theory of historical neo-institutionalism, it seems that AUDA emerged in a context that included both endogenous and exogenous factors favorable to its creation. The endogenous factors are explained by the rivalry for economic and geostrategic leadership among the major African powers at the regional and subregional levels. Here, the main powers in play were South Africa, Libya, Nigeria, Senegal, Egypt, and Algeria. At stake on the national scale was the resolution of political, economic, and social problems. Solutions to these problems were embedded in the renewal of Pan-African discourse, including Mbeki's[5] concept of an

---

[4] Although Taylor states that NEPAD "is one of the most important political events of the turn of the millennium" (Taylor 2003, 120), some leaders, such as Mbeki, have made it into a personal matter.

[5] According to Fantu Cheru, Mbeki's prescriptions reflect the arguments made by "the World Bank and other donors who would like to see South Africa take the leading role to facilitate collective economic liberalisation across the region by

African renaissance and Gaddafi's United States of Africa. At the same time, these discourses reflected the appropriation of liberal culture by African leaders, as well as political and economic analysts.[6]

If endogenous factors helped to shape and frame AUDA's discourse, exogenous factors were the immediate cause of its emergence. In effect, the IFIs exerted symbolic pressure on African leaders by, as I have shown, making clear to them that international conditions were favorable to the emergence of an African initiative, which was necessary in order to keep or even increase aid flows. The fact that the WB specifically pointed out that "partnerships and dialogue are needed to build consensus and support coherent programs," (WB 2000a, 251) may help to explain the imitation we observe in the discourse of African leaders. In schematic terms, African leaders had an interest in adopting discourse similar to that of donors in order to avoid departing from the obvious consensus of the international community[7] and, thus, secure the funding and support necessary to create NEPAD.

In the end, although NEPAD claimed to be an egalitarian partnership among Africa, financial institutions, and Western countries, its immediate cause seems to have been external pressure and conditions rather than any internal analysis of the situation on the continent.

Elements of the Global Strategy

Now that I have shown why the initiative behind AUDA was inspired by external, more than internal, factors – in spite of the ongoing political dynamics in Africa – I turn to the strategic foundations of AUDA. Specifically, I elucidate the similarities and differences across the priority areas identified by AUDA and those of the WB.

---

improving conditions for a more active role by private agents" (quoted in Taylor and Williams 2001, 270).

[6] Taylor and Nel believe that the New Africa (at the dawn of the twenty-first century) is shaped by elites who are involved in deeply liberal projects. These leaders advocate liberal democracy and a market economy. African leaders negotiate with Europeans on their own terms: liberalization, free trade, and globalization. In general, these leaders come from countries that benefit only little from their regions and thus must turn toward the international scene. See Taylor and Nel 2002.

[7] The *Millennium Declaration*, which the United Nations adopted in 2000, is a perfect example of international consensus on the objectives of development (see UN 2000).

The Similarities

There are many points of similarity between the priority areas identified by the WB in 2000 and those chosen by NEPAD in 2001.

The first priority area identified by the WB concerned "improving governance, managing conflict, and rebuilding states" (WB 2000a, 48–82). NEPAD also identified peace, security, and good governance, including a peer evaluation mechanism (NEPAD 2001, 17–19), in its strategy, as preconditions for its success. Thus, AUDA partially repeats the same elements highlighted by the WB as characteristics of a properly functioning state.

However, I must note that South Africa, to which the responsibility for political governance and conflict prevention was assigned, had had limited success in preventing and resolving conflicts, most notably in the Democratic Republic of Congo (DRC). Many experts have charged that military interventions in the DRC were meant less to preserve national unity than to enable networks to profit in the event of total war (Taylor and William 2001). In this light, AUDA's capacity to prevent conflicts remains unconfirmed.

The WB's second priority area consists of "addressing poverty and inequality" (WB 2000a, 83–102). AUDA's analysis of poverty (2001, 28–29) is more superficial than the WB's, although it is identified as one of AUDA's *raisons d'être*. The 7 percent growth rate that the UN proposed and AUDA leaders accepted as necessary to fight poverty "seems excessively ambitious" to the economist Philippe Hugon (2002, 47).

The WB's third priority area consists of "investing in people" (WB 2000a, 103–31), emphasizing two main instruments: health and education. NEPAD (2001, 28–32) repeats the same elements in its strategy.

Identifying its fourth priority area as "lowering infrastructure, information, and finance barriers" (WB 2000a, 132–69), the WB insists on the need to fill gaps in infrastructure and communications, which are drivers of growth. To achieve this, the WB proposes strategies for information and communication technologies, energy, transportation, water, sanitation, and, in general, all infrastructure. Similarly, one of AUDA's main priorities is "bridging the infrastructure gap" (NEPAD 2001, 22–27).

The fifth priority area is "spurring agricultural and rural development" (WB 2000a, 170–207). The WB designed an action plan for agriculture in the twenty-first century, and NEPAD (2001, 33) integrated elements of this plan in its own strategy, mentioning the notions of rural regions, food security, purchasing power, economic growth, climate uncertainty, and regulation.

The sixth priority area consists of "diversifying exports, reorienting trade policy, and pursuing regional integration" (WB 2000a, 208–34). These elements are also repeated by AUDA, which considers regional integration a necessary precondition to fulfilling its goals. Diversifying exports and reorienting trade policy are part of a broader African strategy to support markets.

The final major element of the WB's strategy for Africa consists of "reducing aid dependence and debt and strengthening partnerships" (WB 2000a, 235–58). This is also the last element of AUDA's strategy (NEPAD 2001, 51–55). The success or failure of AUDA, it is said, will depend in large part on the quality of its partnerships with IFIs and other bilateral and multilateral partners.

Whereas Hugon highlights the importance of "questioning [the] international architecture" (2002, 49), AUDA instead reaffirmed the existing architecture in order to avoid differences of opinion with donors. It is true that any development strategy must include such elements as the ones presented previously. However, AUDA's priorities clearly resemble those prescribed by the WB. The priority areas identified are those that favor growth and would turn Africa into a market and an exporter. According to both organizations, these are the means by which development in Africa will occur.

In sum, almost all of AUDA's priority areas are included in the WB's 2000 publication. In fact, the similarities are so obvious that Taylor and Nel argue that the strategic choice made by "the new Africa" consists of challenging the North at its own game of globalization (2002, 171) rather than redefining the rules of the game. Both the programmatic initiative for AUDA and its strategies for achieving its goals seem to have been inspired more by exogenous forces than endogenous ones. I now look at the particularities this project poses compared to earlier initiatives.

Differences

The main differences between AUDA and the IMF and WB initiatives lie in their governance mechanisms. Unlike the institutions that created and oversaw the implementation of earlier projects, NEPAD conceived its own implementation and created three major bodies for its governance.

At the regional level, the first of these bodies is the Heads of State and Government Orientation Committee (HSGOC),[8] consisting of twenty heads of state[9] including the five founding member countries of NEPAD and fifteen rotating members (every two years), usually three from each of the five subregions or following regional consultations within the AU. Some authors (Hope 2002) believe that the success of AUDA's implementation depends on this committee's ability to avoid the harmful effects of bureaucracy, to represent the population (for this, civil society must organize pressure groups and lobby NEPAD), to reconcile AUDA's collective practices with the individual practices of its member states (for example, by having one representative at international negotiations), to strengthen implementation capacities, and to utilize the strategic framework of the fight against poverty. This committee's role is to define the strategic options available by taking inspiration from past developments. Equally important is its role in oversight, evaluation, and establishment of a peer review mechanism, which I present in the next chapter.

The second level of AUDA's governance structure is its Steering Committee, composed of representatives of the heads of state. Its role is to develop the terms of reference for the programs and projects defined by the HSGOC. It is also the organ responsible for overseeing the Secretariat. Notably, NEPAD's structure will change again with the official come into force of the African Union Development Agency (AUDA).

Headquartered in South Africa, the NEPAD Secretariat was the administrative body (third level of governance), responsible for multiple activities, including communication, the coordination of actions at the continental level, and other general administrative functions. In February 2010, the NEPAD Secretariat was replaced by the NEPAD Planning and Coordination Agency (NEPAD Agency), a technical body or specialized agency of the AU.

---

[8] Initially, HSGOC was called the Heads of State and Government Implementation Committee (HSGIC).

[9] Initially, HSGIC had fifteen member states, instead of twenty as HSGOC has now.

Beyond this, the technical responsibilities connected to achieving AUDA's various objectives are divided among the founding countries and distributed on the basis of each country's particular competences. Senegal covers basic infrastructure, the environment, new information and communication technologies, and energy. Human development is entrusted to Algeria. South Africa is responsible for political governance and maintaining peace, stability, and the peaceful resolution of conflicts. Egypt deals with market access and diversifying production, and finally, Nigeria is in charge of good economic governance and capital flows. We see that these technical responsibilities are distributed on the basis of each country's particular competences.

In conclusion, it is clear that the principal particularities of AUDA lie at the institutional level (that of implementation) and not at the strategic level (that of strategy and development). Unlike initiatives that were promoted by the WB, or even other African institutions such as the Lagos Plan of Action, AUDA evolved as a real institution, with an organizational structure (other similar initiatives were simply policies/strategies, without a real distinct institution).

Elements of the Program and Action Plan: An Analysis of Three Sectors

I now compare the action plans proposed at NEPAD's (now the AU Development Agency) creation to those previously implemented or proposed by the WB across three domains that both institutions consider essential: political governance, economic governance, and the fight against poverty.

Democracy and Good Political Governance

African leaders expressed the belief that democracy, respect for human rights, peace, and good governance were preconditions for achieving AUDA's goals. Thus, in NEPAD's founding document, they committed to respecting these principles, stating that "the purpose of the Democracy and Political Governance Initiative is to contribute to strengthening the political and administrative framework of participating countries, in line with the principles of democracy, transparency, accountability, integrity, respect for human rights and promotion of the rule of law" (NEPAD 2001, 17). They further stated that this initiative strengthens the economic governance initiative and that, taken together, these twin initiatives will ultimately contribute to development.

The governance initiative is itself divided into three parts. The first consists of initiating, implementing, and strengthening the fundamental processes of good governance. The second promises to support all measures that encourage the first. The third part institutionalizes leaders' commitments in order to ensure respect for the principles and values of AUDA and advocates a process of mutual learning.

Let us compare the specific targets of AUDA's institutional reforms, which aimed "to strengthen political governance and build capacity to meet these commitments" (NEPAD 2001, 18), with those identified by the WB. While AUDA's first goal is specified as the reform of administrative and civil services, the document does not elaborate on what specific form this goal should take. We may wonder, then, if reform is a goal in and of itself or if it is meant to respond to established, concrete needs. By comparison, the WB document states that public service needs to "adapt to changing circumstances and be made more efficient, cost-effective, and accountable. In most countries this will require a fundamental change in orientation" (WB 2000a, 74). Thus, even if in many ways it seems to have copied the WB's blueprint, AUDA's solutions are less specific than those of the WB.

Strengthening parliamentary oversight is NEPAD's second target in the realm of democracy. Despite the requests of some African Union members of parliament, NEPAD leaders did not submit the initial project for parliamentary consideration before it was formally created. It might therefore seem paradoxical that this measure is included as one of NEPAD's targets. In comparison, the WB maintains that "efforts to build parliamentary expertise, especially of key committees, would also facilitate legislative oversight" (WB 2000a, 70). The similarities between the measures proposed by the WB and those adopted by NEPAD are obvious here as well.

AUDA's third governance target is to promote direct and participatory democracy, which is similar to the WB's proposal for a fully participatory political system. However, this commitment stands in contradiction to certain observed practices. Taylor (2002) contends that the attitude of African elites who promoted NEPAD (AUDA) and yet supported Robert Mugabe, the former president of Zimbabwe – after contested elections – casts doubt on NEPAD's founding principles and ability to carry through reforms, especially in political governance.

Fourth, AUDA insists that effective measures are crucial for combatting corruption and embezzlement. While the fight against embezzlement is, in general, essential to social justice, there is a clear convergence with the WB's discourse: "Anticorruption strategies must be realistic, achievable, and consistently implemented" (WB 2000a, 74).

The final target is the reform of the legal system. Comparison with the WB allows us to see how similar the two programs are. The WB states, "a comprehensive legal sector review can help countries prioritize reforms" (WB 2000a, 71).

Thus, five targets chosen by AUDA do not constitute a wholly innovative solution;[10] they had already been highlighted by other development partners. However, beyond these targets, there are other elements to consider. For example, AUDA members maintain that they are dedicated to "creating and strengthening national, sub-regional, and continental structures that support good governance" (NEPAD 2001, 18). This seems a direct response to the WB, which states that "regional initiatives and institutions can strengthen governance in individual countries" (WB 2000a, 78).

AUDA leaders also emphasize the creation of peer-review mechanisms. Specifically, they write,

The Heads of State Forum of the New Partnership for Africa's Development will serve as a mechanism through which the leadership of the New Partnership for Africa's Development will periodically monitor and assess the progress made by African countries in meeting their commitments towards achieving good governance and social reforms. (NEPAD 2001, 18–19)

This declaration is similar to the recommendation of the WB, which stated that "regional and sub-regional organizations can put pressure on member governments to conform to norms of good governance and democratic behavior" (WB 2000a, 79).

I conclude that AUDA's program for good political governance is very similar to that proposed by the WB. I shall now examine whether this is true of AUDA's second program.

---

[10] Vijay S. Makhan states, "The problems NEPAD was created to solve are well known. Most of the solutions proposed are also familiar to Africa and to the international community, and are widely discussed across many milieus and forums." See Makhan 2002, 5.

Economic Governance, Production Diversification, and Promoting Exports

The AU Development Agency's initiative to improve economic governance consists of an action plan to ameliorate the economic situations in member countries. Believing that "state capacity-building is a critical aspect of creating conditions for development," African leaders in AUDA propose programs "aimed at enhancing the quality of economic and public financial management, as well as corporate governance" (NEPAD 2001, 19). This statement is similar to the WB's that "a strong state is needed and economic policy considerations should inform proposals for political reform" (WB 2000a, 67). It is important to note here that, while the plan proposed by AUDA does not have a direct equivalent in the WB's publication, it parallels existing practices. For example, AUDA's economic governance plan includes a team from several African finance ministries and central banks to audit governance practices. The HSGOC submits to African leaders the recommendations from the audit and, in this way, prioritize the management of public finances and capacity-building.

AUDA also proposes a subregional and regional approach to development. The objective here is to enlarge the market and create an economy of scale that benefits local and foreign investors; as Pierre Moussa writes, "the foreign private sector will invest if it believes, quite simply, that the probability of capital gains are very high and the risks are relatively low" (2002, 39). Institutional strengthening is emphasized as the key to achieving this economic integration. According to Wade,

through massive investments in projects for basic structures and human development, to eventually close the gaps that separate Africa from the developed world, in order to reach full participation in global production and international trade, the engines of economic growth. The goal is to make Africa a partner and no longer a dependent. (quoted in Soumare 2003)

As for market access, I focus on the promotion of exports since this is one of the fundamental elements in the development strategy prescribed by the WB. Table 4.1 presents a comparison of programs by AUDA and the WB to encourage market access. This table clearly shows the degree of similarity between AUDA's action plan and that of the WB, especially in the areas of diversifying and promoting

Table 4.1 *Comparison of AUDA and WB market access programs*

Comparison Criterion	Actions at the African Level (NEPAD/AUDA)	Actions at the International Level (NEPAD/AUDA)	Actions Prescribed by the World Bank
Promotion and diversification of exports	• Promote intra-African trade • Create marketing mechanisms and institutions to develop marketing strategies for African products • Publicize African exporting and importing companies and their products • Reduce the cost of transactions and operations • Promote and improve regional trade agreements, foster interregional trade liberalization • Reduce the cost of transactions and operations	• Negotiate measures and agreements to facilitate access to the world market by African products • Encourage direct foreign investment • Assist in capacity-building in the private sector and strengthen country and subregional capacity in trade negotiations and implementing the rules and regulations of the WTO • Participate in the world trading system and recognize and provide for the African continent's special concerns, needs, and interests in future WTO rules	• Eliminate anti-export bias • Improve standards in certain key import areas • Plan to cut import tariffs • Attract substantial investment in the export sector • Deepen regional integration • Take advantage of the forum for multilateral free trade agreements offered by the WTO • Adopt free trade policies

Source: NEPAD 2001, 166–67; World Bank 2000a, 222–23.

exports and, more generally, economic governance. Is this also true for the fight against poverty?

The Fight against Poverty

AUDA has established goals and a plan of action to aggressively fight poverty. The first objective is to make the fight against poverty part of the macroeconomic and sectorial policies of national governments, although the founding document does not specify how this is to be done. As we have seen, the 2000–2001 WB report identified eradicating poverty as its principal objective, and indicated specifically that "macroeconomic and structural policies that encourage growth and employment are essential for any poverty reduction strategy" (WB 2000a, 99).

AUDA's second objective is "to give special attention to the reduction of poverty among women" (NEPAD 2001, 28), although it largely fails to specify what exactly will be done. One of the few concrete proposals here is the establishment of a special team to investigate the question. Initially, the AU Developmeny Agency relied strongly on the actions proposed by the *Millennium Declaration* and the WB. However, it has recently developed a more holistic approach to gender mainstreaming and women's empowerment, with a view to integrating these concepts into its programmes and processes. One of its flagship programmes is the NEPAD Spanish Fund for African Women's Empowerment (funded by the Spanish Agency for International Development Cooperation), which is reported to have improved living conditions for more than 500,000 direct beneficiaries.

The third objective is to ensure the empowerment of the poor through poverty reduction strategies (NEPAD 2001, 28). Similarly, the WB maintains that "government measures to help households cope with uncertainties must supplement the coping mechanisms used by the poor" (WB 2000a, 102).

AUDA's final objective, which strongly indicates the continuity between the two institutions, is "to support existing poverty reduction initiatives at the multilateral level, such as the Comprehensive Development Framework of the World Bank and the Poverty Reduction Strategy approach linked to the debt relief initiative for Highly Indebted Poor Countries (HIPCs)" (NEPAD 2001, 29). This objective reveals the influence of IFIs on its program of action. Indeed, IFIs consider the Poverty Reduction Strategy Papers essential for any heavily indebted poor country hoping to benefit from debt relief and loans. The founders of NEPAD have therefore converged with the IFIs and included this measure as one of their priorities.

Despite laying out these principles, however, AUDA's action plan to fight poverty is not very detailed. First, it includes a before-and-after evaluation of the various programs outlined. Next, it places a priority on collaboration with institutions within the United Nations system, as well as with the WB, the IMF, and the African Development Bank (AfDB). Such collaboration, it states, will make it possible to "accelerate the implementation and adoption of the Comprehensive Development Framework, the Poverty Reduction Strategy, and related approaches" (NEPAD 2001, 29).

Finally, AUDA has stated that decentralization will generate increased citizen participation, and that this is the best way to guarantee improved services for the poor. However, I should note that the WB states that decentralization will increase local taxes, reducing the state's financial burden.

In conclusion, the present analysis has shown that AUDA's plan of action for poverty reduction largely continues the initiatives of the WB, the IMF, and various UN organizations, rather than breaking away from them. Instead of taking a new direction, AUDA legitimizes the established framework used by these international institutions, suggesting the implementation of existing programs and the acceleration of processes already underway. Thus, AUDA, at its inception, seemed to represent a continuation of the previous initiatives of the IFIs. However, since its creation, AUDA has evolved and developed a distinct dynamic, which will be studied in Chapter 5.

5 | AUDA in the Twenty-First Century

Evolution, Implementation of Key
Programs, Institutional Development,
and Interstate Cooperation

Since 2001, the African Union Development Agency (AUDA), formerly
NEPAD, has faced many challenges and undergone numerous
transformations. It has developed a number of ambitious programs
intended to contribute to the development of Africa (NEPAD 2011). It
has also changed its organizational structure, transforming its Secretariat into the NEPAD Planning and Coordination Agency, a new
technical body of the AU. Now, almost two decades after its creation,
what critical assessment can be made of its evolution, institutional
development, and implementation of certain key programs?

This chapter does not propose a complete evaluation of AUDA's
activities. Rather, relying on the neo-institutional approach (Hall and
Taylor 1996) used thus far, it focuses on institutional transformations
and continuities as well as on interstate cooperation through AUDA. To
this end, I analyze the evolution and implementation of several NEPAD
(now AUDA) projects, paying particular attention to three important
programs first adopted in 2002 in order to analyze their evolutions over
roughly two decades. These are the African Peer Review Mechanism
(APRM),[1] which deals with political and economic governance (NEPAD
Secretariat 2002); the Comprehensive Africa Agriculture Development
Program (CAADP), which deals with the agricultural sector and food
security (NEPAD Secretariat 2010); and the NEPAD Short-Term
Action Plan (STAP), which dealt with regional integration and infrastructure (NEPAD 2003b) until it was incorporated into the Program
for Infrastructure Development in Africa (PIDA) 2010–2040. PIDA also
includes the infrastructure portion of the AU/NEPAD African Action
Plan 2010–2015 (AU and NEPAD 2009). To address the most urgent
infrastructure needs, the Priority Action Plan (PAP) was developed within
PIDA to accelerate the implementation of short- and medium-term

---

[1] The APRM became a specialized agency within the AU.

projects and programs, through 2020 and 2030, respectively. The ongoing immediate priority is defined in the PIDA PAP 2012–2020. This chapter analyzes the transformations, or lack thereof, that have occurred in these three sectors.

Political and Economic Governance: The APRM

The APRM: Good Intentions but a Nonbinding Structure

The APRM was adopted in 2002 (and officially launched in 2003) as NEPAD's main tool for overseeing political governance (NEPAD 2001). It is presented as "Africa's most innovative and ambitious initiative on governance" (APRM 2016a, 1). Its mandate is

to ensure that the policies and practices of participating states conform to the agreed political, economic, and corporate governance values, codes and standards contained in the Declaration on Democracy, Political, Economic, and Corporate Governance. The APRM is the mutually agreed instrument for self-monitoring by the participating member governments. (AU 2002, 1)[2]

In 2014, the AU decided to integrate the APRM as "an autonomous entity within the AU system" (African Union Assembly 2014, 1). In its new status, the APRM is considered a specialized agency within the AU (APRM 2016a).

In terms of governance structure, the APRM is organized at the continental and national levels with specific institutional configurations designed to help it fulfill its mission. Continentally, the APRM organizational structure comprises "an APR Forum[3] composed of the Heads of State and Government of Participating States; an APRM

---

[2] According to the statute adopted in 2016, the mandate is "to promote and facilitate self-monitoring by the Participating States, and to ensure that their policies and practices conform to the agreed political, economic, corporate governance and socio-economic values, codes and standards contained in the Declaration on Democracy, Political, Economic and Corporate Governance; and the African Charter on Democracy, Elections and Governance, as well as other relevant treaties, conventions and instruments adopted by Participating States whether through the African Union or through other international platforms" (APRM 2016b, 7).

[3] This is the supreme decision-making organ, with the chairperson elected on a rotating basis among the five African regions, to serve not more than two years.

Focal Points Committee[4] composed of the national Focal Points of Participating States; an APR Panel of Eminent Persons[5] composed of a minimum of five and a maximum of nine Africans appointed by the APR Forum; and an APRM Continental Secretariat[6] led by a Chief Executive Officer (CEO) appointed by the APR Forum" (APRM 2016b, 11). Nationally, the APRM should consist of "the APRM National Focal Point;[7] the APRM National Governing Council or Commission [NGC];[8] the APRM National Secretariat; and the Technical Research Institutions" (APRM 2016b, 19).

The functions/processes of the APRM are presented in Figure 5.1. The organization functions on a voluntary basis; each African leader is free to choose whether to be evaluated by his or her peers and, ultimately, whether to implement their recommendations. Thus, although it is supposed to encourage "mutual accountability" (AU 2002, 15), it does not have a binding enforcement mechanism for member governments that fail to honor their commitments. Can an institution achieve the results it expects without establishing a mechanism that balances incentives and pressures in a way that ensures that actors respect the rules of the game? Has the APRM enabled a transformation of political and economic governance in Africa? The following section addresses these questions.

The APRM Since the Creation of AUDA

The APRM's track record to date is mixed, though not totally unsatisfactory. I briefly analyze democratic development in Africa since NEPAD's adoption, utilizing the Freedom House combined score of political rights

---

[4] With the status of a ministerial body, the members of the APRM Focal Points Committee represent their heads of state and government. The APRM Focal Points Committee is an intermediary between the APR Forum and the Continental Secretariat.

[5] The "APR Panel shall ensure the integrity, independence, professionalism and credibility of the country review process" (APRM 2016b, 14).

[6] The APRM Continental Secretariat "shall be the Secretariat of the APRM and shall serve the APR Forum, APR Focal Points Committee and APR Panel. Accordingly, the APR Continental Secretariat shall provide the APR Panel with secretariat, technical, advisory, coordination and administrative support for the functioning of the APRM" (APRM 2016b, 16).

[7] The person should be a minister or an assimilated rank in government.

[8] This should be an independent body constituted of respected representatives of all the key sectors in society.

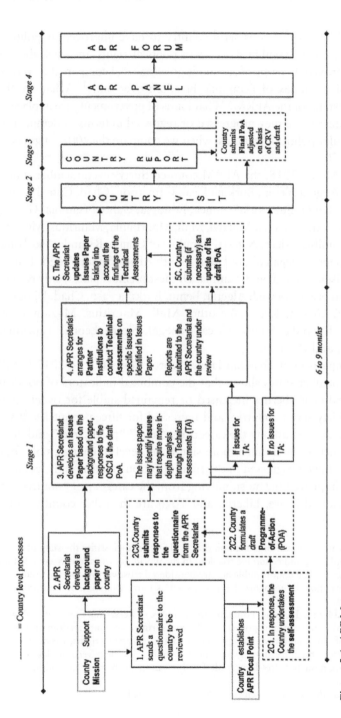

Figure 5.1 APRM processes
Source: NEPAD 2003a, 7.

and civil liberties.[9] I consider a country to have improved its political governance if its combined scores in political rights and civil liberties have improved. In terms of economic governance, I compare the average scores of the Index of Economic Freedom over time.[10] What are the member states of the APRM? What kinds of governments are in place in these states? Have they progressed or regressed in terms of democracy, in particular political freedoms, when we compare the 2002[11] figures to those of 2017?

As of March 2018, the APRM counted thirty-seven member states: Algeria, Angola, Benin, Burkina Faso, Cameroon, Chad, Côte d'Ivoire, Djibouti, Egypt, Equatorial Guinea, Ethiopia, Gabon, Gambia, Ghana, Kenya, Lesotho, Liberia, Malawi, Mali, Mauritania, Mauritius, Mozambique, Namibia, Niger, Nigeria, Republic of Congo, Rwanda, São Tomé and Príncipe, Senegal, Sierra Leone, South Africa, Sudan, Togo, Tanzania, Tunisia, Uganda, and Zambia. Of these member states, only twenty have been peer-reviewed: Algeria, Benin, Burkina Faso, Chad, Djibouti, Ethiopia, Ghana, Kenya, Lesotho, Mali, Mauritius, Mozambique, Nigeria, Rwanda, South Africa, Senegal, Sierra Leone, Tanzania, Uganda, and Zambia.

A comparison of Freedom House scores from 2002 to 2017 for all APRM member states shows that the combined indicators of political rights and civil liberties increased or remained stable for twenty-two out of thirty-seven countries and regressed for fifteen countries. If we focus on changes among the categories "free," "partly free," and "not free," which show a much more significant level of change, only four countries have progressed in the right direction. Tunisia is the country that has improved the most, moving from the category of "not free" to "free." Côte d'Ivoire, Liberia, and Togo are the other countries that

---

[9] This is an American organization that evaluates and classifies the state of civil, political, and economic freedom in the world. Its website is www.freedom house.com. The data it publishes are considered trustworthy and are used by internationally recognized experts, such as Larry Diamond of Stanford University.

[10] Created by the Heritage Foundation, the Index of Economic Freedom evaluates the quality of economic governance by measuring economic freedom on the basis of ten quantitative and qualitative factors (property rights, freedom from corruption, fiscal freedom, government spending, business freedom, labor freedom, monetary freedom, trade freedom, investment freedom, and financial freedom).

[11] This was the year in which the APRM was adopted.

have seen a positive change of category. They have improved their scores enough to move from one category to another, going from a not-free to a partially free regime. Only five countries were downgraded from partially free to not-free regimes, and two countries from free to partially free regimes. The twenty-six remaining countries did not see their categories change in one direction or the other.

As of March 2018, only twenty African countries[12] (about half of APRM members) had completed the APRM process, with the publication of country review reports[13] and National Programs of Action (NPoA).[14] A focus on this subset of countries reveals a relatively stable or slightly positive trend. Twelve out of twenty countries saw their scores improve (Benin, Burkina Faso, Ghana, Nigeria, Rwanda, Senegal, and Sierra Leone) or remain stable (Algeria, Kenya, Mauritius, Uganda, and Zambia). Eight countries saw their scores decrease (Chad, Djibouti, Ethiopia, Lesotho, Mali, Mozambique, South Africa, and Tanzania). These trends suggest that, over the long run, the most committed countries are also those most likely to improve their political governance scores, even if completing the process does not always result in a positive outcome (given the decrease in the score of some countries). In fact, a significant transformation, beyond an incremental improvement of indicators, is the exception.

The trend is similar in the arena of economic governance. When we consider only the Index of Economic Freedom for the twenty countries that have completed the APRM process, the performance of ten countries improved from 2002 to 2017 (Benin, Burkina Faso, Ethiopia, Lesotho, Mauritius, Nigeria, Rwanda, Sierra Leone, Tanzania, and Uganda) and ten decreased (Algeria, Chad, Djibouti, Ghana, Kenya, Mali, Mozambique, Senegal, South Africa, and Zambia).[15] When the

---

[12] Ghana (January 2006); Kenya and Rwanda (July 2006); Algeria, Benin, and South Africa (January 2008); Uganda (June 2008); Burkina Faso and Nigeria (October 2008); Lesotho, Mali, and Mozambique (June 2009); Mauritius (July 2010); Ethiopia (January 2011); Sierra Leone (January 2012); and Tanzania and Zambia (January 2013); Chad, Djibouti, and Senegal (January 2017).

[13] Document prepared by the APRM Secretariat after receiving the self-assessment report and the draft National Program of Action.

[14] Document prepared by each country based on a self-assessment report, to address the problems that were identified. The self-assessment is supposed to be highly participatory but is often very centralized.

[15] Data are missing in 2002 for one country (Sierra Leone).

analysis includes the Index of Economic Freedom for all thirty-three countries (out of thirty-seven) for which data are available from 2002 to 2017, the scores of thirteen countries improve, while twenty countries regress. Only one country is mostly free (Mauritius), five countries are moderately free (Burkina Faso, Côte d'Ivoire, Rwanda, South Africa, and Uganda), twenty-one countries are mostly not free, and ten are repressed. Here also, change is incremental, and the evolution from one economic freedom category to another (free, mostly free, moderately free, mostly not free, and repressed) is rare.

Not only have the changes been limited in categories across both political and economic governance (despite the improved scores of many countries, a positive trend), the changes observed cannot be systematically attributed to the APRM. In fact, in its *Strategic Plan 2016–2020*, the APRM Secretariat is quite critical of its own achievements (APRM 2016a), pointing to the fact that as of May 2016 only seventeen countries have had their country review reports and NPoAs published. Furthermore, "even among the 17 countries that have undergone the full review, the level of compliance with recommendations contained in the National Programs of Actions (NPoAs) leaves a lot to be desired" (APRM 2016a, 12). Many of these countries have not made the US$100,000 minimum contribution required when signing up for review. The APRM Secretariat does not have the capacity to independently monitor the progress reports of the NPoAs submitted to the APR Forum,[16] and the documents are largely drafted by governments with limited participation from civil society.

Despite the mixed results acknowledged by the APRM Secretariat, a few observations should be made. First, the APRM is a voluntary mechanism, and the fact that thirty-six countries have committed to the process contributes to increasing continental integration by setting shared norms and standards of governance. Through the APR Forum composed of the participating Heads of State and Government, African leaders engage with one another, providing feedback on their

---

[16] The APR Forum is "a Committee of Participating Heads of State and Government of the Member States of the African Union who have voluntarily chosen to accede to the APRM": http://aprm-au.org/pages?pageId=APR-forum (accessed April 27, 2018).

mutual governance practices and strategies to improve the implementation of reforms. Second, the fact that the APRM has evolved into an autonomous and specialized agency within the AU demonstrates African leaders' commitment to ensuring its maintenance as well as, more generally, that of continental standards of governance.

Third, the lack of efficient compliance mechanisms partly explains the limited performance of African countries and is not surprising given the quality of economic and political governance of numerous member states involved in the process. The APRM Secretariat is, however, aware of these challenges and is engaged in strengthening its capacities and increasing the levels of ownership and compliance. Finally, the APRM experience demonstrates African countries' willingness to cooperate through continental organizations under noncoercive conditions. They are evaluated without being truly obliged to make any real political and economic reforms, and states therefore retain their sovereignty in determining domestic political and economic outcomes. Over the long run, continentally shared norms could nevertheless have unintended consequences at national levels if new leaders grant or citizens request participation at the anticipated levels. I now turn to an analysis of AUDA's advances in terms of agriculture and food security.

Agriculture and Food Security: The Comprehensive African Agriculture Development Program

The CAADP: A Vision for African Agriculture

Since its creation, AUDA has developed many projects in the agricultural sector, including TerrAfrica, the Fertilizer Support Program, the African Biosciences Initiative, and the Comprehensive Africa Agriculture Development Program (CAADP) (NEPAD 2003a). Drafted by the Food and Agricultural Organization (FAO) of the UN in collaboration with the NEPAD Secretariat, the CAADP founding document gives an overall view of the various issues and challenges that African policymakers must confront in agriculture as well as of opportunities and tactics for solving them (5). The CAADP is "a genuinely Africa-owned and Africa-led framework" (NEPAD 2010, viii) and "reflects the recognition that in Africa agriculture is central to the alleviation of poverty and hunger" (xii). It has four pillars:

(1) land and water management: to extend the area under sustainable land management and expand reliable water control systems;
(2) market access: to increase market access through improved rural infrastructure and other trade-related interventions;
(3) food supply and hunger: to increase food supply and reduce hunger;
(4) agricultural research: to improve agricultural research and systems in order to disseminate appropriate new technologies.

(NEPAD 2010, 5)

In addition to the objectives set by the CAADP, 10 percent of national budgets are intended to be allocated toward carrying them out, and it is expected that African countries will realize a 6 percent growth rate in agricultural productivity. Although the CAADP is a continent-wide solution, implementation requires that its "pillar frameworks" be transferred, adapted, and implemented at the national level. The institutional evolution of the CAADP thus greatly depends on how the national actors in charge of its implementation appropriate and use it. What assessment can we make of the CAADP's implementation?

The Difficult Implementation of the CAADP: Some Successes but Insufficient Appropriation at the National Level, Limited Resources, and Weak Institutional Structure

The results of the CAADP have been mixed, with some success stories and many challenges in coordination and implementation. Internationally, it is recognized as an African instrument of regional cooperation, although it has not been used to its fullest potential in African countries, even among members/signatories.[17]

The relative acceptance of the CAADP internationally is partially explained by the fact that the program was created under strong guidance from the FAO. It is, therefore, not surprising that it is mentioned in the discourse of organizations such as the G8 or the FAO (NEPAD 2010, viii). To take advantage of this recognition, the CAADP created a multidonor fiduciary fund dedicated to its improvement and implementation. Until recently, however, this fund has

---

[17] This is a voluntary commitment made by national actors involved in agriculture to collaborate in implementing the CAADP's pillars.

remained insufficiently financed. Despite this, TerrAfrica – a distinct program created to support CAADP and the Action Plan of the NEPAD Environment Initiative as well as address the challenges related to sustainable land management – financed about thirty-six projects in twenty-six countries through TerrAfrica's Strategic Investment Program (SIP), with close to US$2 billion from leveraged financing.[18]

At the national level, the number of countries involved in the CAADP has substantially increased from 2010 to 2018. By 2010, only twenty-two African countries had signed the CAADP's compact document (Benin, Burkina Faso, Burundi, Cape Verde, Côte d'Ivoire, Ethiopia, Gambia, Ghana, Guinea, Kenya, Liberia, Malawi, Mali, Niger, Nigeria, Rwanda, Senegal, Sierra Leone, Swaziland, Tanzania, Togo, and Uganda) (NEPAD 2010, 9; 2011, 26). In terms of results, however, only eight countries met or exceeded the goal of devoting 10 percent of their budgets to agriculture (Comoros, Ethiopia, Madagascar, Malawi, Mali, Niger, Senegal, and Zimbabwe) (NEPAD Secretariat 2008, 9), and only ten reached the 6 percent growth productivity target (Angola, Ethiopia, Mali, Mozambique, Namibia, Niger, Rwanda, Senegal, Tanzania, and Uganda) (NEPAD Secretariat 2011, 5).

In spite of some agricultural progress in Africa that cannot necessarily be attributed to the CAADP, the program still has to profoundly inspire a more substantial movement that would substantially transform African agriculture – one of its most important missions. Years after its creation, the CAADP still has to demonstrate a transformational impact on agricultural growth in Africa, and several countries have even suffered repeated food crises. Even among those countries that signed the CAADP's compact, few have really used the program's resources to develop their agricultural policies (NEPAD 2010, xvi). The CAADP Secretariat also recognizes that its resources have not measured up to its ambitions, admitting that it "has not been provided with the human or financial resources or legal status to enable it to fulfill its mandate and role" (xv). A 2010 report from NEPAD (now AUDA) noted that the "CAADP's biggest disappointments have been its failure to secure greater understanding and ownership of the CAADP at the country level, and to not achieve more in terms of

[18] NEPAD. "TerrAfrica." NEPAD.org. www.nepad.org/programme/terrafrica (accessed April 27, 2018).

increased investment in the sector by governments and development partners" (NEPAD 2010, viii).

The United Nations Office of Special Adviser on Africa noted in 2015 that "as a result, average public agricultural expenditures have risen by more than 7% per year across Africa since 2003, nearly doubling public agricultural expenditures since the launch of CAADP."[19] By March 2018, however, the situation had changed. At least forty-five countries[20] had signed the CAADP's compact, and a few more were working toward signing it. The number of countries that have signed the CAADP's compact has more than doubled since 2010, with more than three-quarters of African countries now committed. At least forty have developed a National Agricultural Investment Plan, and agriculture is presented as one of the top priorities of each country.

Table 5.1 summarizes the evolution of the CAADP's membership, its processes, and their implementation as of the end of 2015.[21]

The involvement of the majority of African countries contributes to the continental harmonization of African agricultural policies. The CAADP is not only widely accepted by the international community,[22] it is now also widely legitimized by Africa's regional economic

---

[19] Office of the Special Adviser on Africa (United Nations). "Comprehensive Africa Agriculture Development Programme (CAADP)." UN.org. www.un.org/en/africa/osaa/peace/caadp.shtml (accessed April 27, 2018).

[20] Namely, Angola, Benin, Burkina Faso, Burundi, Cameroon, Cape Verde, Central African Republic, Chad, Congo Brazzaville, Côte d'Ivoire, Democratic Rep. of Congo, Djibouti, Equatorial Guinea, Eritrea, Ethiopia, Gabon, Gambia, Ghana, Guinea Bissau, Guinea-Conakry, Kenya, Lesotho, Liberia, Libya, Madagascar, Malawi, Mali, Mauritania, Mauritius, Mozambique, Niger, Nigeria, Rwanda, São Tomé and Principe, Senegal, Seychelles, Sierra Leone, Sudan, Swaziland, Tanzania, Togo, Tunisia, Uganda, Zambia, and Zimbabwe.

[21] "CC1 are countries that signed the compact in 2007–2009; CC2 are countries that signed the compact in 2010–2012; CC3 are countries that signed the compact in 2013–2015; and CC0 are countries that have not yet signed a CAADP compact. CL0 are countries that have not started the CAADP process or are pre-compact; CL1 have signed a CAADP compact; CL2 have signed a compact and formulated a NAFSIP; CL3 have signed a compact, formulated a NAFSIP and secured one external funding source; CL4 have signed a compact, formulated a NAFSIP and secured more than one external funding source" (Namuko et al. 2016, 187).

[22] Including the UN World Food Program (WFP) and FAO.

Table 5.1 *Country classification by period when the CAADP compact was signed and stage of CAADP implementation*

PERIOD WHEN CAADP COMPACT WAS SIGNED				LEVEL OR STAGE OF CAADP IMPLEMENTATION REACHED BY END OF 2015				
2007–2009	2010–2012	2013–2015	Not Signed	LEVEL 0 Not Started or Pre-Compact	LEVEL 1 Signed Compact	LEVEL 2 Level 1 Plus NAIP	LEVEL 3 Level 2 Plus One External Funding Source	LEVEL 4 Level 3 Plus Other External Funding Source
CC1	CC2	CC3	CC0	CL0	CL1	CL2	CL3	CL4
Benin	Burkina Faso	Angola	Algeria	Algeria	Angola	Cameroon	Burundi	Benin
Burundi	Central Afr. Rep.	Cameroon	Botswana	Botswana	Chad	Cape Verde	Gambia, The	Burkina Faso
Cape Verde	Congo, Dem. Rep.	Chad	Comoros, The	Comoros, The	Congo, Rep.	Central Afr. Rep.	Liberia	Côte d'Ivoire
Ethiopia	Côte d'Ivoire	Congo, Rep.	Egypt	Egypt	Eq. Guinea	Congo, Dem. Rep.	Mali	Ethiopia
Gambia, The	Djibouti	Eq. Guinea	Morocco	Morocco	Gabon	Djibouti	Niger	Ghana
Ghana	Guinea	Gabon			Lesotho	Guinea	Sierra Leone	Kenya
Liberia	Guinea Bissau	Lesotho			Madagascar	Guinea	Bissau Togo	Malawi

Sources: ReSAKSS based on IFPRI (2015), WB (2016), and national sources.

communities[23] and individual countries, resulting in the prioritization of agriculture and food security as national-level drivers of economic growth.

Table 5.2 compares the evolution of the share of agriculture in total public expenditure (%) during the pre- and post-CAADP launch periods. Countries are grouped and compared depending on the period when the CAADP was signed and the level of implementation by the end of 2015. The results show a broad but not homogenous progression of the annual average: The countries that signed the CAADP compact earlier and the countries that are more advanced in CAADP implementation seem to outperform the others, even if not systematically. However, none of the categories has reached the target of 10 percent of resources allocated to agriculture, even if a few countries were individually able to do so. Moreover, the countries that have not signed the CAADP continue to underperform.

Although agricultural productivity has increased for the periods 1993–2003 and 2003–2008, no category of countries has reached CAADP's goal of improving agricultural productivity to the annual average growth rate of 6 percent (Table 5.3). Despite disparities, again, the better performers overall are also earlier CAADP signatories and more advanced implementers. Moreover, overall performance has slightly decreased for the period 2008–2015, compared to the two prior periods. Unfortunately, member states that adopt the new vision and policies do not necessarily implement them. African countries seem to be willing to cooperate through continental development organizations such as AUDA in order to find solutions to common problems, without implementing real consequences for noncompliance with the ideals to which they commit.

The CAADP has developed a plan to sustain its momentum by addressing coordination challenges and creating higher levels of national ownership and accountability (NEPAD Agency 2015a). However, the processes remain voluntary and lack enforcement. Therefore,

---

[23] Regional economic communities have also signed the compact: for example, the Common Market for Eastern and Southern Africa (COMESA), the Intergovernmental Authority on Development (IGAD), the Economic Community of Central African States (ECCAS), and the Economic Community of West African States (ECOWAS).

Table 5.2 *Share of agriculture expenditure in total public expenditure (%)*

Region	Annual Avg. Level (1995–2003)	Annual Avg. Change (1995–2003)	2003	Annual Avg. Level (2003–2008)	Annual Avg. Change (2003–2008)	Annual Avg. Level (2008–2014)	Annual Avg. Change (2008–2014)	2014
Africa	3.2	3.4	3.6	3.5	–1.2	3.0	–1.5	2.6
CAADP Compact 2007–2009 (CC1)	3.2	1.8	3.7	4.3	6.5	4.3	0.8	5.8
CAADP Compact 2010–2012 (CC2)	5.3	–1.9	5.1	5.3	2.3	5.9	–0.5	6.0
CAADP Compact 2013–2015 (CC3)	2.0	–7.6	1.6	2.3	12.1	2.1	–12.8	1.0
CAADP Compact Not Yet (CC0)	3.1	6.6	3.5	3.2	–6.5	2.4	0.1	1.9
CAADP Level 0 (CL0)	3.1	6.6	3.5	3.2	–6.5	2.4	0.1	1.9
CAADP Level 1 (CL1)	2.0	8.5	1.5	2.1	12.6	1.9	15.0	0.9
CAADP Level 2 (CL2)	4.2	2.5	4.0	4.1	1.6	4.7	4.2	4.6
CAADP Level 3 (CL3)	5.7	1.6	6.2	7.5	7.5	7.2	–3.6	7.3
CAADP Level 4 (CL4)	3.7	–1.2	3.9	4.3	4.8	4.6	1.6	5.2

Sources: ReSAKSS based on IFPRI (2015), WB (2016), and national sources.

Table 5.3 *Agriculture value added (million, constant 2010 US$)*

Region	Annual Avg. Level (1995–2003)	Annual Avg. Change (1995–2003)	2003	Annual Avg. Level (2003–2008)	Annual Avg. Change (2003–2008)	Annual Avg. Level (2008–2015)	Annual Avg. Change (2008–2015)	2015
Africa	7,183.3	4.79	8,917.0	9,869.0	4.67	12,585.9	3.35	13,939.9
CAADP Compact 2007–2009 (CC1)	13,848.4	7.89	20,618.6	24,249.9	6.74	31,432.6	2.70	33,916.6
CAADP Compact 2010–2012 (CC2)	2,935.0	–0.75	2,925.7	3,152.3	3.42	4,503.5	5.94	5,273.4
CAADP Compact 2013–2015 (CC3)	6,754.3	4.91	7,497.8	7,818.8	2.65	9,516.1	3.58	10,761.9
CAADP Compact Not Yet (CC0)	6,746.6	1.47	7,250.8	7,180.9	1.13	8,474.0	2.50	9,328.6
CAADP Level 0 (CL0)	6,746.6	1.47	7,250.8	7,180.9	1.13	8,474.0	2.50	9,328.6
CAADP Level 1 (CL1)	6,823.7	4.93	7,576.2	7,894.5	2.61	9,607.0	3.60	10,872.3
CAADP Level 2 (CL2)	2,345.3	–5.42	1,876.5	1,965.5	2.99	2,456.2	3.27	2,732.0
CAADP Level 3 (CL3)	1,596.5	2.87	1,684.5	1,973.7	8.19	3,055.4	5.98	3,578.6
CAADP Level 4 (CL4)	12,200.3	7.24	17,659.6	20,756.3	6.46	27,020.8	3.04	29,399.5

Sources: ReSAKSS based on FAO (2016), World Bank (2016), and ILO (2016).

despite the broad adoption of its compact and a handful of success stories, the true impact of the CAADP on transforming agriculture – beyond contributing to shared continental norms related to its importance and incremental improvements in performance indicators – remains to be seen. This is especially true when the tangible indicators identified by the CAADP itself are used to measure progress: Agricultural growth remains weak, and several countries have suffered repeated food crises.

It is thus possible to conclude that almost two decades after NEPAD's adoption, its institutional configurations, financial and human resources, and program implementation have substantially contributed to the creation of a continental agricultural vision, but have also failed to bring about substantial agricultural transformation. Finding effective solutions to the challenges of coordination, accountability, and compliance are key to AUDA's success, and for this, mobilizing resources and strengthening the capacities of its programs and initiatives are critical. I conclude this chapter with a look at AUDA's programs in the areas of infrastructure and regional integration.

Regional Integration and Infrastructure: The Short-Term Action Plan

According to AUDA, establishing adequate infrastructure is an essential element for achieving regional integration (AfDB 2003, 7). For this reason, AUDA has adopted several programs targeting infrastructure and development: the STAP; the Infrastructure Project Preparation Facility (IPFF); the Infrastructure Strategic Action Plan (ISAP); the NEPAD Spatial Development Program (SPD); the AU/NEPAD African Action Plan (AAP) 2010–2015; and the PIDA 2010–2040.[24] This section mainly focuses on the STAP, since it was adopted in 2002 (NEPAD Secretariat 2003b), allowing enough time to evaluate its development and implementation. However, I also discuss the post-STAP period, focusing on PIDA and its Presidential Infrastructure Champion Initiative (PICI), one of the initiatives developed specifically to address the shortcomings of the STAP.

---

[24] A review of the evolution of several of these programs is presented in the *Report on the Programmatic Activities of the NEPAD Agency for the Period July to December 2010 by Chief Executive Officer Dr. Ibrahim Assane Mayaki.*

The STAP: Facilitation, Capacity-Building, Investments, and Studies of Infrastructure and Regional Integration

Created in 2002, the mission of AUDA's STAP is to facilitate, improve, invest in, and study infrastructure projects that contribute to the regional integration of the continent. The AfDB summarizes the program's objectives thus:

(1) facilitation – the establishment of the policy, regulatory, and institutional frameworks to create a suitable body for investment and efficient operations; (2) capacity-building initiatives – to empower the implementing institutions to perform their mandates; (3) investment – in physical and capital projects; (4) studies – to prepare future projects (AfDB 2003, 7).

The STAP experienced significant institutionalization across the continent, with the establishment of nearly 120 regional infrastructure projects in energy, transportation, water, and new information and communication technologies (NICT) (NEPAD 2010, 14). Of these projects, twenty-seven were in the energy sector, eighteen were in NICT, forty-seven were in transportation, and eleven were in the water sector (16). In terms of types of projects, fourteen were capacity-building, forty were investments, eighteen were studies, and thirty-one were for facilitation (16). Importantly, this proliferation of projects does not mean that they were able to achieve the intended levels of institutional development or implementation.

STAP Evolution Since Its Creation: Many Projects, Few Major Achievements

On three occasions, AUDA evaluated the STAP in collaboration with the AfDB: in 2003, in 2004, and in 2009–2010. The 2010 evaluation noted disappointing implementation and lower-than-expected results (NEPAD 2010, 2): Of the 103 projects examined since the 2004 evaluation, only sixteen had been implemented, and seventy-three others had made relatively little progress. Further, no new projects in the capacity-building area had been adopted. These shortcomings can be explained by limited financing, insufficiently structured institutional mechanisms, the ambiguity inherent in project definitions and the division of responsibilities, limited resources, and political and environmental capacities and constraints. The fact that several of the projects initiated were not monitored (there is no information on their development), either by NEPAD or by the subregions charged with their ownership and implementation, illustrates the effective limitations of STAP/NEPAD. Against expectations, the private sector did not spontaneously finance the STAP's infrastructure projects, initially estimated at US$7.13 billion (UN 2006, 2).

In spite of modest advances in several programs,[25] only five out of twenty-seven projects have been fully implemented in the energy sector (NEPAD 2010, 3); two out of eighteen in the information and communications technology sector (5); eight of forty-seven in the transportation sector (7); and none in the sector of transborder water.

One of the major challenges for the STAP is the weakness of its processes for decision-making and implementation. Similar to the programs previously analyzed, AUDA's main role in the STAP is to facilitate, conduct studies, work on capacity-building, and occasionally provide investment. It is thus not surprising that regional economic commissions have occasionally lost interest in certain projects, to the point of failing to monitor them for as long as four years (NEPAD 2010, 7). Better collaboration among AUDA, subregional institutions, and member countries, both in terms of development and implementation, could improve institutions' functioning and increase members' involvement in and appropriations of projects. Furthermore, the programs seem to have been formulated without sufficient consideration of the factors identified by Richard E. Matland[26] as necessary for successful implementation: institutional capacities, financial resources, human and technical resources, the strength of coalitions, and the political context.

Program for Infrastructure Development in Africa (PIDA)

PIDA emerged in 2009 as a project of the African Union Commission, the NEPAD Secretariat, and the AfDB to achieve three main goals: establish a framework to expand African infrastructure, establish an infrastructure investment program, and prepare implementation strategies and processes (AfDB 2009, 4). PIDA aimed to address five main

[25] Between 50% and 80% of projects have progressed, depending on the sector, which means that 20%–50% did not develop at all between 2004 and 2009.
[26] Matland (1995) identifies various factors that condition the success or failure of policies.

Table 5.4 *Stage of PIDA PAP (2012–2020) implementation (2015)*[27]

Stage	Number of Programs	Total Cost (US$ millions)
S1: early concept proposal	8	17,251
S1/S2: in between	1	Not available
S2 : feasibility/needs assessment	14	20,242.5
S2/S3: in between	1	2,150
S2 to S4: in between	1	150
S3: program/project structuring and promotion to obtain financing	11	6,588
S3/S4: in between	11	22,170
S4: implementation and operation	4	8,160
Total	51	76,711.5

Source: World Economic Forum (2015), calculated by the author.

weaknesses in previous frameworks (i.e., STAP), including "incomplete information," "inadequate causal analysis," "lack of politically accepted and technically justified priorities," "poor implementation," and "[lack of] regulatory frameworks and incentives" (AfDB 2009, 4–5). In 2012, at the sixteenth summit of African heads of state and government, PIDA was ratified as a fully fledged framework for infrastructure development.

Implementing the PIDA PAP, a collection of fifty-one backbone projects slated for completion before 2020, are estimate to require US $68 billion (initial estimates), with US$40.3 billion allocated to energy sector development. As of 2015, some progress was made (Table 5.4), but it remains unlikely that the PIDA PAP will be fully implemented by 2020.

To implement all of the intended PIDA programs and projects by 2040, a total of US$360 billion is required, and most of these sources of investment were initially expected to come from the private sector (NEPAD et al. 2012). However, the UN (UN 2014b, 7) remarks that portfolio flows are highly volatile, with few investors having the

---

[27] Out of a total of fifty-one PIPA PAP programs, fifteen are in the energy sector, twenty-four in the transport sector, nine in the transboundary water resource sector, and three in the ICT sector.

capacity to invest in long-term infrastructure projects. Instead, investment often passes through financial intermediaries with short-term incentives. China's investments in Africa's infrastructure seem to have relatively longer-term interests, and additional sources of financing have been proposed by PIDA, such as loan guarantees that have been offered for other projects by the Development Bank of South Africa (DBSA); community levies, such as those implemented by ECOWAS; and partnerships with BRICS nations (Brazil, Russia, India, China, and South Africa), such as the New Development Bank (NEPAD et al. 2012).

Still, PIDA's ability to meet its financing goals remains uncertain. Some initiatives such as the Dakar Financing Summit were launched to secure financing for Africa's infrastructure transformation. Many resources will need to be mobilized by individual countries, which were able to commit US$14 billion to infrastructure development in 2010 (NEPAD et al. 2012), as well as from public–private partnerships. Despite figures put forth by the initial PIDA report, Nicholas C. Niggli and Kodjo Osei-Lah (2014, 20, 23) quote substantially higher figures for the level of investment required – between US$80 billion and US$93 billon per year. Moreover, they identify a US$30 billion - US$40 billion annual funding gap: "These funding gaps, then, threaten the overall viability, success and timely delivery of the programme, with adverse implications for reaching the critical 'tipping points' of infrastructure and services needed for Africa's economic transformation," they remark (Niggli and Osei-Lah 2014, 23–24). Achievement of the PAP alone requires filling a financing gap of US$37 billion, almost equivalent to the entirety of energy sector development projects (Niggli and Osei-Lah 2014, 23).

PIDA relies on regional economic communities (RECs) to be responsible for monitoring and implementing projects, just as with the STAP (NEPAD et al. 2012, 8). However, PIDA is different insofar as it depends on the increasing responsibility of leadership at the national level. Specifically, PIDA calls upon heads of state and government to take on the role of integration as a way of encouraging local ownership (NEPAD et al. 2012).

Along these lines, the AU Assembly endorsed the PICI in January 2011, an initiative proposed by the former South African President Jacob Zuma in order to accelerate development of the most pressing infrastructure projects by selecting presidents to champion a project.

As explained in the 2015 PICI report, "the role of the champions is to bring visibility, unblock bottlenecks, co-ordinate resource mobilization and ensure project implementation. It presents the opportunity for African Heads of State and Government to be actively involved in the development and implementation of projects" (NEPAD Agency 2015b, 6). The presidents of Algeria, Egypt, Kenya, Nigeria, Republic of Congo, Rwanda, Senegal, and South Africa are currently championing regional projects under the PICI.[28] Given its successful implementation, PICI reports that the project led by President Kagame of Rwanda, Unblocking Political Bottlenecks for ICT Broadband and Optic Fibre Projects Linking Neighbouring States, is "a classic example of the success of the PICI and the dedication of its project champions. All the five countries of the East African Community are fully connected via optic fibre and President Paul Kagame has commenced with a second phase of this project through the SMART Africa Initiative" (NEPAD Agency 2015b, 22).

In general, the significance of PICI lies in the new dynamic of accountability and ownership it hopes to bring to the continent through the implementation of infrastructure projects. Designated leaders are expected to report on their progress and be accountable for results, although the individual projects will vary in terms of magnitude and the speed of implementation. The presidents of Algeria and Rwanda have made by far the most progress to date.

This section teaches us that coordination, compliance, and accountability are elusive in Africa's continental development organizations, but not impossible. To conclude this chapter, let us note that AUDA seems to perceive itself as going through a process of long-term

---

[28] The projects are Missing Links on the Trans-Sahara Highway and the Optic Fibre Link between Algeria and Nigeria via Niger by President Abdelaziz Bouteflika of Algeria; the Nigeria-Algeria Gas Pipeline Project (Trans-Sahara Gas Pipeline) by President Muhammadu Buhari of Nigeria; the Dakar-Ndjamena-Djbouti Road/Rail Project by President Macky Sall of Senegal; the North-South Corridor Road/Rail Project by President Jacob Zuma of South Africa (succeeded by President Cyril Ramaphosa in 2018); the Kinshasa-Brazzaville Bridge Road/Rail Project by President Denis Sassou Nguesso of the Republic of Congo; Unblocking Political Bottlenecks for ICT Broadband and Optic Fibre Projects Linking Neighbouring States by President Paul Kagame of Rwanda; Construction of Navigational Line between Lake Victoria and the Mediterranean Sea by President Abdel Fattah el-Sisi of Egypt; and the Lamu Port Southern Sudan-Ethiopia Transport Corridor Project by President Uhuru Kenyatta of Kenya.

institutional development. Its "vision" is probably the element that has received the most support at both the international and continental levels.[29] However, despite some success stories and overall progress, an analysis of some of NEPAD's key programs – the African Peer Review Mechanism, the Comprehensive Africa Agriculture Development Program, the Short-Term Action Plan, and PIDA – shows mixed results and demonstrates that AUDA still has a long way to go if it hopes to reach full and successful implementation. These programs have faced many challenges, including a complex and overlapping institutional configuration,[30] unrealistic mandates and targets,[31] insufficient funding and capacity, occasionally hostile political contexts, and limited participation by the national or subregional actors charged with implementing them.

These challenges are not uniform, and some programs are performing better than others. Initiatives such as the PICI seem to demonstrate the ability of AUDA's leadership to innovate in creating accountability mechanisms at country levels to champion regional infrastructure initiatives. However, this model cannot be generalized to all types of programs and projects, and broader institutional configurations and reforms allowing this type of outcome would determine AUDA's ability to affect development outcomes.

In terms of interstate cooperation, this chapter has shown that states cooperate through AUDA initiatives under conditions of quasi-anarchy, to a certain degree, because they have shared values. However, they also cooperate in order to achieve individual and collective gains, which would be impossible without such collaboration. The notions of shared values and identities are more relevant in the case of the APRM. Leaders engaging in the APRM process do not systematically foresee an immediate tangible or material gain, yet at the same time, they are not substantially constrained if they fail to abide by their commitments. The lack of meaningful enforcement in case of noncompliance facilitates cooperation among African states through

---

[29] This is not surprising since AUDA draws on existing programs.

[30] Several of its programs are not equipped with sufficient incentives or coercive/restrictive institutional mechanisms to guide actors' behavior in the intended direction.

[31] Excessively ambitious, AUDA develops projects and programs that do not sufficiently account for its capacities or resources, or those of its local and subregional partners that are charged with implementing them.

continental or regional organizations. In the case of APRM, leaders have the potential to learn from one another and build a supportive community of peers (such as the APR Forum constituted of heads of state and of government), even if performances to date are varied. Coercion, should it exist, could therefore be perceived as ideational, with the logic of appropriateness and acceptance or rejection by peers, rather than as material or tangible, with significantly dissuasive sanctions.

The materialist or strategic idea of collaborating in order to achieve mutual gains is more obvious in the cases of the CAADP and PIDA. For PIDA, motivations are both ideational and material. In fact, building continental infrastructures would not only help achieve the ideal of continental integration and fundamental values promoted in the ideologies of pan-Africanism and an African renaissance, but would also increase economic opportunities and contribute to development. It is impossible for a given country to achieve such an ambitious continental infrastructure goal without cooperating with other countries and joining efforts to secure resources (financial, technical, human, administrative, coordination, etc.). Moreover, even if some countries seeking to be connected at subregional or continental levels were able to complete their national commitments to infrastructural development, they would still need to cooperate with other states in order to facilitate the cross-border movement of goods and people. In other words, it is almost impossible to build continental infrastructure without the cooperation of most, if not all, of the relevant countries, which helps explain why countries choose to join. It is in both their individual and collective interests, helping to realize their ideal of having an integrated continent where people and goods can easily move from one state or subregion to another.

The case of the CAADP is slightly different from that of PIDA, because countries can achieve their own goals with limited collaboration from others. In such a context, interstate cooperation is mostly driven by self-interest. In fact, the CAADP is an internationally recognized and broadly (even if not sufficiently) supported initiative. Both continental and international players perceive it as the tool to develop African agriculture and tend to provide more resources to the countries engaged in its implementation. These resources include much-needed technical support and access to financial resources. Unless a given leader already has the capacity to mobilize these resources independently, it is in his best interest to be involved in the CAADP process, especially given that there are no meaningful sanctions for noncompliance. Cooperating through AUDA and CAADP therefore allows countries to find common solutions to individual problems without enduring constraining consequences for noncompliance.

Ultimately, whether countries are motivated to cooperate because of shared values, self-interest, or both, the increasingly generalized national adoption of continental policies may, over the long run, contribute to a greater harmonization of values and interests, and thereby advance continental integration.

6 Financing Africa's Development in the Twenty-First Century

Assessment and Perspectives of AUDA's Resource Mobilization Strategy

To achieve its growth target and poverty reduction goals in its initial attempts to meet the MDGs by 2015, NEPAD, now AUDA, developed a resource mobilization strategy (initially aiming at facilitating the mobilization of US$64 billion per year for the continent) consisting of two main initiatives: the Capital Flows Initiative (CFI) and the Market Access Initiative (MAI). The CFI primarily aims to increase domestic resource mobilization, official development assistance (ODA), and private capital flows while seeking "the extension of debt relief beyond its current levels" (NEPAD 2001). The MAI focuses on the removal of nontariff barriers, the diversification of production, and the promotion of the private sector, African exports, and specific sectorial activities.

Although notable efforts have helped increase financial flows to Africa, AUDA has failed to reach its financial targets. Why did AUDA struggle to successfully implement its initial mobilization strategy and secure the necessary funding between 2001 and 2015? What can we learn from AUDA's experience on financing innovation and development in Africa? The goals of this chapter are to understand the ways in which AUDA's resource mobilization strategy evolved and to identify the critical differences between the initial strategy, its effects, and new strategic orientations. The chapter also aims to explain the barriers to and facilitators of the implementation of strategies to mobilize resources in complex African and international contexts, with the goal of improving the implementation process and informing future policy innovation and development.

Basing the analysis on policy implementation theories, especially Matland's (1995) ambiguity-conflict analytical and predictive model (presented in section 2), and international political economy perspectives, this chapter illustrates that NEPAD (now AUDA) was unable to successfully implement its resource mobilization strategy given a complex political-economic context (Bates 1981; Signé 2011; van de Walle

2001). The failure can be attributed to the symbolic nature of implementing the strategy, which would have required a strong coalition to overcome two issues: high levels of policy ambiguity, stemming from overly ambitious programs and problems with underlying assumptions, and high levels of political conflict. This conflict occurred at multiple levels and was exacerbated by the lack of local ownership and appropriation at the national, subregional, and (until recently) continental levels and by divergent interests with some leaders in the international community. Under these circumstances, reducing the degree of ambiguity and conflict while refining the resource mobilization strategy in the post-2015 development context appears to be the best strategy for success.

The first sections of this chapter present the analytical framework, concluding with a broad presentation of the components, potential, and limits of NEPAD's initial resource mobilization strategy (the Capital Flows and Market Access initiatives). The chapter then focuses on the implementation processes and inputs, identifying and discussing some of the key activities, actions, and programs developed or completed from 2001 to 2016 and exploring whether they were implemented according to the initial strategies. The chapter then evaluates the implementation outcomes or outputs, assessing the evolution of domestic and external resource mobilization in Africa since the creation of AUDA and analyzing differences between intentions, implementation, and accomplishments. The goal is to better understand the factors that influence implementation and the reasons that activities conducted under the AUDA framework have not resulted in the anticipated outcomes. The final sections discuss NEPAD's (now AUDA's) evolving resource mobilization strategy, highlighting the new orientation of its leadership, before concluding with remaining challenges and contributions to Africa's development.

Analytical Considerations

Theories of implementation define the analytical framework of this chapter. Top-down policy implementation models (Mazmanian and Sabatier 1989; Pressman and Wildavski 1984) provide an authoritative starting point to identify the traceability of the problem and structure for implementation, as well as the nonstatutory variables affecting implementation. Such models advise clear and consistent goals, limit the extent of change required place the responsibility for implementation on an agency sympathetic with the policy's goals, and regularly neglect prior context and political aspects, as if the implementation process were merely a matter of administrative implementation dependent solely on the availability of resources. Bottom-up policy implementation models (Maynard Moody et al. 1990), instead, view policy from the perspective of the target population and the service deliverers. These models are based on the belief that central decision-making is poorly adapted to local conditions and that flexibility is important to reach goals. However, they are often critiqued as overemphasizing local autonomy and favoring administrative accountability rather than democratic processes and policy leaders' ability to structure local behaviors.

In contrast to these divergent, dogmatic approaches, the comprehensive framework used here is Matland's policy conflict and ambiguity model. Matland systematizes the policy implementation process by connecting levels of policy conflict and policy ambiguity. Policy "conflict" is based on a conception of humans as rational and self-interested in decision-making – traits that result in conflict when interests regularly diverge. Policy "ambiguity" occurs when the goals or means related to a policy are too often lack clarity. When the levels of conflict and ambiguity are low, implementation is administrative and will be successful if sufficient resources are available. When the levels of conflict and ambiguity are high, implementation is symbolic and success depends on the strength of the coalition. When conflict is high and ambiguity low, the implementation is political, and political power is a prerequisite to successful implementation. Finally, when conflict is low and ambiguity high, the implementation is experimental and depends on contextual conditions (see Table 6.1).

To reach the aforementioned research goal, I examine both qualitative and quantitative data.

AUDA's Resource Mobilization Strategy: Capital Flows and Market Access

NEPAD (now AUDA) envisioned two avenues for resource mobilization to fill a US$64 billion (12 percent GDP) annual gap between 2000 and 2015 in order to achieve the 7 percent growth target required to meet the International Development Goals (IDGs): the CFI and the MAI. Although both initiatives are presented, this chapter focuses on the CFI.

Table 6.1 *AUDA ambiguity-conflict matrix: Policy implementation process*

	Low Conflict	High Conflict
Low ambiguity	Administrative implementation (Resources)	Political implementation (Power)
	• Infrastructures • Education • Health • Agriculture • Energy • NICT	• Political governance • Economic governance
High ambiguity	Experimental implementation (Contextual conditions) • AUDA at national levels	Symbolic implementation (Coalition strength) • Resource mobilization

Source: Matrix from Matland, adapted to AUDA implementation by Signé.

Capital Flows Initiative

The CFI can be subdivided into four components: increasing domestic resource mobilization, obtaining debt relief, reforming official development assistance, and undertaking reforms to increase private capital flows.

Domestic resource mobilization centers on capturing untapped resources from within, specifically creating more efficacious tax policies. Relatedly, AUDA has acknowledged that producing conditions conducive to encouraging private sector investment is necessary in order to reverse capital flight (NEPAD 2001, 37). According to Hakim Ben Hammouda and Patrick N. Osakwe (2006), Africa faces two major challenges in mobilizing resources: first, dependence on the export of commodities with highly volatile prices, which causes instability and unpredictability in public budgeting; and second, an inability to raise tax revenues without further increasing the level of tariffs on which the continent already heavily depends.

AUDA also called for debt relief, with the goal of linking fiscal-revenue-proportioned relief with poverty reduction outcomes. To this end, the organization proposed an agreement to be signed by heads of state and government and negotiated with the international community to provide further debt relief to states that participate in the AUDA Economic Governance Initiative. When necessary, this conditional aid agreement would supplement existing channels of debt relief, such as those established through the Paris Club and HIPC initiative. Further, an intracontinental forum was established for discussing strategies for effective governance and qualification.

A major priority of AUDA is to reach unified strategies for achieving common goals. AUDA sought to establish a forum to "develop a common African position on ODA reform (NEPAD 2001, 39)." Donors such as the Development Assistance Committee (DAC) of the OECD come together to form a bilateral partnership with Africa. To effectively utilize ODA flows, AUDA set up working groups, such as the Poverty Reduction Strategy Paper (PRSP) Learning Group, with the assistance of organizations such as the United Nations Economic Commission for Africa (UNECA). To ensure best practices, AUDA also recommended an "independent mechanism for assessing donor and recipient country performance." According to Hammouda and Osakwe (2006), ODA flows have been crucial to development in Africa. In 2004, ODA to the sub-Saharan region totaled US$26 billion.

As a long-term approach, AUDA looked to increase private capital flows (Table 6.2). While it acknowledged that time is necessary for success, several priorities were listed, including the development of a public-private partnership (PPP) capacity-building program through the AfDB and the establishment of a Financial Market Integration Task Force.

Market Access Initiative

AUDA couples the CFI with the MAI, which aims to increase the base of exports, diversify production, and develop greater opportunities for Africa to engage in value-adding industries. Emphasizing economic diversification, the MAI was intended to focus on assisting the informal sector, microenterprises, and small- and medium-sized businesses. Given the critical importance of a conducive business environment to reduce the cost of doing business and facilitate market access, AUDA called upon governments to act, in this case to "remove constraints on business activity and encourage the creative talents of African entrepreneurs" (NEPAD 2001, 37).

Table 6.2 *The Capital Flows Initiative*

Resources	Origin
Increasing domestic resource mobilization	• National savings • Tax collection • Rationalization of government expenditures • Ending capital flight • Creation of special drawing rights for Africa
Debt relief	• Systematic debt relief extension • Indexation with poverty reduction outcomes • Debt relief secured by NEPAD's heads of state for participating countries
ODA reforms	• Increase flow • Improve the efficiency of ODA • Support PRSP with IMF and WB • Tools: Forum, ECA, assessment of donors and recipients, support for multilateral initiatives
Private capital flow	• Change investors' perception of Africa • Increase Public-Private Sectors Partnership

Source: NEPAD 2001.

The MAI established sectorial priorities in agriculture, mining, manufacturing, tourism, and services. For agriculture, specifically, improved productivity was to come through supporting small-scale and female farmers (NEPAD 2001, 41), and increased investment was viewed as necessary to ensure food security. AUDA envisioned Africa as a net exporter of agricultural products and a pioneer in the development of agriscience and technology. To achieve these goals, several elements of intracontinental reform would be necessary: the supply of water must be enhanced through local water management or irrigation facilities, governments must reform the land tenure system, access to credit should be expanded, and government spending in urban areas must be reduced so that spending in rural areas can be increased (NEPAD 2001, 42). Internationally, AUDA reiterates the need to form partnerships, particularly in enabling access to and the transfer of technical skills and expertise and also in learning from other developing countries and counteracting donor fatigue.

In the mining sector, AUDA highlights as key objectives improving mineral resource information flows, developing a business-friendly regulatory framework, and establishing best practices. At the intracontinental level, harmonizing commitments, policies, and regulations can ensure compliance with at least the minimum level of organizational practices while reducing investment risk. Collaboration is necessary to enforce principles of value-addition to natural resources (NEPAD 2001, 43).

Manufacturing is closely tied to the mining and agricultural sectors, particularly when promoting value-addition. Necessary reforms include pursuing membership in international standards organizations and establishing national standards and testing facilities. International standards accreditation infrastructure should be developed regionally whenever possible, so that nations and their international trading partners can share and mutually validate the recognition of results. Internationally, AUDA recommends adopting a framework to balance compliance between the WTO Technical Barriers to Trade agreement and African needs. Facilitating partnerships depends on greater information sharing, particularly with non-African firms, which can be accomplished through the development of organizations such as joint business councils.

The MAI also identified the long-term promotion of exports and the private sector as crucial to development. Again, AUDA stressed that organizations such as chambers of commerce ought to be strengthened, along with the establishment of other entrepreneurial development programs. Simultaneously, NEPAD called for renewed political action to reinvigorate stalled integration initiatives, focusing especially on consideration of a "discretionary preferential trade system" (NEPAD 2001, 46) within the continent and the "alignment of domestic and regional trade and industrial policy objectives" (NEPAD 2001, 46).

Implementation Input and Process: AUDA's Mobilization and Facilitation Efforts

In order to successfully implement its resource mobilization strategy, AUDA has initiated a series of activities, actions, programs, and partnerships, which are grouped here in two categories: strategic activities and partnerships, and development frameworks and sectorial programs. While the strategic activities create the necessary conditions for successfully mobilizing resources, both domestic and international, the development frameworks and sectorial programs are policies that require funding for successful implementation.

Strategic Activities and Partnerships

Three strategic activities aiming to create conditions for better govern-ance and trust of international partners, which are likely to increase domestic resource mobilization, are presented here: the APRM, the mobilization of international support, and the development of partner-ships with NGOs and the private sector.

APRM: Creation of a Conducive Environment

As discussed in Chapter 5, the APRM was established in 2003 by the AU as part of the AUDA framework to ensure adherence by member countries to political, economic, and corporate governance policies. Each member of the AU voluntarily chooses to participate in the APRM, which requires that the country contribute US$100,000 annu-ally to fund the program since it does not rely on external partners (APRM and AU 2012, 23). As part of this initiative, periodic reviews are diligently conducted in five stages (NEPAD 2003).

To date, there have been concerns around some aspects of the APRM. First, the process is not fully transparent. Country-level self-assessments are not always made public; because of this, and despite a participatory process for data collection, few citizens may ever see how their country frames their assessment. Even groups such as UNECA are not given access to all documents (Odeh and Mailafia 2013, 88). Moreover, NPoAs under APRM act as a separate development stra-tegic plan rather than as a targeted list of priorities (AfriMAP 2010).

Within countries, the transparency of the peer-review procedure varies. In Rwanda, for example, government-appointed officials dom-inate the APRM commission, while Benin's APRM commission had only one government official as vice-chair and mostly comprised leaders of civil society organizations (Tungwarara 2010, 10). In Algeria, the government appointed an autonomous, technical review body, which was intended to provide an objective evaluation.

Finally... There is little force behind the APRM, since signatories can easily opt out of the process and the AU lacks the ability to compel participation (Ebegbulem, Adams, and Achu 2012, 275). Ultimately, after conducting a meta-analysis of nine country-specific meta-analyses by separate authors (in AfriMAP 2010), Ozias Tungwarara (2010) concludes that the APRM has generally been dominated by government interests and needs substantial revision.

Mobilizing International Support

According to the NEPAD Secretariat (2004), there was substantial initial progress in moving toward the goals outlined in the 2001 founding document in AUDA's early years.. At first, the main priority was to promulgate the NEPAD (now AUDA) framework as widely as possible in order to obtain institutional buy-in, particularly from international donors. The UN passed a resolution in November 2002 recognizing AUDA as the "framework for engagement with Africa" (United Nations General Assembly 2002), ending the era of the UN New Agenda for the Development of Africa (UN-NADAF) adopted in 1991. As a result, all UN agencies were required to realign and coordinate their programs with AUDA. Within the UN and other intergovernmental organizations, there was evidence of a shift in policy. In April 2003, UN Secretary-General Kofi Annan established the Office of the Special Adviser on Africa (OSAA) with the stated mandate of "coordinating global advocacy in support of NEPAD" and "acting as the focal point for NEPAD within the United Nations Secretariat" (Annan 2003). After the presentation of NEPAD by African leaders at the 2001 G8 summit in Genoa, Italy, representatives of the G8 countries prepared the G8 Africa Action plan, which was presented and accepted at the following year's summit in Kananaskis, Canada.

The renewed commitment to development by wealthy countries was backed by tangible increases in development assistance for the first time in decades. In 2002, at the Financing for Development conference in Monterrey, Mexico, a commitment was made to increase assistance by US$12 billion (NEPAD Secretariat 2004, 63). Later, in Kananaskis, half of the increase was announced as designated for Africa. Moreover, despite a downward trend in external development assistance to Africa in the 1990s, 2001–2002 saw an increase from US$16.2 billion to US$22.2 billion (NEPAD Secretariat 2004, 63; AfDB 2005). Tangible commitments also appeared across various sectors. The WB committed US$500 million toward agricultural research and technology development. African governments agreed to gradually increase investment in agriculture to 10 percent of their national budgets. As of mid-2004, nine infrastructure projects identified by the STAP received funding totaling US$580 million from the AfDB.

More recently, the AUDA initiative has provided countries with the connections to form more narrowly tailored partnerships. For example, South Africa's leadership role in AUDA led to collaboration between their Public Administration Leadership and Management Academy (PALMS) and Japan's International Cooperation Agency (JICA) to offer management-training programs to facilitate South-South cooperation (Honda et al. 2013, 369).

In addition, two other current sources may provide meaningful opportunities to Africans: the New Development Bank (NDB) of the BRICS nations and the OPEC Fund for International Development (OFID). These sources offer balanced alternatives and complements to other sources.

Developing Partnerships with the Private Sector, NGOs, and African Organizations

The African Union Development Agency has partnered with numerous other entities to implement its development vision. Many of the projects associated with NEPAD (now AUDA) actually originated elsewhere and were co-opted. For example, the AfDB is a key AUDA partner and has disproportionately contributed to almost all of AUDA's successes. In 2007, the AfDB had already financed over 200 multinational projects across Africa, including CAADP projects, STAP projects, and the IPFF. After evaluating the outcomes of financed projects, the AfDB found that guidelines and regional frameworks were lacking and were the main reason that only 53 percent of financed projects were deemed satisfactory (Martin 2007, 480).

NEPAD continues to promote the partnership concept as a means of development, yet most partnerships formed are not African-owned. For example, in March 2005, a forum was hosted in South Africa examining the contributions of the private sector. In November 2007, a group of experts organized by OSAA met in New York to discuss concerns about the private sector's response to AUDA (OSAA 2008, 10). In 2012 promoting PPPs became central to the majority of initiatives promoted by AUDA; even then, most initiatives alluded to participation with global private partners (see NEPAD Planning and Coordination Agency, and African Union 2012, 28, 56).

The OSAA lays out serious challenges to private sector involvement in AUDA. The NEPAD Planning and Coordinating Agency (NPCA) was called upon to reverse an "abysmal lack of awareness about NEPAD in organized business in South Africa," which makes sense given the external focus of the first eight years of NEPAD (OSAA 2008, 13). Moreover, in West Africa, no programs existed to promote AUDA among private sector associations, and in most regions, there was no promotion of AUDA projects whatsoever (OSAA 2008, 13).

Development Frameworks and Sectorial Activities

AUDA has developed various frameworks and programs to accelerate resource mobilization and the successful implementation of its strategy in key development sectors: the MAI; the CAADP; the Infrastructure STAP; the PIDA; the AU-NEPAD Capacity Development Strategic Framework (CDSF); the Framework for Engendering NEPAD and Regional Economic Communities; and the AU-NEPAD Health Strategy. The contribution of these programs to NEPAD's (AUDA's) resource mobilization strategy is further discussed later in this chapter.

Market Access Initiative

The MAI highlights the importance of diversifying production and increasing value-added processes, as well as increasing levels of trade across the continent (NEPAD Secretariat 2001, 40). Figure 6.1 shows the value-added growth rates across sectors for developing countries in Africa. It shows that annual growth in manufacturing, industry, agricultural, and services has increased only slightly in the NEPAD era. Overall, NEPAD's success has been marginal at best (Figure 6.2).

Comprehensive Africa Agriculture Development Program

As presented in the previous chapter, the CAADP was designed to fulfill the requirements of eliminating poverty, hunger, and malnutrition, and aligns well with the MAI with regard to the agricultural sector. The CAADP aimed to accelerate the annual agricultural productivity growth rate to six percent by 2015, with technical support from AUDA, and called upon country governments to allocate 10 percent

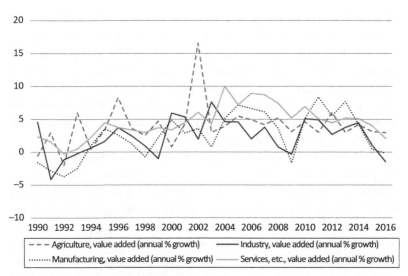

Figure 6.1 Value-added sectorial growth rate for developing countries in sub-Saharan Africa, 1990–2016 (%)

Source: World Bank national accounts data and OECD National Accounts data files. Annual growth rate for sector value added based on constant local currency. Aggregate for developing countries in sub-Saharan Africa based on constant 2010 US$.

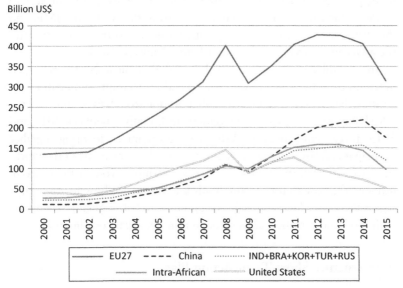

Figure 6.2 Trade flows in Africa with selected partners, 2000–2015 (billion, US$)
Source: AfDB et al. 2017.

of their budgets to the promotion of agriculture. The CAADP had numerous procedural milestones for participating countries: engagement in the preparation and signing of the CAADP compact; a joint commitment by the stakeholders; the drafting and technical review of the National Agriculture and Food Security Investment Plans (NAFSIPs); a business meeting in which stakeholders should endorse and commit to funding; and implementation, including the monitoring and updating of the plan (Dufour et al. 2013).

While the CAADP has proved moderately successful in implementing its policies, several priorities have been neglected. For example, although 70 percent of Africans rely on agriculture for employment, AUDA did not impose binding commitments on signatories nor any substantive guidance on how to reform the underlying problems related to development within the sector, such as land ownership and tenure rules (Chibundu 2008). Moreover, one should be careful not to misconstrue successful metrics, such as agricultural growth, as evidence of change in line with the goals of AUDA, since these indicators sometimes fail to distinguish between commercial agribusiness and small-scale farmers. Ultimately, elements of the CAADP, such as the promotion of new irrigation technologies, were more likely to produce partnerships between the state and foreign capital to increase export crops than to help rural farmers. For example, the Geriza irrigation project in Sudan, which received financial support from the AfDB, the IMF, and the WB, ended up turning indigenous farmers into paid laborers after the government expropriated their land (Omoweh 2004).

An unpublished report in 2011 found that most NAFSIPs lacked nutrition objectives and recommended actions to improve nutrition. As a result, the AU and AUDA, with collaboration from RECs, launched the CAADP Nutrition Capacity Development Initiative. Between 2011 and 2013, three subregional workshops were organized to bring together participants from fourteen to eighteen countries. The goals of the workshop were to increase understanding of nutrition's role in the CAADP framework, how to use existing tools and resources, how to strengthen regional/country-level frameworks, and how to better align policy issues with food and nutrition aims through multisectoral coordination.

Infrastructure Short-Term Action Plan

As presented in Chapter 5, the STAP was launched to create regional infrastructure in the energy, ICT, and water sectors. Initially, approximately 120 projects fell under the STAP umbrella, but by 2009, the number had decreased to 103. AUDA was specifically tasked with facilitating the mobilization of resources for projects, including financial capital (NEPAD 2010, 15).

The 2010–2015 NPCA business plan notes that the STAP has been successful at promoting the NEPAD (now AUDA) brand, fostering greater understanding about NEPAD, and spurring some RECs to attempt to implement projects under NEPAD (NEPAD Planning and Coordination Agency 2010, 9). However, the STAP has been unsuccessful at actually implementing projects. The 2010 review of STAP projects found that only sixteen projects had been completed since the launch of the program, a number identified as "below expectations" (NEPAD 2010, 2). Some STAP projects were already under development prior to the initiative's existence; thus, "it would be a bit disingenuous to state that the private sector got involved in these initiatives *because* of the NEPAD process" (UNECA 2012, 52). The 2010 review committee noted that reasons for the slow progress range from "financing constraints, inadequate mechanisms in project monitoring, [and] projects not being sharply defined." Many RECs had little knowledge of how the projects were developing, particularly those focused on facilitation and capacity-building (NEPAD 2010, 19). One evaluation shows that even though many projects obtained funding, relatively few progressed beyond this stage, particularly in the energy sector.

The 2010 STAP review cited numerous challenges and explanations for its underperformance. Lack of financing is noted nine times within the document, which is unsurprising considering the funding gap of US$23 billion per year (NEPAD 2010, 43). In particular, the NEPAD Secretariat has been unable to mobilize domestic financing, relying on donor support for successful projects (NEPAD 2010, 154). Of the issues with STAP energy projects, three of four of the "severe impact" constraints were at least partially attributable to the NEPAD Secretariat, which was identified throughout the review as having failed to prepare projects, mobilize political support, define roles and responsibilities, and define project frameworks (NEPAD 2010, 124–25).

Program for Infrastructure Development in Africa

PIDA is the framework for infrastructure development in Africa, jointly created by the AU and AUDA, as discussed in Chapter 5.

AU-NEPAD Capacity Development Strategic Framework (CDSF)

The AU-NEPAD CDSF was launched in 2010 in an attempt to integrate capacity development goals across sectors, countries, and regions within Africa. In particular, the CDSF sought to encourage a "culture of responsibility" and awareness of the varying elements of capacity-building, such as the incentives needed to create "constituencies of expertise within ... Africa" (NPCA and AU 2012, 10). To date, the CDSF has been the launchpad for several subinitiatives, such as the Africa Platform for Development Effectiveness. The CDSF also helped to facilitate a common African position for the 2011 Busan Aid Effectiveness Conference and to generate a series of best practices for engaging in South-South cooperation (NPCA and AU 2012, 18–19).

The CDSF was instrumental to the development of the AU-NEPAD CDSP for RECs, which hosted a series of dialogues among the RECs (such as ECOWAS), the World Bank Institute, and the UNDP, on topics ranging from trade integration and best practices for institutional development between RECs (NPCA 2012, 19). Some countries have established mechanisms by which to incorporate NEPAD (AUDA), although it remains unclear how the CDSF fits in with other capacity-building initiatives, particularly those with continent-wide ambitions (Kedir 2011, 331).

Framework for Engendering NEPAD (now AUDA) and Regional Economic Communities

NEPAD (AUDA) has been a strong proponent of the RECs, although it did not pioneer the concept in Africa. Rather, the Lagos Plan of Action (1980) and the Abuja Declaration (1991) laid the foundation for the numerous economic communities that exist today. The NEPAD framework built on these initiatives, including the "regionalization of development" as a precondition for sustainable growth (Martin 2007, 465). RECs have thrived in Africa, at least in name and number. For example, the East African Community (EAC) of Kenya, Uganda, and Tanzania led to the South African Development Community (SADC) in 1992; there is the Commission for East and Central Africa (CECA) and ECOWAS, the sixteen-state community established in 1975 (Chibundu 2008). Although numerous, the efficacy of RECs has been limited, especially beyond ECOWAS. The secretariats of the RECs in question "lack the capacity to promote and facilitate the preparation and implementation of multi-country projects" (NEPAD Secretariat 2004), and even among funded projects, there has been little oversight or monitoring from the RECs. Ultimately, NEPAD's implementation has been poorly coordinated, with few mechanisms for information-sharing across countries, which has likely contributed to the shortcomings of REC integration (Mutangadura 2005, 18).

RECs are central to the partnership model promoted by NEPAD (AUDA), although their benefits are hard to identify. The United Nations Economic Commission for Africa criticizes the partnerships created by AUDA thus far, remarking that relationships between AUDA components, RECs, and nations are "less than strong," making it difficult to implement the AUDA framework (UNECA 2012, 11). Other authors have commented that the REC model may not necessarily produce benefits, even in principle. For example, RECs have created additional bureaucracies, which often act as special-interest groups that resist ceding control to national entities and to the AU or AUDA. Moreover, the multiplicity of interests represented by RECs might undermine Pan-African unity, a factor exacerbated by overlapping memberships that inhibit coordination among RECs themselves and between RECs and Pan-African organizations (Da Silva 2013). Basic development practices seem to be pushed aside as RECs are adopted; for example, some political leaders have reneged on implementing free market policies in favor of more nationalist development ideologies (Mokone 2011, 11).

Ultimately, there is little incentive for RECs and countries to implement AUDA programs (UNECA 2012, 11). Even if there were, structural factors, such as access to financing, would impede success. The potential loss in tax revenues from establishing a customs union, is nonetheless a disincentive to integrate (Martin 2007, 471). Variation in creditworthiness across member countries of the same REC often prevents projects from securing financing. Moreover, an overdependence on external aid leads to numerous, overlapping layers of bureaucracy, which is particularly problematic when multiple donors requiring different conditions are involved (NPCA 2010). Often, the capacity to contribute to a project is disproportionate across REC member states, resulting in stalled projects, particularly when memberships overlap (Martin 2007, 476).

Despite the NEPAD initiative, levels of regional trade remain low both due to failures to fully implement subregional integration through the RECs. Only 12 percent of Africa's exports comprise trade of intraregional goods, less than half the rate of the Association of Southeast Asian Nations (ASEAN).

Another factor in regional trade is the treatment of local indigenous communities. The national borders, drawn during the colonial period, generally ignored local language groups, often combining many different groups within a country and separating others across state borders. The UN agreement on the Rights of Indigenous Peoples, signed by most AUDA nations, gives land rights to cultural groups and allows cross-border migration and trade.

AU-NEPAD Health Strategy

The AU-NEPAD Health Strategy was initially presented at a World Health Organization (WHO) meeting in Harare in 2002 before being subsequently revised through a peer-review process at the 2003 African Expert Consultative Meeting in Pretoria. Section seven of the strategy document (NEPAD Agency 2003) lists numerous priorities, namely creating bodies to report on the effectiveness of the strategy, combating disease, fostering health literacy, reducing pregnancy and childbirth mortality, and mobilizing resources. A development commitment goal was set of US$22 billion per year, presumably meant to come from external partners (NEPAD Agency 2003, 31).

While the concept of African ownership is consistently highlighted across all AUDA programs and initiatives, in practice it is either ignored or structurally impeded. Moreover, the health research that does occur is often problem-specific and driven by external resource availability and the interests of donors. Rather than AUDA providing frameworks, numerous other programs for health-capacity development exist. For example, the Council on Health Research for Development (COHRED) developed a model for evaluating areas that are in need of increased capacity, which ultimately developed into a partnership with AUDA and will be utilized by AUDA's African Science, Technology, and Innovation Indicator (ASTII) project (IJsselmuiden et al. 2012, 231).

The outbreak of Ebola during 2014 and 2016 has brought focus to this problem. Although Ebola was detected years ago in isolated rural

Africa, international attention was only brought to the issue when the disease finally spread to populous regions and across borders. Now substantial international funds go towards developing vaccines and extending health resources to the affected areas.

AUDA's Limited Institutional Funding

AUDA has faced serious operational limitations, both as a standalone agency and subsequently under the umbrella of the AU. For example, in 2003, AUDA received just US$3.4 million in funding from various donors. Although this figure more than doubled to US$7.6 million in 2004, AUDA began FY 2003 with a US$527,766 deficit and ended FY 2004 with a deficit that had swelled to US$1.95 million (NEPAD Secretariat 2004, 56). In 2011, AUDA remained unable to balance its budget, facing a deficit of US$1.12 million after receiving US$13.8 million in payments (NEPAD Agency 2012, 73). The deficit in contributions has resulted largely from African countries' failure to meet their obligations – in 2004 alone, they were US$2.5 million short of what they had committed (NEPAD Secretariat 2004, 57). In an effort to explain its 2011 deficit, AUDA remarked that its budget had a "heavy reliance on development partners" due to inadequate resources from African governments (NEPAD Agency 2012).

Implementation Outputs and Outcomes of the AUDA Resource Mobilization Strategy: Capital Flows Initative

Generally speaking, some improvement in Africa's condition is evident, but there is limited evidence that the AUDA framework is responsible for this improvement. Analysis of the CFI elements demonstrates that although external financial flows have increased, the average rate of GDP growth has inclined only modestly since 2001 (see Figure 6.3 and Table 6.3).

Domestic Resource Mobilization

Numerous authors have remarked on the success of developing countries in mobilizing resources at home (Bhushan 2013; Melamed and Sumner 2011; Mubiru 2010; Sachs and Schmidt-Traub 2013). This

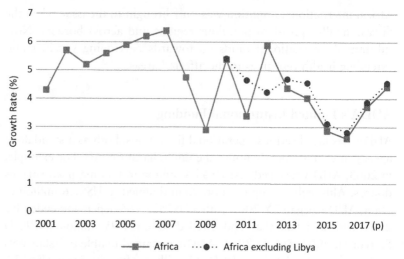

Figure 6.3 GDP growth in Africa, 2001–2018 (%)
Source: Statistics Department, AfDB 2018, 30.

success has been especially evident in tax reforms: Developing countries' tax ratio rose from 20 percent in 2000 to slightly less than 29 percent in 2011 (Greenhill and Prizzon 2012). Aniket Bhushan (2013) notes that while the majority of development financing is mobilized domestically, the poorest states are often in fragile or post-conflict situations, meaning they are unable to rely on domestic resource mobilization to close financing gaps.

In Africa, trade taxes as a component of tax revenues have generally declined since the mid-1990s, while direct taxes have increased, and the change in indirect taxes has been flat. Taxes on trade decreased slightly more than 2 percent between 2004 and 2010 in an effort to meet WTO guidelines. Direct taxation grew the most, from 20.7 percent to 24.2 percent. In Sierra Leone, a single goods and services tax (GST) was adopted in 2010, simplifying tax collection and increasing the tax base. In two years, it increased the tax share of the GDP from 11.7 percent to 14.9 percent (Elovainio and Evans 2013). While countries such as Kenya and Mauritania have a relatively balanced mix of tax types, South Africa relies on direct taxation. The trend of average tax revenues as a share of GDP has been positive since 1990, from 22 percent of GDP in 1990 to 27 percent in 2007. The tax revenue

Table 6.3 *African GDP growth, 2001–2018 (%)*

	2001	2002	2003	2004	2005	2006	2007	2008	2009	2010	2011	2012	2013	2014	2015	2016*	2017[†]	2018[†]
Africa	4.3	5.7	5.2	5.6	5.9	6.2	6.4	4.7	2.9	5.4	3.4	5.9	4.4	4.0	2.9	2.6	3.7	4.4
Africa excluding Libya										5.4	4.7	4.2	4.7	4.6	3.1	2.8	3.9	4.6

*Estimate; [†] Projection.
Source: Statistics Department, AfDB, 2018.

of the upper-middle-income countries in Africa (\$3,856 < income per capita < \$11,905 in 2008) have converged to the tax share of OECD countries (approximately 35 percent according to OECD, 2009) (Mubiru 2010). Total collected tax revenue rose from US\$137.5 billion in 2000 to US\$527 billion in 2012 (AfDB et al. 2014, 65).

Even though tax revenue now comprises more than 20 percent of regional GDP in sub-Saharan Africa, increased taxes on the resource sector have created a disconnect between resource-rich and resource-poor countries (Bhushan 2013). Preexisting low-level institutional capacity, combined with prioritizing resource-driven growth at the expense of a diversified production structure, may be undermining the development of robust institutions (Mavrotas et al. 2011). In addition, increasing revenues via resource extraction is not a reliable form of development financing, as it is prone to unpredictable fluctuations. The data demonstrate that the revenue shocks in 2008, for example, corresponded to global commodity price declines (Mubiru 2010). Problematically, resource-rich economies did not increase their tax revenues as a share of GDP at this time because increased taxation was offset by reductions in other taxes (Greenhill and Prizzon 2012). Despite the problems associated with resource extraction, some countries, such as Botswana, succeeded in utilizing tax revenue to fund public goods (Elovainio and Evans 2013). Namibia has far higher corporate taxes on resource extraction: Diamond mining is taxed at 55 percent, other mining operations at 37.5 percent, and oil and gas extraction at 35 percent (plus an additional profit tax) (Odhiambo and Ziramba 2014).

There is also significant variation in the levels of investment across African states. For example, the AfDB, OECD, and UNECA (AfDB et al. 2014, 55) highlight that Mauritius faces constraints due to its small market size, geographical isolation, and biased investment incentives. A review found that the country should focus on "clarifying legal frameworks for investment ... improving supply-side enablers ... and making more room for private investment in infrastructure markets" (AfDB et al. 2014, 55). In South Africa, institutional investment has soared, with pension assets at 60 percent of GDP, in line with many of the world's most developed countries (UN 2014b, 4). In comparison, Nigeria faces challenges in prioritizing key economic sectors and promoting an open trade policy. Within Lagos, reforms to the land title system are greatly needed in order to improve incentives for investment (AfDB et al. 2014, 56).

According to Fakile et al. (2014), trade taxes account for 30 percent of non-resource tax revenue across Africa, which points to a challenge given that the Economic Partnership Agreements (EPA) and the Doha Round of trade negotiations will require them to further slash taxes without substantially increasing their revenue base from other means (Figure 6.4).

Debt Relief

Debt relief is intended to reduce interest and principal payments in order to divert resources toward development programs. Under AUDA, the HIPC and MDRI initiatives wrote down debt for thirty-five eligible countries. Since the AUDA framework began, countries are increasingly issuing debt in local currencies, which illustrates the degree to which local capital markets have developed. Total debt issued in local currencies increased from $11 billion in 2005 to $31 billion in 2012 (UN 2014b, 13).

In financing the post-2015 agenda, the UN plans to call for an informal forum on sovereign debt restructuring, shifting implicitly away from debt relief, perhaps as a result of increasing criticism about the strategy (UN 2014c, 32–33). Various authors such as Dömeland and Kharas (2009) find that the effects of debt relief on public expenditures are limited at best (see Figure 6.5). Similarly, Chauvin and Kraay (2005, 28) find "very little in the way of significant correlations between debt relief and subsequent changes in growth, investment, total government spending, and tax collection."

Official Development Assistance

The NEPAD Secretariat (2004) noted that success depended on indus-trialized countries meeting their obligation to establish official develop-ment assistance (ODA) commitments to 0.7 percent of gross national income (GNI) under the Monterrey consensus. Despite expansive com-mitments to Africa, from 2004 to 2006 the G8 increased their ODA by less than half of the required amount. ODA to Africa in 2006 neither increased nor decreased, after declining for the first time since 1997 in 2005.

The credibility of the 0.7 percent of GNI developed-country ODA goal has been at issue for years. The goal was originally articulated in

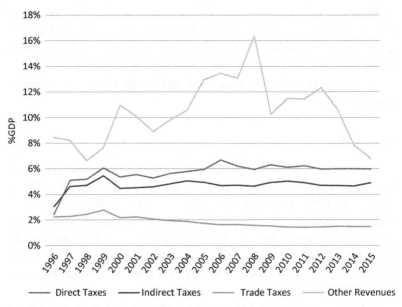

Figure 6.4 Average tax mix of countries in Africa, 1996–2015
Source: AfDB et al. 2016.

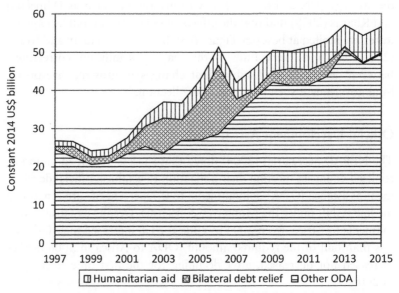

Figure 6.5 Net ODA disbursements to Africa, 1997–2015 (billion, US$)
Source: AfDB et al. 2017.

1969, but not until 2009 did aid flows begin to rise substantively, principally among EU member states, reaching 0.42 percent in 2009 (Nunnenkamp and Thiele 2013). According to the DAC, the goal of doubling aid by 2010, promised in 2005 at Gleneagles, came up US$21 billion short (Dembele 2013). In 2008, aid reached a then-historic level of US$121.5 billion (AfDB and OECD 2010), increasing to US$125 billion in 2012 (AfDB et al. 2014) and US$134.8 billion in 2013. Only five DAC donors contributed at least 0.7 percent of GNI to aid (Denmark, Luxembourg, Norway, Sweden, and the United Kingdom), with the average closer to 0.3 percent of GNI. More troubling, aid flows decreased by 2 percent to the least developed countries, with sub-Saharan Africa taking on a decrease of 4 percent in total aid to US $26.2 billion (UN 2014b, 11).

The 2008 financial crisis produced numerous changes in how developed countries address ODA. Countries are now increasingly interested in linking ODA to commercial and foreign policy incentives, seeking to harmonize their own goals (i.e., selling fighter jets) with those of developing countries (i.e., building security) and to promote private-sector development in the process (Greenhill et al. 2013).

Private Capital Flows

Amadou Sy (2014) remarks that the nature of capital flows has shifted: Private flows now supersede aid flows (see Figures 6.6 and 6.7 and Tables 6.4 and 6.5), mostly as a result of greater investment from BRICS nations, the source of 25 percent of Africa's overall foreign direct investment (FDI). Moreover, the UN (2014b, 6) suggests that South-South cooperation provides beneficial opportunities for linkages between countries with similar levels of technical capacity and skill, which could ultimately lead to improved investment. According to the UN (2014b, 6), FDI is increasingly directed toward the services and manufacturing sectors, which aligns with the founding priorities of AUDA.

Some authors are particularly concerned with the way that FDI inflows (Figure 6.6) are affecting Africa in the age of partnerships. "Some of these new arrangements could actually be exploitative – in other words, they may not be mutually beneficial. Instead, they may create opportunities for these new foreign partners to plunder Africa's resources and leave the continent essentially underdeveloped," notes Mwangi S. Kimenyi (2014, 32).

Curbing Illicit Flows

AUDA has prioritized curbing the massive rate at which capital disappears illicitly from Africa each year. Estimates vary, but the amount lost through tax evasion, illicit enterprises (e.g., drug trafficking), and corruption in developing countries overall is estimated at between US $529 billion and US$778 billion each year (WB 2013). In the developing world, sub-Saharan Africa accounted for 7 percent of global illicit flows between 2001 and 2010, which was lower than the shares of developing Asia (61 percent), the Western Hemisphere (15 percent), and the Middle East and North Africa (10 percent), and equivalent to the share of developing Europe (WB 2013). But, still, such illicit outflows of capital have a pernicious impact on development.

Moving Ahead: AUDA's Evolving Strategy

Over time, the AUDA strategy has shifted, both in terms of how resources are to be mobilized and how they are to be used. Seerp Wigboldus et al. (2011) comprehensively review development strategies between 1950 and 2010, and while their efforts do not focus specifically on AUDA, they nonetheless provide context for understanding the initiative's evolution. In the 1990s, perspectives from the new institutional school broadened the role of capacity-building efforts by looking to the sector level rather than the agency level (e.g., private, public, and NGO). Between 1990 and 2010 (the NEPAD framework development and implementation era), more attention was given to technical cooperation, local ownership and participatory approaches, results-based management, and needs assessment. From 2010 to the present, public-private partnerships have been central to development plans and frameworks, as a focus on regional integration to solve cross-border issues (Wigboldus et al. 2011, 4).

UNECA divides the AUDA framework into four distinct eras based on leadership, examining the successes, failures, and opportunities moving forward (UNECA 2012, 9–14). From 2001 to 2005, NEPAD (now AUDA) was taking its first steps under the leadership of Professor

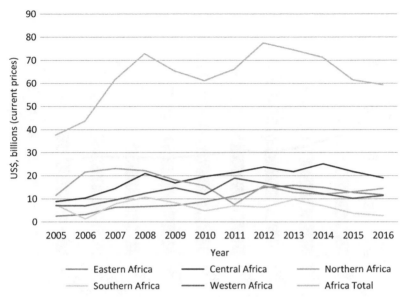

Figure 6.6 Flow of FDI to Africa, 2005–2016 (billion, US$)
Source: UNCATD FDI Statistics.

Wiseman Nkuhlu, and during this period there were numerous initial successes in the various NEPAD priority areas. Resource mobilization occurred with a primary focus on interacting with wealthy external partners, such as G8 countries, in order to increase aid flows and debt relief (UNECA 2012, 9). This external focus, however, was perceived as a top-down approach in contrast to AUDA's emphasis on African ownership.

Between 2005 and 2007, external financial support remained a key component of NEPAD's resource mobilization strategy. During that period, AUDA's financing efforts mostly focused on attracting resources from external actors, especially the WB, G8, and OECD (UNECA 2012, 12). By 2007, NEPAD had lost a substantial degree of African political capital, as some of its champions (including former President Abdoulaye Wade of Senegal) had become very critical of the limited progress that had been made.

Between 2008 and 2009, under the direction of Ambassador Olu-korede Willoughby, there were renewed efforts to integrate NEPAD into the African Union. One key conclusion drawn from the tenth

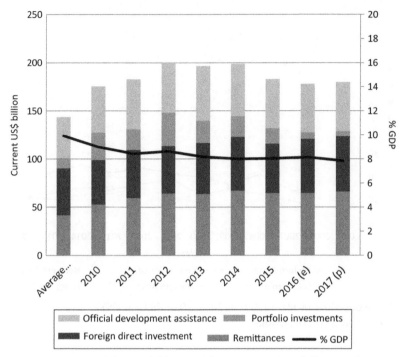

Figure 6.7 External financial flows to Africa, 2000–2017 (billion, US$)
Source: AfDB et al. 2017.

meeting of the Africa Partnership Forum in Tokyo was that reversing the lack of development between 2005 and 2008 would require greater alignment with existing development strategies, such as the Millennium Development Goals (MDGs) (UNECA 2012, 12). Since Dr. Ibrahim Mayaki took over NEPAD in 2009, the priority for financing development was still focused externally. For example, the 2012 NPCA Business Plan highlights seven initiatives under the communication, partnership, and resource mobilization section (NPCA 2012, 19); three of these explicitly focus on G8 or G20 countries, three on intracontinent cooperation, and one initiative, preparing a policy brief, on domestic resource mobilization.

As one of the key partners relied on for financing initiatives, the AfDB exerts tremendous influence over the AUDA framework. The *African Economic Outlook 2010*, an AfDB and OECD publication, was one of the first comprehensive documents to contextualize the idea that Africa shifts its sources of development finance. The report

Table 6.4 Flows of FDI to Africa, 2005–2016 (billions, current US$)

	2005	2006	2007	2008	2009	2010	2011	2012	2013	2014	2015	2016
Eastern Africa	2.6	3.2	6.3	6.7	7.1	8.8	11.2	14.9	15.9	15.0	12.8	11.7
Central Africa	8.9	10.4	14.5	21.0	16.9	19.7	21.4	23.8	21.8	25.1	21.8	19.1
Northern Africa	11.6	21.6	23.1	22.2	18.1	15.7	7.5	15.6	12.7	12.0	13.1	14.5
Southern Africa	7.4	1.3	7.9	10.6	8.4	4.8	7.0	6.4	9.7	6.9	3.7	2.7
Western Africa	7.1	7.0	9.6	12.4	14.8	12.0	18.9	16.8	14.5	12.2	10.2	11.4
Africa Total	37.7	43.6	61.4	72.8	65.3	61.1	66.0	77.5	74.6	71.3	61.5	59.4

Source: UNCATD FDI Statistics.

Table 6.5 *External financial flows to Africa, 2005–2017 (billions, US$)*

	Average 2005–2009	2010	2011	2012	2013	2014	2015	2016*	2017[†]
Remittances	41.74	53.09	59.64	64.32	63.73	67.23	64.77	64.59	66.16
Portfolio investments	10.53	28.50	21.62	34.32	23.03	21.31	15.73	6.50	5.18
Official development assistance	42.60	47.81	51.59	51.76	56.81	54.30	51.04	50.16	50.87
Foreign direct investments	48.70	45.99	49.83	49.37	53.10	55.98	51.26	56.47	57.54
% GDP	9.9	9.0	8.4	8.6	8.2	8.0	8.0	8.2	7.9
Total	143.57	175.39	182.68	199.77	196.67	198.82	182.79	177.72	179.75

*Estimate; [†]Projection.

Source: AfDB et al. 2017, 45.

presents empirical data regarding the success of public finance in Africa, focusing on various types of tax revenue and providing strategies for increasing it (AfDB and OECD 2010). In 2014, other development partners continued to affirm the change, and as part of the post-2015 agenda, the UN declared national governments fully responsible for funding their own core economic and social functions through domestic resource mobilization (UN 2014c, 28). While the mobilization of domestic resources has always been a AUDA priority, it is now considered central to Africa's development success.

The AfDB seems to have outlined a second growth strategy for post-2015 African development: integration into global value chains. By undertaking structural economic reforms in order to better participate in the globalized economy, African countries can position themselves to take advantage of increased transfer benefits and economic growth (AfDB et al. 2014, 182). It appears that reforms needed to take advantage of global value chains are merely good development practices harmonized with country-specific policies. For example, countries are encouraged to assess opportunities within a value chain, identify which structural bottlenecks need to be reformed, and develop contextualized policy solutions. In many cases, reducing trade barriers is a precondition for integration into a global value chain, while the benefits of opening borders translates to all industries and helps diversify domestic economies (AfDB et al. 2014, 186).

While AUDA may be valuable as a normative and administrative framework, it has not suitably addressed the challenges of the political reforms needed to increase financing for development. While the political and governance components of AUDA have had some success in supporting democratic transitions, economic reforms have proven more difficult to accomplish given the behavior of numerous African leaders. Patrick Chabal (2002) explains that contemporary African politics are characterized by "neo-patrimonialism and disorder": Despite formal political structures, power is exercised through the interplay between the formal and informal sectors, a factor exacerbated where power is personalized. This damages the backbone of AUDA's financing strategy: domestic resource mobilization.

Numerous factors have been highlighted here to explain the limited implementation of AUDA, namely, its excessive dependence on external financial resources and programs and limited financial contribution by its own members. Since its creation, AUDA's biggest accomplishments have been its recognition as a development partner by African regional institutions and international organizations and its integration into the AU. AUDA has made much more progress on development, compared to the previous Lagos Action Plan, by partnering with numerous institutions to foster the implementation of existing programs or the creation of joint ones, instead of trying to reinvent the wheel. However, despite refining its resource mobilization strategy and successfully pursuing substantial efforts and accomplishments, AUDA has not been able to reach most of its financial targets. In fact, the post-9/11 context of the war against terrorism, combined with successive financial and economic crises, has reduced the will and capacity of many of its partners, including the G8, which had initially committed to sufficiently financing AUDA. Given the inherent complexity of international resource mobilization, the discourse is now shifting toward domestic resource mobilization, a sector in which it is difficult to assess AUDA's impact.

Moreover, AUDA's limited appropriation and ownership by African heads of state and by civil society undermine the organization's ability to deliver. Although symbolic implementation remains a complex challenge under normal circumstances, AUDA should take the appropriate course of action to reverse undesirable results. It should work toward adopting more credible goals; increasing its level of legitimacy, ownership, and appropriation by its constituents; reducing the high levels of policy ambiguity and political conflicts among its shareholders; developing stronger national, continental, and international coalitions of supporters; strengthening its own institutional design; and developing a more effective outreach strategy to better mobilize financial resources and successfully implement its programs. The current AUDA leadership has reinvigorated the organization since 2009, but member states and the international community can and should do much more by promoting ownership, accountability, and support.

7 | The Way Forward to Transforming Africa by 2030/2063

Resource Mobilization, Financing, and Capacity-Building Strategies for Effective Delivery of the Sustainable Development Goals and African Union Agenda 2063

NEPAD (as of July 2018, officially renamed the African Union Development Agency) is the leading development agency of the AU, in charge of implementing the newly adopted African Union Agenda 2063 (Agenda 2063) and coordinating the implementation of the Sustainable Development Goals (SDGs) at the continental level. At present, policymakers and scholars are exploring innovative implementation, financing, and capacity-building strategies to achieve the SDGs by 2030 as well as Agenda 2063.[1] The SDGs evolved in the context of the unmet Millennium Development Goals (MDGs) for most African countries. As discussed in Chapter 3, the UN adopted the MDGs in order to make "the right to development a reality for everyone" (UN 2000), with eight goals specified and slated for achievement between 1990 and 2015.[2] To date, however, most sub-Saharan African countries have been unable to achieve the MDGs, although several countries have reached some targets. As the global community looks ahead to the SDGs, it is critical to develop strategies to overcome obstacles that have hindered achievement of the MDGs, including capacity-building and resource mobilization. As stated by former US President Barack Obama, "the security and prosperity and justice that we seek in the world cannot be achieved without a strong and prosperous and self-reliant Africa" (Obama 2014).

---

[1] Portions of this chapter are drawn from a paper I wrote for the German Marshall Fund of the United States and the OCP Policy Center, to whom I express my gratitude: www.gmfus.org/publications/mobilizing-resources-africa (accessed April 27, 2018).

[2] (1) Eradicating extreme poverty and hunger; (2) achieving universal primary education; (3) promoting gender equality and women's empowerment; (4) reducing child mortality rates; (5) improving maternal health; (6) combating HIV/AIDS, malaria, and other diseases; (7) ensuring environmental sustainability; and (8) developing a global partnership for development.

This chapter provides a comprehensive strategy to help African and international decision-makers successfully mobilize financial resources and effectively build capacity for improved implementation of the SDGs. It discusses the relevance and efficient use of a wide range of tools that development actors can adopt, depending on their specific context and goals. Actors evaluated include African countries and regional institutions, North-South country cooperation, South-South country cooperation, international financial institutions, and key stakeholders such as the private sector, civil society organizations, research centers, and think tanks.

Agenda 2063

In 2015, the African Union adopted Agenda 2063, "a strategic framework for the socio-economic transformation of the continent over the next 50 years" (AU n.d.), aiming at making "the 21st Century as the African Century" (African Union Commission 2015a, 1). Rooted in Pan-Africanism and the African renaissance, Agenda 2063 seeks to foster the implementation of initiatives for economic growth and development. African leaders "rededicate ourselves to the enduring Pan African vision of 'an integrated, prosperous and peaceful Africa, driven by its citizens and representing a dynamic force in the international arena'" (African Union Commission 2015a, 1). The program has adopted seven key goals for 2063:

1. A prosperous Africa, based on inclusive growth and sustainable development;
2. An integrated continent, politically united, based on the ideals of Pan-Africanism and the vision of Africa's renaissance;
3. An Africa of good governance, democracy, respect for human rights, justice and the rule of law;
4. A peaceful and secure Africa;
5. An Africa with a strong cultural identity, and a common heritage, values and ethics;
6. An Africa whose development is people driven, relying on the potential offered by its people, especially women and youth, and caring for children;
7. An Africa as a strong, united, resilient, and influential global player and partner. (African Union Commission, 2015a, 2)

The relationship between Agenda 2063 and AUDA has evolved over time. In January of 2015 when Agenda 2063 was officially adopted, the Executive Council of the African Union requested that AUDA "work closely within the framework of Agenda 2063 (African Union Executive Council Twenty-Sixth Ordinary Session, 8). In June 2016, the Executive Council of the African Union commended the NEPAD Planning and Coordinating Agency (NPCA) and the African Union Commission for the pair's excellent work related to development of the First Ten-Year Implementation for Agenda 2063 (African Union Executive Council Twenty-Seventh Ordinary Session 2016, 1). In January 2016, the Executive Council requested that the Commission expedite NEPAD's integration into the AU in order to avoid program overlap and duplication (African Union Executive Council Twenty-Eighth Ordinary Session 2016, 11). By the end of the same year, NEPAD's annual report illustrated the institution's leadership in resolving the question of its integration into Agenda 2063, with a report entitled "Accelerating the African Union's Agenda 2063," wherein NEPAD outlined its strategy for fostering African development.

The First Ten-Year Implementation for Agenda 2063 (covering 2014–2023) specifically outlines the role of AUDA related to Agenda 2063, as envisioned by the AU (African Union 2015b). This document describes the expected roles to be played by a broad community of actors and institutions in implementing Agenda 2063. The African Union Commission was presented as the body that would "follow up the formulation and adoption of decisions on Agenda 2063" (African Union Commission 2015b, 27), while both the African Union Commission and AUDA "will follow up on the implementation of continental programmes/projects" as well as on "the formulation of policies and frameworks for the assessment of RECs and national capacities at the inception and mid-term review of every 10 Year Plan." In the same document, the section related to NEPAD was still unclear, although leaning toward a central technical role for Agenda 2063: "NEPAD/ NPCA: Yet to be defined but appears apparent in the face of the principle of leveraging the strengths of existing institutions could play a lead technical role for Agenda 2063" (92).

Finally, in January 2017 the AU officially designated AUDA its official development agency: "NEPAD should be fully integrated into the Commission as the African Union's development agency, aligned with the agreed priorities and underpinned by an enhanced results-monitoring framework" (African Union Assembly 2017).

Sustainable Development Goals

The formulation of SDGs has been characterized by the diverse participation of many stakeholders, including individuals through mechanisms such as the United Nations Development Group, among others; NGOs; the High-Level Panel of Eminent Persons on the Post-2015 Development Agenda, the Sustainable Development Solutions Network, the United Nations Global Compact, the United Nations Regional Commissions, the United Nations System Chief Executives Board for Coordination (CEB), the United Nations Secretary-General and the broader UN system, and UN member states through intergovernmental processes, including through the United Nations Conference on Sustainable Development (Rio+20 Conference) (UN 2014c).

The agreement at the Rio+20 Conference to formulate a next round of global goals resulted in the creation of the General Assembly Open Working Group on Sustainable Development on January 22, 2013, which was tasked with developing a concrete proposal for action. On September 10, 2014, the United Nations General Assembly adopted resolution A/RES/68/309, which states, "the proposal of the Open Working Group on Sustainable Development Goals [including seventeen goals and 169 targets] contained in the report shall be the main basis for integrating sustainable development goals into the post-2015 development agenda" (UN 2014b). The seventeen Sustainable Development Goals currently guiding discussions among stakeholders are as follows:

Goal 1. End poverty in all its forms everywhere;
Goal 2. End hunger, achieve food security and improved nutrition, and promote sustainable agriculture;
Goal 3. Ensure healthy lives and promote well-being for all at all ages;
Goal 4. Ensure inclusive and equitable quality education and promote lifelong learning opportunities for all;
Goal 5. Achieve gender equality and empower all women and girls;

Goal 6. Ensure the availability and sustainable management of water and sanitation for all;

Goal 7. Ensure access to affordable, reliable, sustainable, and modern energy for all;

Goal 8. Promote sustained, inclusive, and sustainable economic growth, full and productive employment, and decent work for all;

Goal 9. Build resilient infrastructure, promote inclusive and sustainable industrialization, and foster innovation;

Goal 10. Reduce inequality within and among countries;

Goal 11. Make cities and human settlements inclusive, safe, resilient, and sustainable;

Goal 12. Ensure sustainable consumption and production patterns;

Goal 13. Take urgent action to combat climate change and its impacts;

Goal 14. Conserve and sustainably use the oceans, seas, and marine resources for sustainable development;

Goal 15. Protect, restore, and promote sustainable use of terrestrial ecosystems, sustainably manage forests, combat desertification, halt and reverse land degradation, and halt biodiversity loss;

Goal 16. Promote peaceful and inclusive societies for sustainable development, provide access to justice for all, and build effective, accountable, and inclusive institutions at all levels;

Goal 17. Strengthen the means of implementation and revitalize the global partnership for sustainable development. (UN 2014a)

These SDGs (and their targets) will require substantial financial resources, which can be obtained through innovative mechanisms, strategies, and tools, as will be seen.

Financing and Building Capacities for the SDGs and Agenda 2063

Sources of development financing can largely be broken into five distinct categories: ODA from countries that are members of the Development Assistance Committee (DAC) of the OECD; non-DAC country aid flows and private donor flows; private investment; domestic resource mobilization; and emerging (nontraditional) sources, such as "global solidarity" levies on currency transactions.

Traditionally, the development agenda has relied on direct transfers to public entities rather than on financial innovations. However, non-traditional forms of fundraising – such as lotteries, diaspora bonds, and loan guarantees – raised $57.1 billion between 2000 and 2008, and they have proved more lucrative than attempting to identify new sources of ODA (Girishankar 2009, 3–4). These mechanisms should be viewed as a complement, rather than as a replacement, for traditional forms of aid (Baliamoune-Lutz 2013, 9).

If most of the relevant actors (African countries and regional organizations; developed countries; developing countries; international institutions; and key stakeholders, including the private sector, civil society organizations, think tanks, and research centers) take the appropriate courses of action, positive change can occur. This could result in improved capacity-building, efficient resource mobilization, successful implementation of goals, and shared prosperity. In order to address previous limitations, special attention should be given to tax reform, private sector promotion, goals and metric monitoring, capacity-building, and efficient coordination between actors, as I explain later in the chapter.

African Countries: Creating Conditions for Resource Mobilization

African countries bear the primary responsibility for resource mobilization. Throughout the past century, weak institutional capacity and limited accountability, combined with poor management and misuse of financial resources, have damaged relations between African governments and donors. Although the situation improved at the beginning of the twenty-first century, conditions in many countries are not yet conducive to enabling a massive increase of capital flows and foreign direct investment (FDI). In order to overcome these barriers and secure enough external and domestic resources, African countries should rebuild trust in government among citizens, donors, and the private sector. African countries can achieve this goal by implementing strategies to strengthen the financial management capacity of the state and create effective public administration, improve domestic tax-collection systems, promote private sector development, create a market-friendly environment, reinforce subregional and regional integration, and expand the banking sector.

Strengthening the Financial Management Capacity of the State and Creating Effective Public Administration

It is necessary that African countries implement public management reforms in order to ensure that governments are catalytic, community owned, competitive, mission driven, results oriented, customer focused, enterprising, anticipatory, decentralized, and market oriented (Gaebler and Osborne 1992). Although each country should develop its own trajectory toward reform, it should also try to learn from successful and unsuccessful peer experiences. Inefficient government and public administration result in mistrust from donors or investors, while also reducing the effectiveness of the funding intended to achieve SDGs and Agenda 2063. Special attention to failed, weak, fragile, and post-conflict states is needed to rebuild the capacity for basic financial management and deliver basic services.

Moreover, African countries should strengthen the standards for accountable governance and the equitable redistribution of public resources to prevent domestic conflicts (e.g., Boko Haram in Nigeria and rebel groups in Central African Republic) resulting from ineffective, clientelist, and self-serving management of public funding. In this way, countries can preserve their resources for SDGs and Agenda 2063. Countries ranked lowest in terms of budget transparency are generally low-income and authoritarian regimes and often dependent on aid and resource rents. Data from the Open Budget Survey,[3] which examines budget transparency, participation, and oversight, show that change is possible[4] and is driven by both internal and external actors. In Angola, international institutions' insistence on transparency, especially through the HIPC initiative,[5] resulted in a tangible increase in the availability of budget information. In Rwanda, technical assistance

---

[3] The International Budget Partnership administrated the Open Budget Survey biannually between 2006 and 2012, measuring budget transparency and accountability in 100 countries. For more information, see: www.survey .internationalbudget.org/#download.

[4] Countries such as Angola, Democratic Republic of Congo, Liberia, and Rwanda have made significant progress.

[5] The HIPC Initiative is a comprehensive debt relief strategy launched by the IMF and the WB in 1996 to reduce to a sustainable level the external debt of countries with high levels of poverty and unsustainable debt burdens. As of March 2015, thirty-five out of the thirty-nine eligible countries had received full debt relief.

from international agencies also increased the available budget data (De Renzio and Masud 2011, 607–16).

In all cases, clear, consistent, and actionable plans are required to implement reforms successfully. Countries should take responsibility for developing local and national development frameworks, such as the National Economic Empowerment Development Strategy (NEEDS) framework in Nigeria, which encourages investment and provides a path for economic diversification.[6]

Urban-rural divides can present particular challenges to domestic resource mobilization. Countries should promote the use of the formal financial sector, including integrating assets held in the informal sector, such as livestock, into the formal financial system; developing accessible credit at varying levels of consumption; insuring deposits; and expanding the use of technology (Gayi 2008).

Improving Domestic Tax-Collection Systems

A major determinant of increased domestic resource mobilization is a country's ability to collect taxes. Countries should continue their tax-collection reform efforts, particularly by investing in human and technological capital. Collaborating with international institutions, such as Tax Inspectors Without Borders, can be helpful in facilitating the transfer of knowledge (OECD 2013), while automation can reduce the potential for graft (Gayi 2008, 46) and improve the depth of collection efforts (Mubiru 2010, 4). Countries should also work to simplify existing tax structures. For example, adopting a single value-added tax (VAT) or goods and services tax (GST), as in Sierra Leone, can simplify collection and create a more predictable tax environment (Elovainio and Evans 2013, 7).

More broadly, countries should seek to expand the share of revenue comprised of property taxes, particularly in urban areas, since Africa's urban population is expected to increase from 294 million to 742 million between 2000 and 2030 (Mubiru 2010, 5). Additionally, countries should revoke concessions granted to corporations in order to attract investment, which are difficult to renegotiate and prone to benefit special interests at the expense of new investment projects.

---

[6] See, for example, Adegbite and Adetiloye 2013, 213; Akume and Abdullahi 2013, 240; Elovainio and Evans 2013; and Joshua et al. 2013, 72.

For example, in 2005, 55 percent of total tax revenue was lost in Burundi due to tax exemptions (Gayi 2008, 46). Eliminating subsidies, particularly in the energy sector, can enable resources to flow to the most beneficial development projects.

Promoting Private Sector Development

Greater private sector engagement does not serve citizens without the development of robust institutions. Countries should engage in substantive governance reforms to encourage greater transparency and accountability (UN 2014c). Recommendations include building on existing processes and mechanisms, establishing benchmarks, creating oversight bodies, and producing written reports addressing national and international stakeholders. In particular, countries should ensure that FDI inflows promote the domestic industry by encouraging the development of linkages between sources of FDI and local component manufacturers. For example, South Africa created the Motor Industry Development Program in 1995, seeking to link the assembly plants of BMW, Daimler Chrysler, Volkswagen, Toyota, and Renault to local auto component producers (Flatters 2005, 1).

Creating a Market-Friendly Environment

Attracting investment requires a broad commitment to institutional development. Countries should make substantive reforms to judicial systems to enable more effective enforcement of regulations and property rights. Countries should also make reforms to reduce the risk associated with transacting with smaller enterprises and increase access to credit, as well as to combat the excessive liquidity of African banks that has been caused by perceptions of high risk and low opportunity (Dahou et al. 2009, 32). Ultimately, countries should promote stronger intellectual property rights, which encourage innovation, research and development, and e-commerce (AU 2014, 8).

Countries should seek to reverse some of the harms of capital flight by offering a period of amnesty for those who relocate assets back to the country of origin, regardless of whether the capital was obtained or transferred illegally (Gayi 2008, 47). For example, in an attempt to boost the dirham, strengthen foreign reserves, and mobilize resources for the state budget in 2014, Morocco granted amnesty to all account holders involved in capital flight if they paid a onetime fee and repatriated assets to Moroccan banks. Similarly, in 2004 South Africa collected over 2 billion rand (roughly $310 million in 2004 dollars) in revenue from an amnesty period, which provided those who were guilty of having illegally transferred capital out of the country an opportunity to pay either a 5 or 10 percent fine, depending on whether they returned their assets to the country (Seeraj 2010).

For businesses, the lack of a mutually beneficial relationship with the state is often the result of overcomplicated procedures. For example, in Uganda and Zambia, these barriers include corruption and bureaucracy; in Togo, complex registration processes hinder participation (Mubiru 2010, 4). Complicated procedures are particularly problematic in the globalized economy. Countries should reduce supply-chain barriers to trade by simplifying border administration and investing in transport and communications infrastructure, especially taking advantage of the preferential treatment afforded to developing nations under the 2013 Bali Package. Basic reforms would enable increases in exports and imports, amounting to 63 percent and 55 percent, respectively (Cattaneo et al. 2013). Countries should also seek to increase the volume of tax payments from smaller enterprises, particularly those currently in the informal sector, by reducing the barriers to incorporation and providing incentives, such as legal title to assets (Gayi 2008, 45).

Reinforcing Subregional and Regional Integration

Often, impoverished states attempt to compete by undercutting their neighbors. While healthy competition is valuable, however, development incentives are less effective when they drag down neighboring nations. Thus, countries should cooperate and agree on unified policies for incentivizing development. Preventing a subsidy or tax holiday "race to the bottom" is crucial for least developed countries (LDCs), who may have little left with which to compete (Fjeldstad 2013; Nunnenkamp and Rainer 2013, 75–98). Countries should also continue to reduce trade tariffs and other barriers to encourage more diverse economic integration and trade (Mubiru 2010, 6). Two recent initiatives are showing progress toward regional integration: the Single Air African Transport Market (SAATM) and the African Continental Free Trade Area (AfCFTA).

The Free Movement of People, the Single Air African Transport Market (SAATM), and the African Union Passport

Individual governments and regional bodies have already begun to implement policies to facilitate the free movement of people, which is critical for fostering business across nations. Out of the fifty-five countries, African visitors can now travel without a visa or obtain a visa on arrival in at least thirty. Perhaps most important, in 2016 the AU launched the African passport, and, though it is presently available only to high-ranking African officials, the AU hopes, and AU officials have vowed, to create the conditions necessary to extend it to all African citizens by 2020.

However, these strategies towards increased freedom of movement have not been universally praised. Some analysts voice their concerns over the feasibility of the African passport's widespread use given the greatly varying capabilities of African states and their access to the required biometric technology. Similarly, individual countries diverge in their willingness to adopt the African passport, as the move entails foregoing substantial visa revenues, which are important sources of income for many. Some critics have also raised concerns over the potential strengthening of terror groups and organized crime given increasingly open borders.

Despite these concerns, the continent is also trying to promote free movement of people through other endeavors. For example, the Single Air African Transport Market (SAATM), launched at the Assembly of Heads of States and Governments of the African Union in January 2018, is hoped to be a tool to lower prohibitively high travel costs, as it will allow Africa's sky to work under a common regulatory framework. The SAATM will encourage more regular flights between African cities, rather than trips that often involve layovers in the Middle East or Europe. As a flagship project of the African Union's Agenda 2063, the SAATM aims to liberalize and unify the African skies, enhance connectivity, and foster the development of the aviation sector, tourism, and trade. In particular, a study by the International Air Transport association found that "if just 12 key African countries opened their markets and increased connectivity, an extra 155,000 jobs and $1.3 billion in annual GDP would be created in those countries."

If implemented successfully, the SAATM could mirror the European Union's Internal Market for Aviation, which has increased air safety as well as improved competition among airlines, which in turn has lowered airfares. So far, twenty-three countries have signed the solemn commitment to the SAATM; notable signatories include economic powerhouses South Africa, Nigeria, Kenya, Côte d'Ivoire and Ethiopia. For the SAATM to be truly successful, though, all member countries must adopt it. The AU Commission is now working towards creating an African sky infrastructure in countries that have signed on the initiative by 2023 as well as working to get the remaining thirty-two AU countries to get on board.

The African Continental Free Trade Area (AfCFTA)

What Is the AfCFTA and How Did It Come About?

The AfCFTA creates a single continental market for goods and services as well as a customs union with free movement of capital and business travelers. The African Union agreed in January 2012 to develop the AfCFTA. It took eight rounds of negotiations, beginning in 2015 and lasting until December 2017, to reach agreement.

The AU and its member countries hope the AfCFTA will accelerate continental integration and address the overlapping membership of the continent's regional economic communities (RECs). Many African countries belong to multiple RECs, which tends to limit the efficiency and effectiveness of these organizations.

The EAC and the Economic Community of West African States have made some progress toward achieving subregional economic integration. But most RECs are underperforming, with a low level of compliance by member states, which has delayed successful integration.

What Will the AfCFTA Do, Exactly?

One of its central goals is to boost African economies by harmonizing trade liberalization across subregions and at the continental level. As a part of the AfCFTA, countries have committed to remove tariffs on 90 percent of goods. According to the UN Economic Commission on Africa, intra-African trade is likely to increase by 52.3 percent under the AfCFTA and will double upon the further removal of nontariff barriers.

By promoting intra-African trade, the AfCFTA will also foster a more competitive manufacturing sector and promote economic diversification. The removal of tariffs will create a continental market that allows companies to benefit from economies of scale.

Countries, in turn, are likely to be able to accelerate their industrial development. By 2030, Africa may emerge as a $2.5 trillion potential market for household consumption and $4.2 trillion for business-to-business consumption.

Who stands to gain the most? African nations with large manufacturing bases, such as South Africa, Kenya and Egypt, would receive the most immediate benefits.

What Key Challenges Lie Ahead for the AfCFTA?

The AU hopes to create a single common market embracing all countries in Africa. However, only forty-four countries have signed the AfCFTA's establishing framework to date. And just thirty nations have signed the Free Movement Protocol – signifying the free movement of people, right of residence, and right of establishment.

The most prominent nonsignatory of the AfCFTA is Nigeria, which has one of the largest economies in Africa. Nigerian President Muhammadu Buhari has justified his decision by claiming that he needed more time to consult with unions and businesses to assess the risks an open market would pose to his country's manufacturing and small-business sectors. Buhari may be cautious, but it's very likely that the prospect of a continent-wide market eventually will prompt Nigeria to join the AfCFTA.

The AfCFTA also faces the difficult task of fostering cooperation among a multitude of national and regional actors with trade interests that will diverge at times. I discuss these challenges in my book, *Innovating Development Strategies in Africa: The Role of International, Regional and National Actors*, where I argue that ensuring each country benefits and establishing strong compliance mechanisms are critical to success.

The heterogeneous size of African economies, the existence of numerous bilateral trade agreements with the rest of the world, overlapping REC memberships, divergent levels of industrial development, and varying degrees of openness also pose challenges to the AfCFTA.

So What's Next?

African leaders have agreed to have the AfCFTA come into effect within eighteen months after its signing in March 2018. For this to occur, at least twenty-two countries must ratify the agreement formally. Some observers consider that the time frame may be too short, especially given the need for debate and negotiations within each signatory nation.

Countries and RECs still have to complete negotiations on competition, dispute-resolution mechanisms, intellectual property rights, and investments, among other issues. They should also agree on regulatory frameworks for service-trade liberalization (to facilitate market access), submit tariff concessions schedules for trade in goods (specifying the timeline and nature of products that will be liberalized), and make progress in the signing of the free-movement protocol.

The final critical steps for the AU will be to persuade the remaining countries to join, to create a secretariat to coordinate the implementation, and to provide enough resources to ensure the AfCFTA's success.

Expanding the Banking Sector

Lack of access to financing is a major factor constraining the growth of domestic industries in Africa. In order to overcome this impediment, countries should direct ODA into expanding telecommunications infrastructure, which is crucial for improving access to finance for small- and medium-sized enterprises (UN 2014c), as well as reducing transaction costs for all parties. Governments should also incentivize local social security, pension funds, and insurance companies to invest in local bonds for infrastructure development. The development of bonds to be sold on international capital markets could also prove effective. Bonds are an attractive prospect to investors, since they have low barriers to market entry and exit compared to FDI (Dahou et al. 2009, 32). Moreover, a robust bond program has the potential of reducing dependence on aid, grants, and other outside guarantees (Mu et al. 2013). For example, in Côte d'Ivoire, the investment rate has increased from 8 percent of GDP during the country's recent civil war to 16.5 percent by 2015, in part due to a successful issue of a $750 million Eurobond in July 2014. The country has also secured other international sovereign bonds offerings: US$1 billion in 2015; US$1.25 billion and €625 million in 2017; and €1.7 billion in 2018[7]:

Nontraditional forms of banking and finance are increasingly prevalent across Africa, and greater effort is needed to harness these mechanisms. For example, countries should encourage microfinance institutions to become part of the formal financial system so they can scale up operations and be integrated with tax-collection systems, as well as provide services to more individuals (Dahou et al. 2009, 23). African governments should issue diaspora bonds to finance long-term infrastructure development projects and tap into the large population of overseas migrants. For example, Burundi was able to mobilize $1.5 million in the first year of a pilot real estate development program by offering investment opportunities tailored to Burundians residing abroad (Gayi 2008, 46). Countries should enable banks to offer foreign currency accounts to residents, which would reduce transaction costs for remittances and insulate account holders from domestic currency shocks (Gayi 2008, 46).

North-South Cooperation: Resource Mobilization through Multiple Channels

North-South cooperation remains a key axis for external resource mobilization to finance SDGs and Agenda 2063 in Africa. The United States, the United Kingdom, and France remain the largest donors to the African continent, contributing $9.1 billion, $4.1 billion, and $3.4 billion, respectively (AfDB et al. 2014, 62). However, commitments from European countries, which make up a large share of ODA, are projected to decline substantially, with 2015 levels not reaching the previous peak contribution level in 2010. However, funds from European Development Finance Institutions (EDFIs) are likely to continue to increase (63). In 2001, EDFIs invested just over $2 billion in the continent, while in 2012 investment increased to over $8 billion. As they act as catalysts for private sector investment, EDFIs are an excellent opportunity for countries to diversify their ODA contributions (63).

---

[7] Cleary Gottlieb. March 22, 2018: "Côte d'Ivoire's € 1.7 billion sovereign bond offering." Available online: https://www.clearygottlieb.com/news-and-insights/news-listing/cote-divoires-1-7-billion-sovereign-bond-offering (consulted on July 30, 2018)

Official Development Assistance

Developed countries should continue their efforts to reach or exceed the aid target of 0.7 percent of GNI as soon as possible, or to redefine their goals to ensure that the goals are realistic and followed through with successful implementation (UN 2014c, 29). The credibility of the ODA goal originally articulated in 1969 – 0.7 percent of GNI from developed countries – has been an issue for years. It was not until 2009 that aid flows began to increase substantially, and even then the increase was almost exclusively limited to EU member states, which together reached an average of 0.42 percent in 2009 (Nunnenkamp and Rainer 2013). According to the DAC, the doubling of official aid by 2010 promised in 2005 at the Gleneagles summit was $21 billion short (Dembele 2012, 190). Nonetheless, the WB remarks that ODA, when evaluated per capita, has been maintained, if not increased, in the least developed countries (WB 2013, 15). In fragile states, ODA comprises 40 percent of total financial flows (WB 2013, 16).

Developed countries should reach their ODA target, a declining resource, so that recipients can use it as efficiently as possible. Donors should focus on using ODA to finance global public goods, such as by targeting climate-related efforts in African regions affected by droughts. Ultimately, ODA should allow recipient countries to build capacity and move toward utilizing domestic resources as soon as possible (Sachs and Schmidt-Traub 2013, 8; Snoddy 2005, 8); aid should be utilized as a means to an end, not as an end in itself, particularly in the context of government capacity (Baliamoune-Lutz 2013, 9). Recipient countries should more closely align and target ODA to domestic priorities, such as by ensuring that ODA develops domestic capacity in tax collection and thereby provides a greater return on investment. In addition, developed countries should continue to support multilateral development banks and institutions, such as the African Development Bank, which offer credit guarantees and innovative financing mechanisms, since they are insulated from political interference and could better enable developing nations to finance immediate needs (WB 2013, 25).

Ensuring Aid Effectiveness

DAC countries have a role in ensuring that aid is effective. One of the best ways that donor countries can do this: They can make aid contingent on the results of governance reforms (as recommended by the NEPAD Secretariat), insist on robust monitoring programs, or offer loan guarantees (as explained previously). Without contingencies, aid can perversely reduce the impetus to develop robust institutions, to the detriment of the recipient country (Baliamoune-Lutz 2013, 9).

Global Value Chains

Developed countries should encourage corporations to integrate developing countries into global value chains. Globalization has enabled countries to participate in the international production network without possessing full upstream capability in domestic industry. For example Morocco, Egypt, and South Africa act as vehicle manufacturing hubs for international car companies (AfDB et al. 2014, 142).

Financial Transactions Tax (FTT) and Solidarity Mechanisms

Countries should further explore innovative financing mechanisms to offset declining political will to provide ODA. For example, countries within the EU should work to ratify an EU-wide financial transactions tax to be used for development assistance, enabling all countries to contribute proportionally, and reducing financial instability across the EU, while simultaneously contributing approximately €200 billion per year, which could be contributed to development goals (Nunnenkamp and Rainer 2013, 11; WB 2013, 25). In a similar vein, developed countries should implement surcharges on items such as fuel consumption, institute airline travel levies, and establish lotteries to finance development, as is already done in Belgium and France (Girishankar 2009, 3–4).

South-South Cooperation: Strengthening Relationships

Although the idea of South-South cooperation is not new – the G-77 and ACP already exist – the renewed interests of emerging countries such as China, India, and Brazil, but also African countries such as South Africa and Morocco, are providing the African continent with a unique opportunity to secure additional resources for the post-2015 development agenda. According to Sanoussi Bilal, the estimated absolute foreign aid assistance provided in 2010 was $3.9 billion from China, $680 million for India, $472 million from Russia, more than $400 million from Brazil, and $143 million from South Africa. BRICS, advanced developing countries, and non-DAC donors should strengthen their relationships with African countries, mobilize additional resources (Bilal 2012) and increase investments in Africa.

The Case of Morocco's Readmission to the African Union: A New Dynamic for Africa's Transformation?

The Kingdom of Morocco, although only recently readmitted to the AU (January 2017, after leaving in 1984 following the decision of the Organization of African Unity to admit Western Sahara (former Spanish possession claimed by Morocco) and seat their delegation.), has long been a supporter of AUDA and Africa's transformation. Additionally, the recent approval of Morocco's membership (June 2017) by ECOWAS leadership (Economic Community of West African States, made of fifteen African countries) is reinforcing regional and continental dynamics started earlier.

During the period 2001–2003, Morocco contributed its expertise to the drafting of the NEPAD (now AUDA) Environment Plan of Action and organized meetings with its secretary of state for environment[8] to increase awareness of AUDA's environmental components.

In 2003, the Moroccan foreign minister announced the decision of HM King Mohammed VI to contribute 300 000 € to the world digital solidarity fund, making Morocco a founding member of the fund and a supporter of AUDA's goals to reduce the digital gap.[9]

Morocco has also contributed to the implementation of the NEPAD (now AUDA) Sustainable City Programme, which is also supported by UN-HABITAT. Under this program, Morocco's National Local Agenda 21 Programme has provided technical support to prepare a city profile, an important step in making Rabat a "Sustainable NEPAD City."[10]

---

[8] Available on the website of the United Nations: www.un.org/ esa/africa/ support/Morocco.htm.

[9] Available on the website of the Permanent Mission of the Kingdom of Morocco to the United Nations Office and other international organizations in Geneva: www.mission-maroc.ch/en/pages/273.html.

[10] Available on the website of UN-Habitat: http://mirror.unhabitat.org/ content.

In the UN Secretary-General's 2014 report on the New Partnership for Africa's Development,[12] Morocco was presented as the only country from North Africa to have registered a "solid growth of 24 percent, to \$3.5 billion" in FDI inflows.

Morocco is also participating in the Program for Infrastructure Development in Africa (PIDA). The AU[12] has recently reported its agreement with the REC the Arab Maghreb Union (AMU) to implement the PIDA projects registered under AMU. The meeting was held in Rabat with the participation of the African Union Commission, NEPAD Agency, African Development Bank, and AMU. These seven projects include the "facilitation of transport and transit along the Trans-Maghreb highway; harmonization of the legal and regulatory framework for ICTs in the Maghreb countries; the creation and securing of a Maghreb high-speed telecommunications network based on optical fiber; the electric transmission line of North Africa; the Trans-Saharan Nigeria-Algeria gas pipeline; the aquifer system of the northern Sahara; and the aquifer system of Lullemeden and Taoudent/Tazrouft."

A 2014 report[13] published by the Moroccan Ministry of Economy and Finance, entitled "Moroccan-African Relations: The Ambition of 'New Borders,'" reaffirmed the Kingdom of Morocco's support for NEPAD. Morocco confirmed its will to "play a leading role in triangular cooperation" (receiving funding from donors and investing in African countries), defending the "interests of the least developed countries," "being the second African investor in Africa and the first African investor in West Africa," providing "support for the training of African professionals, sharing expertise and advanced technical assistance and the implementation of infrastructure projects in priority sectors," and providing humanitarian assistance.

Morocco has not waited to rejoin the AU to engage with the rest of the continent in terms of both bilateral and multilateral perspectives.

[11] United Nations, Report of the Secretary-General, 2014. New Partnership for Africa's Development: Twelfth Consolidated Progress Report on Implementation and International Support. A/69/161. New York: United Nations.

[12] Available on the website of the African Union: www.african-union.africa-newsroom.com/press/a-joint-meeting-with-the-arab-maghreb-union.

[13] Kingdom of Morocco, Ministry of Economy and Finance, Directorate of Financial Studies and Forecasts. 2014. *Moroccan-African Relations: The Ambition of "New Borders."* Rabat: Kingdom of Morocco.

Its established leadership in triangular cooperation, associated with its leadership in key sectors (tourism, agriculture, investment, etc.), could make a significant difference in the implementation of continental development strategies, e.g., SDGs, NEPAD, and Agenda 2063. As stated by Karns and Mingst (2010), "regionalism does not just happen. Deliberate policy choices by states' leaders are key to increasing the flow of economic and political activities."

BRICS, Advanced Developing Countries, and Non-DAC Donors

New development donors have a large role to play in ensuring that Africa achieves SDGs. The BRICS countries should work within new institutions for South-South cooperation, such as the New Development Bank and Asian Infrastructure Investment Bank (UN 2014c, 26), as well as increase their foreign aid assistance. Non-DAC and BRICS countries should continue to work with existing entities, such as the Office of the Special Adviser on Africa (OSAA) support the development and implementation of international standards for sustainable development, including funding initiatives and the formation of policy options favorable to Africa. For example, the Export-Import Bank of China has funded projects that other actors have refused to fund due to environmental concerns, while supporting extractive industries and allegedly corrupt regimes (Strange et al. 2013). The potential for these relationships to create mutually beneficial outcomes is great, but these relationships should emphasize partnerships to avoid exploitation.

International Institutions: Supporting Realistic and Measurable Goals

The OECD, DAC, and IFIs, especially the WB and IMF, continue to play key roles in mobilizing resources for the SDGs and Agenda 2063 in Africa. From providing products and services to working with countries to set goals and metrics, international institutions are crucial links to the development process. Successful achievement of the SDGs and Agenda 2063 within Africa requires these institutions to adapt to the needs of developing countries.

Products and Services

IFIs should provide better-tailored, well-integrated, multilevel, cross-sectorial, and high-impact financial products and services (such as low-interest loans, interest-free credit, grants, guarantees, debt relief, private equity, and investment funds) that best meet the specific needs of the poorest countries, post-conflict and fragile states, and middle-income countries. This should include projects on regional infrastructure integration, public administration, human development, agriculture, and the inclusion of vulnerable groups.

Goals and Metrics

IFIs should continue to support clear goals and metrics to better measure progress and encourage more output-based aid. Attention should be paid to measuring the aid inflow from nontraditional donors, such as non-DAC countries or private sources (Greenhill and Prizzon 2012, 23).

Goals and metrics should be developed as inclusively as possible, both by the countries that will implement them and by international institutions. From an exogenous perspective, the tools developed by international institutions would provide a comparative and global perspective to African countries.

International organizations should act as connectors for the needs of countries and donors. Given the rise of non-DAC donors, Baliamoune-Lutz (2013, 8) recommends a market-based system where countries can offer project proposals, enabling them to choose from various donors and forms of aid based on their specific needs. The DAC should establish common reporting requirements for creditors and donors in order to monitor and evaluate progress more effectively (Baliamoune-Lutz 2013; Birdsall 2004, 22).

Financial Assistance

International institutions should increase funding to regional bodies, in particular the AU, which needs external financial assistance to operate at full capacity. Currently, the AU is unable to provide sufficient resources to organizations such as AUDA given its own level of resources and effectiveness (Landsberg 2012, 61). For example, many AUDA regional infrastructure projects that would have facilitated trade among countries and fostered economic growth were not successfully implemented due to insufficient resources.

At the national level, international institutions should offer guarantees rather than direct funding to mitigate the increased perception of risk that stymies private sector involvement in infrastructure development. For example, the WB was able to utilize US $41.5 million of international funding to provide a US$166 million guarantee, which ultimately gave the government of Kenya access to US$623 million in credit to finance projects in the energy sector (WB 2013, 21). In addition, the greater provision of debt relief, which is intended to reduce interest and principal payments so that resources can be spent on development programs, is crucial for many highly indebted countries. At a minimum, developed countries and IFIs should continue to commit to relieving the debt of countries that have yet to qualify under the HIPC initiative (WB 2013, 16).

Finally, international institutions should not ignore their roles in helping to develop human capital, specifically by expanding programs that facilitate the transfer of knowledge and capacity building. For example, Tax Inspectors Without Borders has been an effective pilot initiative, enabling domestic resources to be mobilized by establishing positive norms and best practices (OECD 2013, 27).

The United Nations Office of the Special Adviser on Africa and AUDA

In 2002, a resolution adopted by the United Nations General Assembly endorsed "the recommendation of the Secretary-General that the New Partnership for Africa's Development ... should be the framework within which the international community, including the United Nations system, should concentrate its efforts for Africa's development" (United Nations General Assembly 2002, 3). A year later, UN Secretary-General Kofi Annan created the Office of the Special Adviser on Africa, with a special adviser directly accountable to the secretary-general. Three of its six key functions are directly associated with NEPAD:

The Office of the Special Adviser on Africa:

(a) Supports the General Assembly and the Economic and Social Council in their deliberations on Africa;
(b) Coordinates and guides the preparation of Africa-related reports and inputs, in particular support for the New Partnership for Africa's Development (NEPAD) by the United Nations system and the international community, including the private sector and civil society;
(c) Coordinates the interdepartmental task force on African affairs, to ensure a coherent and integrated approach for United Nations support for Africa, including following up on the implementation of all global summit and conference outcomes related to Africa;
(d) Initiates reports on critical issues affecting Africa, and in particular on the interrelated issues of peace and development;
(e) Coordinates global advocacy in support of NEPAD;
(f) Acts as the focal point for NEPAD within the United Nations Secretariat at Headquarters. (United Nations Secretary-General 2003, 1–2)

Additionally, the document declared, "The Office of the Special Adviser on Africa shall provide backstopping to the Secretary-General in promoting a coordinated, system-wide response in support of Africa's development, particularly the implementation of NEPAD (now AUDA), through the United Nations System Chief Executives Board for Coordination" (United Nations Secretary-General 2003, 2).

In 2012, a new resolution adopted by the General Assembly established "a United Nations monitoring mechanism to review commitments made towards Africa's development" and requested "the Office of the Special Adviser on Africa to serve as the secretariat for the review, in coordination with relevant entities of the United Nations system" (United Nations General Assembly resolution A/RES/66/293, 3). Since its creation, the Office for the Special Adviser on Africa has been instrumental in advocating for AUDA and Africa within the UN system as well as globally, providing policy analysis and monitoring and reporting to AUDA on implementation and international support.

Other Key Stakeholders in Resource Mobilization

Although numerous additional actors can substantially contribute to successful resource mobilization on the continent, three are of particular interest for the purposes of this chapter: citizens, the private sector, and think tanks/research centers.

Citizens and Civil Society Organizations

Citizens should contribute to domestic resource mobilization by being responsible taxpayers (the upper and middle classes). They should ensure the transparent management and vertical accountability of their government by fully participating in their countries' livelihood and electoral processes, and by favoring candidates strongly committed to preventing the misuse of both domestic and external resources, such as Ory Okolloh's Ushahidi program in Kenya.

Civil Society Organizations (CSOs) can be instrumental to policy design and formulation and should be heavily involved in the process because they can provide details about bottom-up needs for success, such as resources needed to meet local imperatives. Moreover, it is essential that small, often marginalized groups participate; otherwise their interests will be ignored. CSOs should use their flexibility and agility to be responsive to local requirements. For example, the Rehabilitation of Arid Environments Trust in Kenya enabled the restoration of grasslands by installing electric fences that divided the areas into communal and private fields, ultimately resulting in increased agricultural productivity. Additionally, CSOs should actively participate in service delivery. For example, outside of Africa, CSOs helped reduce the incidence of HIV/AIDS in Thailand by forming a national coalition and coordinating their efforts. With the promise of a coordinated CSO framework, the Thai government was willing to contribute funding in 1992 that caused rates of HIV prevalence among new army conscripts to decline from 7 percent to less than 1.5 percent between 1992 and 2002 (United Nations Millennium Project 2005, 131). The same role for civil society should be encouraged in Africa.

Private Sector Contributions

National and multinational corporations should be responsible taxpayers, rather than using fiscal arrangements or corrupting governments to prevent or evade tax contributions. Multinationals should also favor local suppliers and producers when conducting business in Africa, such as using local franchise models (as Coca Cola does) to overcome barriers posed by poor infrastructure (Lucci 2012, 7). Firms could help create solutions to overcome the lack of infrastructure in the region. For example, the Namibian Ministry of Health and Social

Services was able to partner with the United Africa Group to ensure the delivery of pensions and grants to rural beneficiaries – a prime example of a successful public-private partnership (United Nations Millennium Project 2005, 141).

Such engagement with development priorities can also be advantageous for corporations. Firms should harness the opportunity to be socially responsible and transparent as part of their business strategies, such as by explaining to consumers how production processes advance development goals (prime examples include Vodafone, Unilever, and Microsoft) (Lucci 2012, 2). There is also a business case for supporting the SDGs as well: The Business & Sustainable Development Commission argues that, globally, the SDGs can open new market value worth more than $12 trillion by 2030, while at the same time creating up to 380 million jobs. Indeed, the commission states, sustainable business models could unlock create up to 85 million new jobs by 2030 in Africa alone.[14] Firms should also capitalize on the benefits of positive community engagement. Business leaders who recognize the importance of a corporate philosophy of "giving back" and "doing good" can reap the rewards of improved satisfaction and worker productivity (Lucci 2012, 6). Corporations should engage in the development of public-private partnerships in order to overcome the difficulty of operating in limited markets. For example, to better provide electricity to parts of rural Chile, in 1994 the Chilean government financed infrastructure through competitive subsidies to ensure development while relying on the private sector to deliver services (United Nations Millennium Project 2005, 140).

Corporate social responsibility (CSR) is most directly observable within the corporate hierarchy, and private sector entities should be encouraged to fund employee wellness campaigns that address major health issues among others. For example, Anglo American introduced an HIV testing and treatment program for its employees and their families, which ultimately reduced absenteeism in South Africa (Lucci 2012, 7). Such programs also contribute to broader public health goals within the region. Corporations should endorse and pledge to adhere

[14] Brookings Africa Growth Initiative. Foresight Africa. Top priorities for the continent in 2018. Washington DC: Brookings. Available online: https://www.brookings.edu/wp-content/uploads/2018/01/foresight-2018_full_web_final2.pdf (consulted on June 30, 2018). See at the page 46 of the report the viewpoint of Mark Malloch-Brown and Paul Polman)

to international standards for worker and human rights, such as the 2000 UN Global Compact, whether country-level guidelines are less restrictive or not (United Nations Millennium Project 2005, 142).

Companies can also contribute to the broader goals of development organizations by providing valuable data and feedback, such as by making public information about their contributions to national development and their adherence to international reporting standards. This information will help governments, international donors, NGOs, and citizens measure rates of private sector development. Companies should participate in efforts to harmonize CSR standards, such as those by the International Integrated Reporting Council (IIRC) (Callan 2012; Lucci 2012, 9–10).

Firms can also proactively participate in development by reaffirming their commitment to free, fair, and open markets. Companies should take public stances on fighting corruption by refusing to pay bribes and being as transparent as possible. For example, companies should publish the taxes they pay so that citizens can hold governments accountable for how they use revenues (United Nations Millennium Project 2005, 143). One successful example of such a private-sector-run program is the Extractive Industries Transparency Initiative (EITI) (Lucci 2012, 6).

Finally, businesses should not be overlooked as entities that can shape the development agenda. Firms should help form and participate in sector-level associations that can help unify development efforts by proposing policies, pledging funds, or backing initiatives. Companies have the potential to benefit by increased access to supply-chain partners and greater access to markets.

Think Tanks and Research Centers

The role of researchers and think tanks is increasingly relevant following the lackluster performance of the UN MDGs in Africa. Researchers should focus on developing metrics for evaluating country-specific performance and providing decision-makers with policy options and innovative solutions to the most pressing problems. Think tanks should mediate the relationship between governments and citizens in order to build a strong civil society by independently informing policy debates and evaluating ongoing policy proposals (McGann 2005, 3). By staying tapped into the policy sphere, researchers can provide timely, high-quality, evidence-based recommendations about pressing issues, especially about complex topics like domestic resource mobilization.

Research centers should engage in outreach to increase public awareness of policy issues, contributing to a more informed and educated electorate and greater general public understanding (McGann 2005, 3). Think tanks and research centers should adopt the roles of research and development, relying on country-level operations to interface laterally with developed countries. For example, product development partnerships, such as that of the European and Development Country Clinical Trial Partnership, have focused on strengthening capacity while simultaneously driving research and development (PATH 2014, 9).

Conclusion: Sustaining External Resources and Increasing Domestic Resource Mobilization

Despite important progress made by numerous countries, Africa has yet to fully achieve the MDGs by the end of 2015, partly due to an inability to mobilize sufficient financial resources to achieve these ambitious goals. Prospects for achieving the SDGs by 2030 and Agenda 2063 remain uncertain. The ability to effectively and systematically mobilize domestic resources and manage them efficiently to achieve development goals remains a key factor for successful implementation of the SDGs and Agenda 2063 in Africa. Above all, comprehensive, contextual, realistic, and coherent resource mobilization strategies exist and should be adopted by each country, subregion, and continent, with consideration of the lessons learned from past failures and successes. Although Africans bear the primary responsibility for their future, international actors can and should play a major role in helping to achieve the financial resource targets necessary for the successful implementation of the SDGs and Agenda 2063.

Conclusion

Continental Development Since the Creation of AUDA: Theoretical and Practical Implications

This book has made broad theoretical, methodological, and practical contributions to the fields of international relations, comparative politics, and African studies. In 2001, the founders of NEPAD (now the African Union Development Agency, or AUDA) proclaimed the innovative nature of their initiative and set extremely ambitious goals in terms of development, regional economic integration, and the eradication of poverty. In 2018, almost two decades after the creation of AUDA, Africa is the world's second-fastest-growing region, with substantial socioeconomic transformation.

In this study, I have addressed three questions: How and why did AUDA emerge? Does AUDA constitute change or continuity with respect to the earlier initiatives of the IMF and the WB? What critical assessment can we make both at the level of its evolution or institutional development and the implementation of certain key programs? And, finally, what are the implications for interstate cooperation through continental organizations for development in Africa?

To answer the first two questions, if we consider our neo-institutional analysis of institutional emergence, change, and continuity (at the levels of discourse, strategies, and programs), we draw several conclusions.

The Emergence of the African Union Development Agency

As for the historical process[1] that led to AUDA's emergence, we have observed that since the 1980s, the WB and the IMF have applied development policies and strategies centered on structural adjustment programs. Initially focused on reforming macroeconomic policies in order to encourage growth, these strategies ultimately failed and received widespread criticism, including by UN organizations such

---

[1] In conformity with the inductive method adopted for this demonstration.

as UNICEF, by the middle and end of the 1980s. At that time, a reorientation of the adjustment programs occurred, which began to incorporate human concerns along with strictly economic ones in order to limit the reforms' negative impacts on the poor. The WB increasingly included human and social issues in its discourse. However, "adjustment with a human face" also failed to provide an effective solution for sustainable growth and development in Africa. The number of people living in poverty remained the same or even increased, and African leaders remained passive in the policies they adopted.[2] In light of this, the WB began to call the Washington Consensus somewhat into question and shifted towards poverty eradication as the principal objective of its development strategy. This evolution took place as the UN adopted the *Millennium Declaration*, which sought to improve the well-being of individuals, eradicate poverty and inequality, and put all countries on the path to sustainable development. Financial institutions and international organizations formulated strategies with this goal in mind, and African leaders[3] were expected to apply them if they wanted to lift their countries out of the abyss separating them from the rest of the world. Out of this context of international consensus on the need for collective action, AUDA was born.[4]

AUDA (until July 2108 known as NEPAD) was the result of a merger between two competing projects: the MAP and the Omega. The MAP, which emphasized international partnerships, Africa's place in globalization, and political and economic governance, was promoted by South African President Thabo Mbeki, Nigerian President Olusegun Obasanjo, Algerian President Abdelaziz Bouteflika, and Egyptian President Hosni Mubarak. The Omega Plan, proposed by Senegalese President Abdoulaye Wade, paid particular attention to development aid, infrastructure, agriculture, health, and education. These two plans merged on July 3, 2001 to form the New African Initiative, renamed NEPAD on October 23, 2001, when it was

---

[2] The failure of SAPs created a "critical juncture" for the WB and the IMF. These conditions demanded a reorientation of the discourses and practices of development.

[3] The new policies and development strategies proposed by IFIs correspond to a "bifurcation" with respect to their former practices. A new trajectory, determined by the old one, was adopted.

[4] The concept of "path dependence" helps to explain AUDA's origin. The change in orientation of IFIs' policies also created a critical juncture favorable to AUDA's emergence. But this concept alone is not sufficient for a meaningful explanation.

adopted by the Organization of African Unity (today the AU). In July 2018, NEPAD officially became the "African Union Development Agency, or AUDA."

AUDA's founders considered the institution innovative in relation to all earlier actions and presented the initiative as an endogenous one. However, the comparison of discourses, strategies, and programs presented here has revealed a different reality.

Changes and Continuities between AUDA's and IFIs

The comparison of discourses has shown that the initiative had exogenous causes. Indeed, most key elements of AUDA's discourse, in particular those relating to the project's origin, can be found in the advice given by the WB and the UN – AUDA uses the same rhetoric as these international organizations.[5] The discourse-variable shows that there is more continuity than change between the WB's discourse and AUDA's.

I then looked for similarities and differences between the strategies applied and recommended by the WB and those adopted by AUDA. This comparison showed that the content and priorities presented in AUDA's strategies were often direct replicas of those of the WB. These strategies include improving good political and economic governance by strengthening institutions; promoting peace and security; eradicating poverty; investing in the population and in infrastructure; promoting agriculture and rural development; liberalizing trade policies; leveraging development aid and financing; and forming national, regional, and international partnerships. Indeed, AUDA's strategies seem directly inspired by the WB publication *Can Africa Claim the Twenty-First Century?* (WB 2000a). The main differences we have seen concern the mechanism of AUDA's functioning. Thus, we can say that AUDA's strategies continue those of the WB.

Regarding programs of action, I focused on three specific areas: political governance and democracy, economic governance, and the

---

[5] Two explanations are possible. Sociological institutionalism explains the adoption of a similar discourse by pointing out that African leaders, suffused with the liberal culture transmitted by international economic organizations and by donors, changed cultural references. Rational choice institutionalism holds that the leaders adopted the same language in anticipation of their partners' behavior; the imitation can thus be explained through African leaders' quest to maximize profits and obtain funding.

fight against poverty. The actions NEPAD prioritized in supporting democracy and good governance – reforming public services and administration; strengthening parliamentary control, participatory democracy, and the fight against corruption; and reforming the legal system – can all be found in the WB's previous recommendations. Thus, NEPAD's political measures represented continuity with the WB's initiatives.

The actions taken by NEPAD for economic governance and market access were also similar to those of the WB. In addition, NEPAD sought to challenge the WB within its own domain, notably regarding goals for production diversification and promoting exports. The fight against poverty led to a similar scenario. I may add that NEPAD did not have a real plan of action to fight poverty; it is satisfied with simply accepting the various existing international programs in this domain. These programs belong to the WB, the IMF, the UNDP, and the UN. NEPAD thus continues the policies of these institutions.

All in all, the various elements of discourse examined serve to validate my two hypotheses. First, African leaders did take a more active stance in formulating and implementing development programs for the continent. Their political attitude was thus something new, and the race for leadership among NEPAD's founders exemplifies this.

Second, the discourses, strategies, and programs of NEPAD were largely similar to those of the WB. Thus, contrary to what some African leaders claim, there has been no strategic innovation. These elements constitute continuations of WB and the IMF initiatives[6] in terms of specific development policies and strategies.

NEPAD Almost Two Decades Later: Institutional Evolution and Development, the Implementation of Key Programs, and Future Challenges

Today, although AUDA can boast some successes, much more is needed for the achievement of its initial mission (or of its goals as presented in the founding framework) as discussed in the chapter 5. In terms of institutional evolution and development, it underwent a

---

[6] By these I mean the recent changes observed within IFIs. As an example from the IMF, the Enhanced Structural Adjustment Facility (ESAF) became the Poverty Reduction and Growth Facility. Within the WB, the Policy Framework Paper and the Structural Adjustment Credit became, respectively, the PRSP and the Poverty Reduction Support Credit. See Cling et al. 2006.

significant transformation in February 2010 when it was further integrated into the African Union. The NEPAD Secretariat was replaced by
the NEPAD Planning and Coordination Agency (also known as the
NEPAD Agency), a technical body or specialized agency of the AU.
Although NEPAD is recognized by its international partners and is
accepted in Africa, it is struggling to receive financing at the international level and to convince states and subregional organizations
to adopt and implement its programs. I have analyzed three major
NEPAD programs: the APRM (NEPAD 2001), the CAADP (NEPAD
2010), and the NEPAD STAP (NEPAD 2003b), all of which reveal
underwhelming results.

Since its founding, NEPAD has gradually become more institutionalized, although its final configuration is different from the initial intentions of its decision-makers. Nevertheless, it still faces many challenges,
which have contributed to the disappointing results of the programs
analyzed. There are, for example, the issue of its appropriation both at
the level of African states and African civil society; the degree of participation of the various actors involved in its implementation; the manner
in which it functions, giving member states little incentive to behave well
and including few restrictions to punish them if they do not; its limited
mobilization of financing; and finally, the need to adjust its organizational configuration and to strengthen its institutional capacities in
order to successfully realize its vision, its mission, and its programs.

What Conclusions Can Be Drawn about the Development of Institutions in Africa?

It is useful to propose theoretical conclusions regarding the main
concerns of the neo-institutional school of thought – the origin and
evolution of institutions and the relationships between institutions and
actors – whenever conducting a study of Africa and, even more so, of
NEPAD. As for the origin of institutions, it would appear that it is
difficult, though not impossible, to innovate within a highly structured
institutional context in Africa.[7] The emergence of an institution such as
NEPAD corresponds to a complex dynamic that blends historical
processes, the calculated intentions and strategies of actors, and structural and institutional constraints (Chabal 2002).

---

[7] See Signé 2010 and Signé 2011.

The evolution or development of institutions does not necessarily correspond to the intentions of the political actors who create or promote them (Pierson 2000), but rather, the results from a particular constellation of structural, contextual, strategic, and ideational factors that must be observed empirically.

Regarding the ways in which institutions affect actors' behavior, since its creation NEPAD has multiplied its programs and action plans, with limited results. This raises the question of the relationships between institutions and actors and between programs and their implementation. Indeed, how can we explain that the actors responsible for implementing these programs do not produce results in conformity with initial intentions or objectives? In the case of NEPAD, the explanations include: excessively ambitious objectives that do not account for actual capacities; limited or nonappropriated involvement by national and local decision-makers charged with implementation; inadequate institutional configurations; a political context often not suited to policies; an excessively outward-looking attitude; numerous programs without appropriate prioritization; human capital that is still insufficient; and the complexity of policies to be implemented (Matland 1995). If they truly hope to make this project a success, NEPAD's (AUDA's) leaders will have to review these variables.

Continental Coordination and Interstate Cooperation in Africa: International Relations and Interdisciplinary Contributions

Understanding NEPAD and its impact on interstate cooperation in Africa requires understanding the individual and collective motivations, aspirations, identities, and interests of such countries engaging with each other at the individual or continental level. What drives interstate cooperation for development in Africa at a continental level? Why do African states cooperate through NEPAD? What roles are played by ideas, ideologies, identities, power dynamics, interests, institutions, and leadership, and how do they relate to each other in such forms of cooperation? How much influence does NEPAD have on domestic politics, and what explains the variation of its impact across issues and over time? Employing a single approach may not allow us to understand the full complexity of a phenomenon. The analysis of NEPAD shows that institutional genesis and evolution involve multiple factors – in this case, the ideologies of Pan-Africanism and African renewal, shared ideas and visions regarding African problems and solutions, and a specific policy framework of programs, projects, and institutions to achieve its vision.

I have therefore followed in the footsteps of Robert O. Keohane (2008, 714) who considers the multiple approaches within international relations to be "complementary rather than alternative," and I have taken a cue from Hall and Taylor (1996), Paul Pierson (2004), and my own prior work (2010), in favoring the mutual reinforcement of the various approaches characteristic of the new institutional school in comparative politics. I have sought to carry out the project expressed by Steven Smith (2008) when he wrote, "International relations [to which I add comparative politics] needs to focus on the relationship between the material and the ideational" (729).

From an ideational/constructivist perspective, NEPAD has contributed to the establishment of a modern African zeitgeist. The ideas, values, and ideologies promoted by NEPAD were themselves integrated into Agenda 2063, a document that embodies Pan-African ideology. The ideals of Pan-Africanism and an African renaissance remain integral to the success of the AU, even if the vision of Pan-African identity is emphasized less now than it was at the birth of NEPAD.

NEPAD has tried to increase cooperation and develop policy coordination among African states through the ideational process of reframing and redefining problems to create a common continental perception and understanding of root causes and, most importantly, of future solutions. The pattern of impact on African countries' developmental policies is uneven, ranging from near inertia to partial absorption or accommodation, but thus far falling short of full transformation. These impacts have primarily been made through a process of behavioral rule absorption, rather than systematic, intentional, and fully integrated adoption. Ideational factors are therefore critical to understanding the origin and extent of interstate cooperation in Africa. They are, however, insufficient for understanding the full scope of cooperation and need to be complemented by other variables.

From a materialist/realist perspective, the level of the integration of NEPAD's initiatives into national policies also depends on the interest of state elites, who may or may not favor cooperation. Countries are more likely to cooperate on issues and in sectors from which they receive technical or financial support, especially support that does not constrain their own autonomy or which they believe is most urgent or necessary. Given the existing power dynamics, South Africa, Nigeria, and Senegal, each a founding member of NEPAD, also generally have expressed different aspirations for their involvement and implementation, as compared to those countries that were not involved in NEPAD's creation. The founding members have also played a leading role in initiating policies. The levels of motivation and aspiration also differ from one cluster to another. Some sectors are better represented in policies than others, creating an asymmetry reflective of power dynamics. The materialist/realist perspective allows us to explain the dynamics of power or interest behind specific policies, but also the variation across countries' and subregional communities' levels of participation.

From an institutional/liberal perspective, many African countries have expressed the belief that continental cooperation through NEPAD is likely to generate mutual benefits, and prevent threats, including marginalization by the international community. However, the capacity actually to create coordinating institutions differs significantly from one country to another. South Africa, Cape Verde, and Mauritius all have strong institutional capacities and well-organized central governments, in comparison to states embroiled in or emerging from conflict, such as the Central African Republic or the Democratic Republic of Congo. Through institutional reforms, NEPAD's strong leadership has facilitated coordination at the continental level and has increased state participation in its initiatives, but challenges remain given the organization's interdependency with multiple other regional institutions and decision-making bodies. While many African countries share an understanding of the cause(s) of their problems, reaching a consensus on solutions and the strategies to implement them continues to be a major challenge. This is not very surprising given the variety of problems, institutions, and actors involved and the heterogeneity of countries each of which may have a different agenda for solving its own problems.

In conclusion, given the multiplicity of ideas, interests, institutions, actors, and programs, studying continental institutions such as NEPAD requires an approach capable of incorporating all relevant factors. The idea is not just to say what matters, but how and under what conditions. Without "eclectic theorizing" this would be a "mission impossible" for any scholar seeking a comprehensive understanding. Specific approaches are, of course, relevant for specific research questions. As I stated in my previous book (2017), "the merit of this eclectic approach is to propose, through the complementarity of variables, a more comprehensive and valid explanation of the relationship between international, regional, and national actors ... This is even more so when the analysis bears on the African continent" (Signé 2017, 174).

References

Abrahamsen, Rita. 2017. "Africa and International Relations: Assembling Africa, Studying the World." *African Affairs* 116 (462): 125–39. doi: 10.1093/afraf/adw071.

Adegbite, Esther Olufunmilayo, and Kehinde Adekunle Adetiloye. 2013. "Financial Globalisation and Domestic Investment in Developing Countries: Evidence from Nigeria." *Mediterranean Journal of Social Sciences* 4 (6): 213–23.

Adler, Emanuel, and Haas, Peter M. 1992. "Conclusion: Epistemic Communities, World Order, and the Creation of a Reflective Research Program." *International Organization* 46 (1): 367–90.

African Development Bank. 2003. *Project Implementation Review of the NEPAD Infrastructure Short Term Action Plan (STAP)*. Tunis: African Development Bank.

2005. *AfDB Group Annual Report 2004*. Abuja: African Development Bank.

2009. *NEPAD Infrastructure Project Preparation Facility Project Information Memorandum*. Tunis: African Development Bank.

2012. *Financing PIDA Projects Brief*. Tunis: African Development Bank.

2018. African Economic Outlook. Tunis: African Development Bank.

African Development Bank, and Organization for Economic Co-operation and Development. 2010. *African Economic Outlook 2010*. Paris and Tunis: OECD and African Development Bank. https://sustainabledevel opment.un.org/content/documents/AEO2010_part1_p76.pdf (accessed April 27, 2018).

African Development Bank, Organization for Economic Co-operation and Development, and United Nations Development Programme. 2014. *African Economic Outlook 2014: Global Value Chains and Africa's Industrialisation*. Tunis: African Development Bank.

2016. *African Economic Outlook 2016: Sustainable Cities and Structural Transformation*. Tunis: African Development Bank.

2017. *African Economic Outlook 2017: Entrepreneurship and Industrialization*. Tunis: African Development Bank.

African Peer Review Mechanism. 2016a. *APRM: A Vision and Plan for the Future. Strategic Plan 2016–2020.* Johannesburg: APMR Secretariat.

2016b. "Statute of the African Peer Review Mechanism." Johannesburg: African Peer Review Mechanism.

African Peer Review Mechanism, and African Union. 2012. *Annual Report: African Peer Review Mechanism 2011.* Addis Ababa: African Peer Review Mechanism, and African Union.

African Union. n.d. "Agenda 2063." African Union. www.au.int/web/en/agenda2063 (accessed April 27, 2018).

n.d. "CFTA – Continental Free Trade Area." https://au.int/en/ti/cfta/about (accessed April 27, 2018).

2002. *AHG/235 (XXXVIII), Annex 2. NEPAD. APRM.* Durban: African Union.

2014. "Common African Position (CAP) on the Post-2015 Development Agenda." January 31. www.uneca.org/sites/default/files/uploaded-documents/Macroeconomy/post2015/cap-post2015_en.pdf (accessed April 27, 2018).

2016. "A Joint Meeting with the Arab Maghreb Union Agrees on the Need to Accelerate the Implementation of PIDA Projects in the Region." www.au.int/web/sites/default/files/pressreleases/31609-pr-pr_-_uma-pida-rabat_en.pdf (accessed April 27, 2018).

African Union, and Program for Infrastructure Development in Africa. 2017. *The Single African Air Transport Market: An Agenda 2063 Flagship Project SAATM – flying the AU agenda 2063.*

African Union Assembly. 2014. *Assembly of the Union Twenty-Third Ordinary Session. Decision on the Integration of the APRM into the African Union Doc. EX.CL/851(XXV). Decision No: Assembly/AU/Dec.527(XXIII).* www.au.int/web/sites/default/files/decisions/9661-assembly_au_dec_517_-_545_xxiii_e.pdf (accessed April 27, 2018).

2017. *Assembly of the Union Twenty-Eighth Ordinary Session. Draft Decisions, Declarations, Resolution and Motion.* www.hrw.org/sites/default/files/supporting_resources/assembly_au_draft_dec._1_-_19_xxviii_e.pdf (accessed April 27, 2018).

African Union Commission. 2015a. *Agenda 2063. The Africa We Want.* Addis Ababa: African Union Commission. www.un.org/en/africa/osaa/pdf/au/agenda2063.pdf (accessed April 27, 2018).

2015b. *First Ten-Year Implementation Plan 2014–2023.* Addis Ababa: African Union Commission.

African Union Commission, and NEPAD Planning and Coordination Agency. 2017. *Continental Agribusiness Strategy Framework Document: Driving Africa's Inclusive Growth.*

African Union Executive Council Twenty-Sixth Ordinary Session. 2015. *Decisions and Recommendation of the Twenty-Sixth Ordinary Session of the Executive Council. EX.CL/Dec.851–872(XXVI).* January. Addis Ababa: African Union. www.au.int/web/sites/default/files/decisions/9666-ex_cl_dec_851_-_872_xxvi_e.pdf (accessed April 27, 2018).

African Union Executive Council Twenty-Seventh Ordinary Session. 2015. *Decisions and Recommendation of the Twenty-Seventh Ordinary Session of the Executive Council.* June. Addis Ababa: African Union. www.au.int/web/sites/default/files/decisions/31762-ex_cl_dec_873_-_898_xxvii_e.pdf (accessed April 27, 2018).

African Union Executive Council Twenty-Eighth Ordinary Session. 2016. *Decisions and Recommendation of the Twenty-Ninth Ordinary Session of the Executive Council.* EX.CL/Dec.898–918(XXVIII) Rev. 1. January. Addis Ababa: African Union. www.au.int/web/sites/default/files/decisions/29513-ex_cl_dec_898_-_918_xxviii_e.pdf (accessed April 27, 2018).

African Union Executive Council Twenty-Ninth Ordinary Session. 2016. *Decisions and Recommendation of the Twenty-Ninth Ordinary Session of the Executive Council.* EX.CL/Dec.919–925 and 928–938(XXIX). July. Addis Ababa: African Union. www.au.int/web/sites/default/files/decisions/31275-ex_cl_dec_919_-_925_and_928_-_938_xxix_e.pdf (accessed April 27, 2018).

African Union, and NEPAD. 2009. *The AU/NEPAD African Action Plan 2010–2015: Advancing Regional and Continental Integration in Africa.* Addis Ababa: African Union and NEPAD.

AfriMAP. 2010. *The African Peer Review Mechanism: A Compilation of Studies of the Process in Nine African Countries.* Johannesburg: Open Society Initiative for Southern Africa. www.opensocietyfoundations.org/sites/default/files/aprm-overview-english-20100720_0.pdf (accessed April 27, 2018).

Agénor, Pierre-Richard, and Karim El Aynaoui. 2014. "Politiques Publiques, Transformation Industrielle, Croissance et Emploi au Maroc : Une Analyse Quantitative." OCP Policy Center Research Paper RP-14/03. www.ocppc.ma/sites/default/files/OCPPC-RP1404-2_0.pdf (accessed April 27, 2018).

Akume, Albert T., and Yahaya M. Abdullahi. 2013. "NEPAD and Governance Question in Nigeria: Progress and Challenges." *Journal of Research in National Development* 10 (3): 234–43.

Amaïzo, Yvez Ekoué. 2001. "De l'OUA à l'Union Africaine: les chemins de l'interdépendance." *Afrique contemporaine* 197: 97–145.

Amin, Samir. 1976. *Unequal Development.* New York: Monthly Review Press.

Amuwo, Kunle. 2002. "Globalization, NEPAD, and the Governance Question in Africa." *African Studies Quarterly* 6 (3): 65–82.

Annan, Kofi. 2003. "Secretary-General's Bulletin: Office of the Special Advisor on Africa." New York: United Nations Secretariat. www.un.org/en/ga/search/view_doc.asp?symbol=ST/SGB/2003/6 (accessed April 27, 2018).

Arrighi, Giovanni. 1994. *The Long Twentieth Century: Money, Power, and the Origins of Our Times*. London: Verso.

Aynaoui, Karim El, and Aomar Ibourk, eds. 2018. *Les enjeux du marché du travail au Maroc*. Rabat, Morocco: OCP Policy Center. www.ocppc.ma/sites/default/files/Final%20%20Le%20March%C3%A9%20du%20Travail%20Marocain.pdf (accessed April 27, 2018).

Baliamoune-Lutz, Mina. 2013. "ODA and the Quest for Innovative Sources of Financing Development." Robert Schuman Centre for Advanced Studies Policy Paper no. 2013/06. http://cadmus.eui.eu/bitstream/handle/1814/27497/RSCAS_PP_2013_06.pdf?sequence=1 (accessed April 27, 2018).

Bates, Robert H. 1981. *Markets and States in Tropical Africa: The Political Basis of Agricultural Policies*. California: University of California Press.

Béland, Daniel. 2002. "Néo-institutionnalisme historique et politiques sociales: une perspective sociologique." *Politique et Sociétés* 21 (3): 21–39.

Berahab, Rim. 2016. "Structure des échanges entre le Maroc et l'Afrique : une analyse de la spécialisation du commerce." OCP Policy Center Research Paper RP-16/07. www.ocppc.ma/sites/default/files/OCPPC-RP1607v2.pdf (accessed April 27, 2018).

——— 2017. "Relations between Morocco and Sub-Saharan Africa: What Is the Potential for Trade and Foreign Direct Investment?" OCP Policy Center Policy Brief PB-17/04. www.ocppc.ma/sites/default/files/OCPPC-PB1704vEn.pdf (accessed April 27, 2018).

Berger, M., J. Murugi, E. Buch, C. IJsselmuiden, M. Moran, J. Guzman, M. Devlin, and B. Kubata. 2009. "Strengthening Pharmaceutical Innovation in Africa." Council on Health Research for Development (COHRED and NEPAD). http://policycures.org/downloads/COHRED-NEPAD_Strengthening_Pharmaceutical_Innovation_AfricaREPORT.pdf (accessed April 27, 2018).

Berger, Peter L., and Thomas Luckmann. 1966. *The Social Construction of Reality: A Treatise in the Sociology of Knowledge*. New York: Doubleday.

Berman, Sheri. 1998. "Path Dependency and Political Action, Re-Examining Response to the Depression." *Comparative Politics* 30 (4): 379–400.

Bhorat, Haroon. 2014. "The Post-2015 Development Agenda: What Are the Priorities for Africa?" In *Foresight Africa: Top Priorities for the Continent in 2014*, 16–18. Washington, DC: The Brookings Institution.

Bhushan, Aniket. 2013. "Domestic Resource Mobilization and the Post-2015 Agenda." *GREAT Insights* 2 (3): 22–23.

Bikam, Abdelkhalek El, Afang Ndong Zita, and Kourouma Oumar. 2017. "African Union: What Are the Possible Options for Strategic Autonomy?" OCP Policy Center Policy Brief PB-17/29. www.ocppc.ma/sites/default/files/OCPPC-PB1729vEn_0.PDF (accessed April 27, 2018).

Bilal, Sanoussi. 2012. "What Is the Rise of South-South Relations About? Development, Not Aid." *Mondiaal Nieuws Papers* 70. http://ecdpm .org/wp-content/uploads/2013/10/What-is-Rise-South-South-Relations-about-Development-not-Aid-Bilal.pdf (accessed April 27, 2018).

Birdsall, Nancy. 2004. "Seven Deadly Sins: Reflections on Donor Failings." Center for Global Development Working Paper no. 50. www.cgdev.org/sites/default/files/2737_file_WP50_rev12_05_2.pdf (accessed April 27, 2018).

Bourguignon, François, Daniel Cohen, and Alain Liepetz, eds. 2000. *Développement*. Paris: La Documentation française.

Callan, Margaret. 2012. "What Do We Know about Private Sector Contributions to Development?" DevPolicyBlog, Development Policy Centre. http://devpolicy.org/what-do-we-know-about-private-sector-contributions-to-development20120110/ (accessed April 27, 2018).

Cantin, Étienne. 2002. "Le Système de Bretton Woods." In *Relations internationales*, edited by Alex Macleod, Evelyne Dufault, and Guillaume Dufour, 21–25. Quebec: Athéna.

Cardoso, Fernando. 1978. *Dépendance et développement en Amérique latine*. Paris: Presses Universitaires de France.

Carr, Edward H. 1964. *The Twenty Years' Crisis, 1919–1939: An Introduction to the Study of International Relations*. 2nd ed. New York: St Martin's Press.

Cattaneo, Olivier, Gary Gereffi, Sebastien Miroudot, and Daria Taglioni. 2013. "Joining, Upgrading, and Being Competitive in Global Value Chains: A Strategic Framework." World Bank Policy Research Working Paper no. 6406. http://documents.worldbank.org/curated/en/2540014 68336685890/pdf/wps6406.pdf (accessed April 27, 2018).

Chabal, Patrick. 2002. "The Quest for Good Government and Development in Africa: Is NEPAD the Answer?" *International Affairs (Royal Institute of International Affairs)* 1944–78 (3): 447–62.

Chang, Ha-Joon. 2002. *Kicking Away the Ladder: Development Strategy in Historical Perspective*. Lenders: Anthem Press.

Chauvin, Nicolas Depetris, and Aart Kraay. 2005. "What Has 100 Billion Dollars Worth of Debt Relief Done for Low-Income Countries?" http://siteresources.worldbank.org/DEC/Resources/ChauvinKraayWhatHas DebtReliefAccomplishedSept2005.pdf (accessed April 27, 2018).

Chenntouf, Tayeb. 2005. "NEPAD in the Twenty-First Century: An Answer to the Educational, Cultural and Scientific Challenges?" In *Africa and Development Challenges in the New Millennium: The NEPAD Debate*, edited by Jimi O. Adesina, Yao Graham, and Adebayo Olukoshi, 196–216. London: Zed.

Chibundu, Maxwell O. 2008. "NEPAD and the Rebirth of Development Theory and Praxis." http://papers.ssrn.com/sol3/papers.cfm?abstract_id=1122443 (accessed April 27, 2018).

Clausewitz, Carl Von. 1979. *On War*. Edited and translated by M. Howard and P. Paret. Princeton: Princeton University Press.

Cling, Jean-Pierre, Mireille Razafindrakoto, and François Roubaud, editors. 2006. *New International Poverty Reduction Strategies*. London: Routledge.

Collier, Paul. 2007. *The Bottom Billion*. Oxford: Oxford University Press.

Cooper, Frederick. 2001. "What Is the Concept of Globalization Good For? An African Historian's Perspective." *African Affairs* 100 (399): 189–213.

Cornia, Giovanni Andrea, Richard Jolly, and Frances Stewart. 1987. *Adjustment With a Human Face, Volume 1, Protecting the Vulnerable and Promoting Growth*. New York: Oxford University Press.

Cornia, Giovanni Andrea, Rolph van der Hoeven, and Thandika Mkandawire, eds. 1992. *Africa's Recovery in the 1990s: From Stagnation and Adjustment to Human Development*. New York: St. Martin's Press.

Coussy, Jean. 2004. "Le succès du NEPAD, un paradoxe." Montreal: Centre d'études et de recherche internationales.

Cox, Robert. 1987. *Production, Power, and World Order: Social Forces in the Making of History*. New York: Columbia University Press.

Dahou, Karim, Ismael Omar Haibado, and Mike Pfister. 2009. "Deepening African Financial Markets for Growth and Investment." Paper distributed at the Ministerial and Expert Roundtable of the NEPAD-OECD Africa Investment Initiative, November 11–12. www.oecd.org/development/investmentfordevelopment/43966839.pdf (accessed April 27, 2018).

Da Silva, Igor Castellano. 2013. "From OAU to AU: 50 Years of African Continentalism." *Mundorama* 67. www.mundorama.net/2013/03/30/from-oau-to-au-50-years-of-african-continentalism-by-igor-castellano-da-silva/ (accessed April 27, 2018).

de Beer, Jeremy, Izabella Sowa, and Kristen Holman. 2014. "Frameworks for Analysing African Innovation: Entrepreneurship, the Informal Economy and Intellectual Property." In *Innovation & Intellectual Property: Collaborative Dynamics in Africa*, edited by Jeremy de Beer, Chris Armstrong, Chidi Oguamanam, and Tobias Schonwetter, 32–58. Claremont: University of Cape Town Press.

Defarges Philippe Moreau. 1996. *Les organisations internationales contemporaines*. Paris: Seuil.

Dembele, Demba Moussa. 2012. "Africa's Developmental Impasse: Some Perspectives and Recommendations." *Africa Development* 37 (4): 179–96. www.ajol.info/index.php/ad/article/view/87489/77171 (accessed April 27, 2018).

De Renzio, Paolo, and Harika Masud. 2011. "Measuring and Promoting Budget Transparency: The Open Budget Index as a Research and Advocacy Tool." *Governance* 24 (3): 607–16.

De Waal, Alex. 2002. "What's New in the New Partnership for Africa's Development." *International Affairs* 78 (3): 463–75.

Diamond, Larry, and Michal Plattner. 2010. *Democratization in Africa: Progress and Retreat*. Baltimore: Johns Hopkins University Press.

Di Maggio, Paul, and Walter Powell. 1991. *The New Institutionalism in Organizational Analysis*. Chicago: The University of Chicago Press.

Dömeland, Dörte, and Homi Kharas. 2009. "Debt Relief and Sustainable Financing to Meet the MDGs." In *Debt Relief and Beyond: Lessons Learned and Future Challenges*, edited by Carlos A. Prima Braga and Dörte Dömeland, 117–40. Washington, DC: World Bank.

Dufour, Charlotte, Johanna Jelensperger, and Elvira Uccello. 2013. "Mainstreaming Nutrition in Agriculture Investment Plans in Sub-Saharan Africa: Lessons Learnt from the NEPAD CAADP Nutrition Capacity Development Initiative." *SCN News* 40: 61–68.

Duruflé, Gilles. 1988. *L'ajustement structurel en Afrique (Sénégal, Côte d'Ivoire, Madagascar)*. Paris: Karthala.

Easterly, William. 2006. *The White Man's Burden: Why the West's Efforts to Aid the Rest Have Done So Much Ill and So Little Good*. New York: Penguin.

Ebegbulem, Joseph C., John A. Adams, and Ayuk A. Achu. 2012. "The Challenges of Integrating Africa into the Globalised World through New Partnership for Africa's Development (NEPAD)." *International Journal of Humanities and Social Sciences* 2 (6): 270-78. http://ijhssnet.com/journals/Vol_2_No_6_Special_Issue_March_2012/25.pdf (accessed April 27, 2018).

ECDPM, ESRF, and LARES. 2014. "Independent Assessment of the CAADP Multi-Donor Trust Fund." Discussion Paper No 148. http://ecdpm.org/wp-content/uploads/DP-158-Independent-Assessment-CAADP-Multi-Donor-Trust-Fund-2014.pdf (accessed April 27, 2018).

Economist. 2000. "Hopeless Africa." *The Economist*. May 11. www.economist.com/node/333429 (accessed April 27, 2018).

2011a. "Africa's Impressive Growth." *The Economist*. January 6. www.economist.com/blogs/dailychart/2011/01/daily_chart (accessed April 27, 2018).

2011b. "The Hopeful Continent: Africa Rising." *The Economist*. December 1. www.economist.com/node/21541015 (accessed April 27, 2018).

Elovainio, Riku, and D. Evans. 2013. "Raising and Spending Domestic Money for Health." Centre for Global Health Working Group Papers: Working Group on Financing Paper 2. www.chathamhouse.org/sites/files/chathamhouse/public/Research/Global%20Health/0513_health finance.pdf (accessed April 27, 2018).

Emmanuel, Arghiri. 1972. *Unequal Exchange: A Study of the Imperialism of Trade*. New York: Monthly Review Press.

Evans, Peter, Dietrich Rueschemeyer, and Theda Skocpol. 1985. *Bringing the State Back In*. New York: Cambridge University Press.

Fakile, Adeniran Samuel, Folajimi Festus Adegbie, and Olusola Samuel Faboyede. 2014. "Mobilizing Domestic Revenue for Sustainable Development in Africa." *European Journal of Accounting Auditing and Finance Research* 2 (2): 91–108.

Fankam, Jeanine. 2004. "NEPAD: une opportunité pour le Cameroun." *Cameroun Tribune*, May 26.

Felts, Arthur A., and Philip H. Jos. 2000. "Time and Space: The Origins and Implications of the New Public Management." *Administrative Theory and Praxis* 22 (3): 519–33.

Finnemore, Martha, and Kathryn Sikking. 1998. "International Norm Dynamics and Political Change." *International Organization* 52 (4): 887–917.

Fjeldstad, Odd-Helge. 2013. "Taxation and Development: A Review of Donor Support to Strengthen Tax Systems in Developing Countries." World Institute for Development Economics Research Working Paper no. 2013/010. www.econstor.eu/dspace/bitstream/10419/80886/1/736 072497.pdf (accessed April 27, 2018).

Flatters, Frank. 2005. "The Economics of MIDP and the South African Motor Industry." Paper presented at TIPS/NEDLAC South Africa Trade and Poverty Programme (SATPP) Policy Dialogue Workshop, Johannesburg, November 2. http://qed.econ.queensu.ca/pub/faculty/flat ters/writings/ff_economics_of_midp.pdf (accessed April 27, 2018).

Fourie, Pieter, and Brendan Vickers. 2003. "African Economic Pragmatism, NEPAD, and Policy Prostitution." *Africa Insight* 33 (3): 11–19.

Frank, Gunder. 1966. *The Development of Under-Development*. Boston: New England Free Press.

1979. *Dependent Accumulation and Underdevelopment*. New York: Monthly Review Press.

Gaebler Ted, and David Osborne. 1992. *Reinventing Government: How the Entrepreneurial Spirit Is Transforming the Public Sector*. Reading: Addison-Wesley Publishing Co.

Gankou, Jean-Marie. 1985. *L'investissement dans les pays en développement: le cas du Cameroun.* Paris: Economica.

Gaye, Sérigne-Bamba. 2002. "Décentralisation, réseaux de politique publique et construction du référentiel sectoriel à travers la réforme de la fiscalité locale au Sénégal." Doctoral thesis, Laval University, Québec.

Gayi, Samuel K. 2008. "Mobilizing Domestic Financial Resources for Africa's Development." *African Technology Development Forum Journal* 4 (4): 36–51. www.atdforum.org/IMG/pdf__Mobilizing_domestic_resources_Gayi.pdf (accessed April 27, 2018).

Gazibo, Mamoudou, and Jane Jenson. 2004. *La politique comparée, fondements, enjeux, et approches théoriques.* Montreal: Presses de l'Université de Montréal.

Geo-Jaja, Macleans A., and Garth Mangum. 2001. "Structural Adjustment as an Inadvertent Enemy of Human Development in Africa." *Journal of Black Studies* 32 (1): 30–49.

Gill, Stephen. 1990. *American Hegemony and the Trilateral Commission.* Cambridge: Cambridge University Press.

editor. 1993. *Gramsci, Historical Materialism and International Relations.* Cambridge: Cambridge University Press.

Gilpin, Robert. 1981. *War and Change in World Politics.* Cambridge: Cambridge University Press.

Girishankar, Navin. 2009. "Innovating Development Finance: From Financing Sources to Financial Solutions." World Bank Policy Research Working Paper, no. 5111. http://elibrary.worldbank.org/doi/pdf/10.1596/1813-9450-5111 (accessed April 27, 2018).

Greenhill, Romilly, and Annalisa Prizzon. 2012. "Who Foots the Bill after 2015? What New Trends in Development Finance Mean for the Post-MDGs." Working paper 360. London: Overseas Development Institute. http://sustainabledevelopment.un.org/content/documents/768odi.pdf (accessed April 27, 2018).

Greenhill, Romilly, Annalisa Prizzon, and Andrew Rogerson. 2013. "The Age of Choice: Developing Countries in the New Aid Landscape." Working paper 364. London: Overseas Development Institute. www.odi.org/sites/odi.org.uk/files/odi-assets/publications-opinion-files/8188.pdf (accessed April 27, 2018).

Griesco, Joseph M. 1988. "Anarchy and the Limits of Cooperation: A Realist Critique of the Newest Liberal Institutionalism." *International Organization* 42 (3): 485–507.

Grotius, Hugo. 1984. *The Law of War and Peace.* Birmingham: Legal Classics Library, Division of Gryphon Editions.

1995. *The Law of Prize and Booty.* Buffalo: Hein.

Group of Eight. 2002. *G8 Africa Action Plan.* Kananaskis: Group of Eight.

Hall, Peter. 1986. *Governing the Economy, The Politics of State Interven-
    tion in Britain and France*. New York: Oxford University Press.
    1989. *The Political Power of Economic Ideas: Keynesianism Across
    Nations*. Princeton: Princeton University Press.
Hall, Peter, and Rosemary Taylor. 1996. "Political Science and the Three
    New Institutionalisms." *Political Studies* 44 (5): 936–57.
Hamilton, Alexander. 1997. "Report on Manufacturers." In *The Theoret-
    ical Evolution of Economy: A Reader*, edited by George T. Crane and
    Abla Amawi, 37–47. New York: Oxford University Press.
Hammouda, Hakim Ben, and Patrick N. Osakwe. 2006. *Financing Devel-
    opment in Africa: Trends, Issues and Challenges*. Addis Ababa: Afri-
    can Trade Policy Centre, United Nations Economic Commission for
    Africa. www.sarpn.org/documents/d0002563/ATPC_financing_Africa_
    Des2006.pdf.
Hanouz, Margareta Drzeniek, and Caroline Ko. 2013. "Enabling African
    Trade: Findings from the Enabling Trade Index." In *The Africa Com-
    petitiveness Report 2013*, by World Economic Forum, 41–68. Geneva:
    World Economic Forum.
Hansen, Randal, and Desmond King. 2001. "Eugenic Ideas, Political Inter-
    ests, and Policy Variance: Immigration and Sterilization Policy in Britain
    and the United States." *World Politics* 53 (2): 237–63.
Hardin, Garrett. 1968. "The Tragedy of the Commons." *Science* 162 (3859):
    1243–48.
Hasenclever, Andreas, Peter Mayer, and Volker Rittberger. 1997. *Theories
    of International Regimes*. Cambridge: Cambridge University Press.
Hausmann, Ricardo, Jason Hwang, and Dani Rodrik. 2007. "What You
    Export Matters." *Journal of Economic Growth* 12 (1): 1–25.
Hobbes, Thomas. 1968. *Leviathan*. New York: Penguin.
    1985. *Leviathan*. Edited by C. B. MacPherson. Harmondsworth: Penguin.
    1986. *Leviathan*. Harmondsworth: Penguin.
Honda, Shunichiro, Hiroshi Kato, and Yukimi Shimoda. 2013. "South-South
    and Triangular Cooperation for Sub-Saharan Africa's Development:
    With Special Emphasis on Knowledge Exchange and Co-Creation."
    In *For Inclusive and Dynamic Development in Sub-Saharan Africa*.
    JICA Research Institute. www.jica.go.jp/jica-ri/publication/booksandre
    ports/jrft3q00000029aw-att/TICAD_JICA-RI-1300-Chapter13-v3.pdf
    (accessed April 27, 2018).
Hope, Kempe Ronald. 2002. "From Crisis to Renewal: Toward a Successful
    Implementation of the New Partnership for Africa's Development."
    African Affairs 101 (404): 387–402.
Houdaigui, Rachid El, ed. 2017. *African Union: What Are the Possible
    Options for Strategic Autonomy?* Rabat, Morocco: OCP Policy Center.

www.ocppc.ma/sites/default/files/Rapport%20APSACO%20AN.pdf (accessed April 27, 2018).

Hugon, Philippe. 2002. "Le NEPAD: nouvelle chance pour l'Afrique." *Afrique contemporaine* 204: 42–51.

Igué, John. 2002. "Le NEPAD, initiative de la dernière chance?" *La revue international et stratégique* 46 (2): 103–6.

IJsselmuiden, Carel, Debbie L. Marais, Francisco Becerra-Posada, and Hassen Ghannem. 2012. "Africa's Neglected Area of Human Resources for Health Research: The Way Forward." *South African Medical Journal* 102 (4): 228–33.

Ikenberry, G. John. 2000. *After Victory: Institutions, Strategic Restraint, and the Rebuilding of Order after Major Wars.* Princeton: Princeton University Press.

International Air Transport Association (IATA). 2018. "IATA Welcomes Single African Air Transport Market but Says Effective Implementation is Key." www.iata.org/pressroom/pr/Pages/2018-01-28-01.aspx (accessed April 27, 2018).

Jespersen, Eva. 1992. "External Shocks, Adjustment Policies, and Economic and Social Performance." In *Africa's Recovery in the 1990s: From Stagnation and Adjustment to Human Development,* edited by Giovanni Andrea Cornia, Rolph van der Hoeven, and Thandika Mkandawire, 9–50. New York: St. Martin's Press.

Jones, Vivian C., and Brock R. Williams. 2012. "US Trade and Investment Relations with Sub-Saharan Africa and the African Growth and Opportunity Act." Congressional Research Service Report RL31772. Washington, DC: Congressional Research Service. https://fas.org/sgp/crs/row/RL31772.pdf (accessed April 27, 2018).

Joshua, Samuel Gambo, Okpanachi Joshua, and Danpome Gosele Moses. 2013. "Rural Savings Institutions and Economic Empowerment in Nigeria: An Analysis." *International Journal of Arts and Commerce* 2 (3) 71–80.

Kant, Immanuel. 1991. "Perpetual Peace: A Philosophical Sketch." In *Political Writings,* translated by H.B. Nisbert, edited by Hans Reiss Hans, 93–130. 2nd ed. Cambridge: Cambridge University Press.

Karns, Margaret P., and Karen A. Mingst. 2010. *International Organizations: The Politics and Processes of Global Governance.* London: Lynne Rienner Publishers.

Katzenstein, Peter J. 2005. *A World of Regions: Asia and Europe in the American Imperium.* Ithaca: Cornell University Press.

Katzenstein, Peter, and Rudra Sil. 2008. "Eclectic Theorizing in the Study and Practice of International Relations." In *The Oxford Handbook of International Relations,* edited by Christian Reus-Smit and Duncan Snidal, 109–30. Oxford: Oxford University Press.

Katzenstein, Peter J., Robert O. Keohane, and Stephen.D. Krasner. 1998. "International Organization and the Study of World Politics." *International Organization* 52 (4): 645–85.

Kedir, Abbi M. 2011. "Donor Coordination in Fragile States of Africa: Capacity Building for Peace and Poverty Reduction." *World Journal of Entrepreneurship, Management and Sustainable Development* 7 (2/3/4): 307–56.

Kennedy, Paul. 1987. *The Rise and Fall of the Great Powers: Economic Change and Military Conflict from 1500 to 2000.* New York: Random House.

Keohane, Robert O. 1984. *After Hegemony: Cooperation and Discord in the World Politics Economy.* Princeton: Princeton University Press.

1989. *International Institutions and State Power: Essays in International Relations Theory.* Boulder: Westview.

1990. "International Liberalism Reconsidered." In *The Economic Limits to Modern Politics*, edited by J. Dunn, 165–94. Cambridge: Cambridge University Press.

2008. "Big Questions in the Study of World Politics." In *The Oxford Handbook of International Relations*, edited by Christian Reus-Smit and Duncan Smidal, 708–15. Oxford: Oxford University Press.

Keohane, Robert O., and Joseph S. Nye, Jr. 2001. *Power and Interdependence.* 3rd ed. New York: Longman.

Kindleberger, Charles P. 1976. "Systems of International Economic Organization." In *Money and the Coming World Order*, edited by David P. Calleo, 15–39. New York: New York University Press.

Kingdom of Morocco, Ministry of Economy and Finance, Directorate of Financial Studies and Forecasts. 2014. *Moroccan-African Relations: The Ambition of "New Borders."* Rabat: Kingdom of Morocco.

Kimenyi, Mwangi S. 2014. "Harnessing Africa's Emerging Partnerships." In *Foresight Africa: Top Priorities for the Continent in 2014*, 32–35. Washington, DC: The Brookings Institution.

Koelbe, Thomas. 1994. "The New Institutionalism in Political Science and Sociology." *Comparative Politics* 27 (2): 231–43.

Krasner, Stephen D. 1978. *Defending the National Interest: Raw Materials Investments and US Foreign Policy.* Princeton: Princeton University Press.

1982. "Structural Causes and Regime Consequences: Regimes as Intervening Variables." *International Organization* 36 (2): 185-205.

1999. *Sovereignty: Organized Hypocrisy.* Princeton: Princeton University Press.

Landsberg, Chris. 2012. "The African Union and the New Partnership for Africa's Development (NEPAD): Restoring a Relationship Challenged?" *African Journal on Conflict Resolution* 12 (2): 49–71.

Lecours, André. 2002. "L'approche néo-institutionnaliste en science politique: unité ou diversité?" *Politique et Sociétés* 21 (3): 3–19.

L'Écuyer, François. 2002. "Qui a besoin du NEPAD en Afrique?" In *Le G8 et l'Afrique, crise et reconstruction*. Montréal: Alternatives, Réseau d'action et de communication pour le développement international.

Lichbach, Mark Irving, and Alan S. Zuckerman. 1997. *Comparative Politics: Rationality, Culture, and Structure*. Cambridge Studies in Comparative Politics. Cambridge: Cambridge University Press.

Lo, Moubarack. 2016. "Relations Maroc-Afrique subsaharienne : quel bilan pour les 15 dernières années?" OCP Policy Center Research Paper RP-16/10. www.ocppc.ma/sites/default/files/OCPPC-RP1610v2.pdf (accessed April 27, 2018).

Locke, John. 1980. *The Second Treatise of Government*. Edited by C. B. MacPherson. Indianapolis: Hackett.

Loriaux, Michel. 2003. "France: A New 'Capitalism of Voice'?" In *States in the Global Economy, Bringing Domestic Institutions Back In*, edited by Linda Weiss, 101–20. New York: Cambridge University Press.

Loxley, John. 2003. "Imperialism and Economic Reform in Africa: What's New About the New Partnership for Africa's Development (NEPAD)?" *Review of African Political Economy* 30 (95): 119–28.

Lucci, Paula. 2012. "Post-2015 MDGs: What Role for Business?" Overseas Development Institute Working Paper. www.odi.org/sites/odi.org.uk/files/odi-assets/publications-opinion-files/7702.pdf (accessed April 27, 2018).

Luke, David, and Babajide Sodipo. 2015. "Launch of the Continental Free Trade Area: New Prospects for African Trade?" *ICTSD Bridges Africa*, Vol. 4, No. 6, International Centre for Trade and Sustainable Development.

Machiavelli, Niccolo. 1970. *The Discourses*. Translated by L. J. Walker. Harmondsworth: Penguin.

1985. *The Prince*. Translated by H. C. Mansfield. Chicago: University Press.

Makhan, Vijay S. 2002. "L'Union africaine et le NEPAD: un nouveau départ pour l'Afrique?" *Afrique contemporaine* 204: 5–10.

Makinde, Diran. 2014. "African Orphan Crops Consortium: A NEPAD-Led Initiative." In *Viewpoints: Africa's Future ... Can Biosciences Contribute?* edited by Brian Heap and David Bennett, 57–63. Cambridge: Banson/Biosciences for Africa.

March, James, and Olsen Johan. 1984. "The New Institutionalism: Organizational Factors in Political Life." *American Political Science Review* 78 (3): 734–49.

Mars, Inc. 2014. "AOCC Infographic." Mars, Inc. www.mars.com/global/african-orphan-crops.aspx.

Martin, Septime. 2007. "Regional Economic Communities within Nepad: What Prospects for Sustainable Economic and Social Development in Africa?" Tunis: African Development Ban. www.afdb.org/fileadmin/uploads/afdb/Documents/Knowledge/Conference_2007_anglais_19-part-IV-3.pdf (accessed April 27, 2018).

Marx, Karl, and Friedrich Engels. 1975. *Marx and Engels Collected Works,* vol. V. *April 1845–April 1847.* London: Lawrence.

Matland, Richard E. 1995. "Synthesizing the Implementation Literature." *Journal of Public Administration Research and Theory* 5 (2): 145–75.

Mavrotas, George, Syed Mansoob Murshed, and Sebastian Torres. 2011. "Natural Resource Dependence and Economic Performance in the 1970–2000 Period." *Review of Development Economics* 15 (1): 124–38.

Mayaki, Ibrahim Assane, "CFTA: Moving African Integration Further Forward," *The New Times,* April 5, 2018, www.newtimes.co.rw/opinions/cfta-moving-african-integration-further-forward (accessed April 27, 2018).

Maynard-Moody, Steven, Michael Musheno, and Dennis Palumbo. 1990. "Street-Wise Social Policy: Resolving the Dilemma of Street-Level Influence and Successful Implementation." *The Western Political Quarterly* 43 (4): 833–48.

Mazmanian, Daniel A., and Paul A. Sabatier. 1989. *Implementation and Public Policy with a New Postscript.* Lanham: University Press of America.

Mbaku, John Mukum. 2004. "NEPAD and Prospects for Development in Africa." *International Studies* 41 (4): 387–409.

McGann, James G. 2005. "Think Tanks and Policy Advice in the US." Foreign Policy Research Institute. www.kas.de/wf/doc/kas_7042-1522-1-30.pdf?050810140439 (accessed April 27, 2018).

Mearsheimer, John J. 2001. *The Tragedy of Great Power Politics.* New York: Norton.

Melamed, Claire, and Andy Sumner. 2011. "A Post-2015 Global Development Agreement: Why, What, Who?" In *UNDP/ODI Workshop,* 26–27. www.odi.org.uk/sites/odi.org.uk/files/odi-assets/publications-opinion-files/7369.pdf (accessed April 27, 2018).

Mengoub, Fatima Ezzahra. 2018. "Agricultural Investment in Africa: A Low Level . . . Numerous Opportunities." OCP Policy Center Policy Brief PB-18/02. www.ocppc.ma/sites/default/files/OCPPC-PB1802.pdf (accessed April 27, 2018).

Millennium Partnership for the African Recovery Programme. 2001. "The Millennium Partnership for the African Recovery Programme, Draft 3a." Pretoria, South Africa. http://archive.unu.edu/africa/africa day/files/2001/MilleniumAfricaPlan.pdf (accessed April 27, 2018).

Mokone, Mokote. 2011. "The World Bank, NEPAD and Africa's Development." WIReDSpace. http://mobile.wiredspace.wits.ac.za/handle/10539/9823 (accessed April 27, 2018).

Mokri, Karim El. 2016. "Le défi de la transformation économique structurelle : une analyse par la complexité économique." OCP Policy Center Research Paper RP-16/08. www.ocppc.ma/sites/default/files/OCPPC-RP1608.pdf (accessed April 27, 2018).

Mokri, Karim El, and Tayeb Ghazi. 2016. "Africa-Atlantic Integration: Can the Economy Unite What Geology Has Divided?" OCP Policy Center Policy Brief PB-16/19. www.ocppc.ma/sites/default/files/OCPPC-PB1619vEn.pdf (accessed April 27, 2018).

Montpetit, Éric. 2002a. *Misplaced Distrust: Policy Network and the Environment in France, the United States and Canada*. Vancouver: University of British Columbia Press.

2002b. "Pour en finir avec le lobbying: comment les institutions canadiennes influencent l'action des groupes d'intérêts." *Politique et sociétés* 21 (3): 91–112.

2003. "Public Consultation in Policy Network Environments: The Case of Assisted Human Reproduction in Canada." *Canadian Public Policy* 29 (1): 95–110.

Moravcsik, Andrew. 1997. "Taking Preferences Seriously: A Liberal Theory of International Politics." *International Organization* 51 (4): 512–53.

1999. "Is Something Rotten in the State of Denmark? Constructivism and European Integration." *Journal of European Public Policy* 6 (4): 669–81.

2003. "Theory Synthesis in International Relations: Real Not Metaphysical." *International Studies Review* 5(1): 131–36.

Morgenthau, Hans J. 1993. *Politics among Nations: The Struggle for Power and Peace*. Revised by Kenneth W. Thompson. New York: McGraw-Hill.

Moussa, Pierre. 2002. "L'investissement privé étranger en Afrique: atouts et obstacles." *Afrique contemporaine* (204): 5–80.

Moyo, Dambisa. 2009. *Dead Aid: Why Aid Is Not Working and How There Is a Better Way for Africa*. New York: Farrar, Straus and Giroux.

Moyo, Theresa. 2002. "The Resource Mobilisation Strategy of the New Partnership for Africa's Development: A Critical Appraisal." In *New Partnership for Africa's Development, NEPAD: A New Path?*, edited by Peter Anyang' Nyongo'o, Aseghedech Ghirmazion, and Davinder Lamba, 182–208. Nairobi: Heinrich Böll Foundation.

Mu, Yibin, Peter Phelps, and Janet Gale Stotsky. 2013. "Bond Markets in Africa." International Monetary Fund Working Paper no. 13/12. www.imf.org/external/pubs/ft/wp/2013/wp1312.pdf (accessed April 27, 2018).

Mubiru, Alex. 2010. "Domestic Resource Mobilisation across Africa: Trends, Challenges, and Policy Options." Committee of Ten Policy Brief. African Development Bank. www.afdb.org/fileadmin/uploads/afdb/Documents/Publications/C-10%20Note%202%20English%20(final)_for%20posting%202.pdf (accessed April 27, 2018).

Mutangadura, Gladys. 2005. "Assessment of Progress in Implementing NEPAD in Southern Africa." *Africa's Sustainable Development Bulletin* 1:14–19. Addis Ababa: UNECA-Sustainable Development Division.

NEPAD. n.d. "About NEPAD: Governance." NEPAD.org. www.nepad.org/content/about-nepad#gov (accessed April 27, 2018).

2001. *The New Partnership For Africa's Development (NEPAD)*. Abuja: NEPAD.

2003a. "The African Peer Review Mechanism (APRM)." http://aprm-au.org/sites/default/files/aprm_base_0.pdf.

2003b. *Guidelines for Countries to Prepare for and to Participate in the African Peer Review Mechanism (Aprm)*. Document AHG/235 (XXXVIII), Annex II. Johannesburg: NEPAD. https://issafrica.s3.amazonaws.com/site/uploads/GUIDEREVIEW.PDF (accessed April 27, 2018)

2010. *Project Implementation Review of the NEPAD Infrastructure Short Term Action Plan*. Johannesburg: NEPAD.

NEPAD Agency. 2003. "NEPAD Health Strategy." www.sarpn.org/documents/d0000612/ (accessed April 27, 2018).

2012. *NEPAD 2011 Annual Report*. Johannesburg: NEPAD.

2015a. *The CAADP Results Framework [2015–2025]*. Johannesburg: NEPAD Agency.

2015b. *Presidential Infrastructure Champion Initiative (PICI) Report*. Johannesburg: NEPAD Agency.

2018. "NEPAD News January 2018." www.nepad.org/download/file/fid/7861%20 (accessed April 27, 2018).

NEPAD Planning and Coordination Agency, and United Nations Economic Commission for Africa. 2014. *Mobilizing Domestic Financial Resources for Implementing NEPAD National and Regional Programmes & Projects- Africa Looks Within*.

NEPAD, Program for Infrastructure Development in Africa, African Development Bank, and African Union. 2012. *Programme for Infrastructure Development in Africa Interconnecting, Integrating and Transforming a Continent*. www.afdb.org/fileadmin/uploads/afdb/Documents/Project-and-Operations/PIDA%20note%20English%20for%20web%200208.pdf (accessed April 27, 2018).

NEPAD Secretariat. 2001. *The New Partnership for Africa's Development*. Johannesburg: African Union.

2002. *The New Partnership for Africa's Development: The African Peer Review Mechanism (APRM). AHG/235 (XXXVIII) Annex II.* Durban: NEPAD.

2003a. *Comprehensive Africa Agriculture Development Program.* Johannesburg: NEPAD.

2003b. *NEPAD Infrastructure Short-Term Action Plan (STAP): Review of Implementation Progress and the Way Forward.* Johannesburg: NEPAD.

2004. *NEPAD Annual Report 2003/2004.* African Union. www.eisa.org .za/aprm/pdf/NEPAD_%20Annual_Report_2004.pdf (accessed April 27, 2018).

2008. *CAADP Annual Report 2008.* Johannesburg: NEPAD.

2010. *CAADP Review: Renewing the Commitment to African Agriculture.* Johannesburg: NEPAD Planning and Coordinating Agency.

2011. *Report on the Programmatic Activities of the NEPAD Agency for the Period July to December 2010 by the Chief Executive Officer, Dr. Ibrahim Assane Mayaki.* Addis Ababa: NEPAD.

Niggli, Nicholas C., and Kodjo Osei-Lah. 2014. "Infrastructure Provision and Africa's Trade and Development Prospects: Potential Role and Relevance of The WTO Agreement on Government Procurement (GPA)." WTO Staff Working Paper. www.econstor.eu/bitstream/ 10419/104767/1/803270313.pdf (accessed April 27, 2018).

Nkoyokm, Jacqueline. 2002. "Mobiliser la Société Civile pour la Nouvelle Initiative Africaine." In *Le G8 et l'Afrique, crise et reconstruction.* Montréal: Alternatives, Réseau d'action et de communication pour le développement international.

North, Douglass. 1990. *Institutions, Institutional Change and Economic Performance.* New York: Cambridge University Press.

NPCA (NEPAD Planning and Coordination Agency). 2010. *NPCA Business Plan: 2010–2014.* Johannesburg: NEPAD Agency.

2012. *NEPAD Agency Business Plan 2012: Towards a Second Decade of NEPAD Programmes for Sustainable Development Results in Africa.* Midrand: NEPAD Agency.

2016. *MoveAfrica Initiative: Moving Goods & Facilitating Trade.* Mdirand: NEPAD Agency.

NPCA (NEPAD Planning and Coordination Agency), and African Union. 2012. *Africa's Capacity Development Strategic Framework.* Midrand: NEPAD Planning and Coordinating Agency. www.africa-platform.org/ sites/default/files/resources/booklet_final_english_16_10_2013_mail_ web_b.pdf (accessed April 27, 2018).

Nunnenkamp, Peter, and Rainer Thiele. 2013. "Financing for Development: The Gap between Words and Deeds since Monterrey." *Development Policy Review* 31 (1): 75–98.

Obama, Barack. 2014. "Remarks by the President in Town Hall with the Washington Fellowship for Young African Leaders, Omni Shoreham Hotel, Washington, D.C." July 28. The White House Office of the Press Secretary. https://obamawhitehouse.archives.gov/the-press-office/2014/07/28/remarks-president-town-hall-washington-fellowship-young-african-leaders (accessed April 27, 2018).

Odeh, M. A., and M. D. Mailafia. 2013. "The African Union and Public Sector Reforms under the New Partnership for Africa's Development (NEPAD)'s African Peer-Review Mechanism." *Journal of Social Sciences and Public Policy* 5 (1): 77–98.

Odhiambo, Ojijo, and Emmanuel Ziramba. 2014. *Mobilising Domestic Resources for Development Financing in Namibia? Constraints and Opportunities*. International Policy Centre for Inclusive Growth Working Paper no. 127. www.ipc-undp.org/pub/IPCWorkingPaper127.pdf (accessed April 27, 2018).

OECD (Organization for Economic Co-operation and Development). 2013. "Final Report on the Feasibility Study into the Tax Inspectors Without Borders Initiative." June 5. www.oecd.org/tax/tax-global/TIWB_feasibility_study.pdf (accessed April 27, 2018).

——— 2014. "CRS Aid Statistics." http://stats.oecd.org; http://dx.doi.org/10.1787/data-00285-en (accessed April 27, 2018).

Office of the Special Adviser on Africa (United Nations). 2008. *The Private Sector's Institutional Response to NEPAD: Review of Current Experience and Practices*. New York: OSAA.

Ohaer, Roland. 2018. "SAATM LAUNCH: Sustenance Will Drive Tremendous Benefits for African Operators, States." *Aviation & Allied Business*. www.aviationbusinessjournal.aero/2018/2/19/saatm-launch-sustenance-will-drive-tremendous-benefits-for-african-operators,-states.aspx (accessed April 27, 2018).

Olson, Mancur. 1965. *The Logic of Collective Action*. New York: Schocken Books.

Omoweh, Daniel A. 2004. "Does Nepad Address the Land and Resource Rights of the Poor?" In *Securing Land and Resource Rights in Africa: Pan-African Perspectives*, Programme for Land and Agrarian Studies, 95–104. Cape Town: Programme for Land and Agrarian Studies.

Ould-Abdallah, Ahmedou. 2002. "L'Afrique à l'heure de la mondialisation: une nouvelle initiative pour le développement en Afrique." *La revue internationale et stratégique* 2 (46): 97–102.

Palier, Bruno, and Giuliano Bonoli. 1999. "Phénomènes de path dependency et réformes des systèmes de protection sociale." *Revue française de science politique* 49 (3): 399–420.

PATH. 2014. "The Role of Research and Innovation for Health in the Post-2015 Development Agenda: Bridging the Divide between the Richest and Poorest Within a Generation." Washington, DC: COHRED, Global Health Technologies Coalition, International AIDS Vaccine Initiative, and PATH. www.ghtcoalition.org/pdf/The_role_of_research_and_inno vation_in_the_post_2015_development_agenda.pdf (accessed April 27, 2018).

Pease, Kelly-Kate S., and David P. Forsythe. 1993. "Human Rights, Humanitarian Intervention, and World Politics." *Human Rights Quarterly* 15 (2): 290–314.

Permanent Mission of the Kingdom of Morocco to the United Nations Office and other International Organizations in Geneva. n.d. "Morocco Commits 300,000 Euros to the World Digital Solidarity Fund." www.mission-maroc.ch/en/pages/273.html (accessed April 27, 2018).

Perroux, François. 1961. *L'Économie du XXeme siècle*. Paris: Presses Universitaires de France.

Pfister, Mike. 2009. "Taxation for Investment and Development: An Overview of Policy Challenges in Africa." Presented at the Ministerial Meeting and Expert Roundtable of the NEPAD-OECD Africa Investment Initiative. www1.oecd.org/investment/investmentfordevelopment/4396 6821.pdf (accessed April 27, 2018).

Pierson, Paul. 2000. "The Path to European Integration: A Historical Institutionalism Analysis." *Comparative Political Studies* 29 (2): 123–63.

2004. *Politics in Time: History, Institution, and Social Analysis*. Princeton: Princeton University Press.

Pressman, Jeffrey L., and Aaron Wildavsky. 1984. *Implementation*. 3rd ed. Berkeley: University of California Press.

Radelet, Steven. 2006. "A Primer on Foreign Aid." Center for Global Development Working Paper no. 92. www.cgdev.org/publication/primer-for eign-aid-working-paper-92 (accessed April 27, 2018)

Ricardo, David. 1965. *Principles of Political Economy and Taxation*. New York: Dutton.

Risse, Thomas. 2000. "'Let's Argue!': Communicative Action in World Politics." *International Organization* 54: 1.

Robinson, Jackson Onome. 2013. "Unmaking the Third World via the New Partnership for African Development (NEPAD): Experience and Future Action Areas." *International Journal of African and Asian Studies* 3: 19–27.

Rostow, Walt. 1970 [1963]. *Les étapes de la croissance économique*. Paris: Seuil.

Russett, Bruce Martin. 1993. *Grasping the Democratic Peace*. Princeton: Princeton University Press.

Sachs, Jeffrey. 2005. *The End of Poverty: How We Can Make It Happen in Our Lifetime*. New York: Penguin.

Sachs, Jeffery D., and Guido Schmidt-Traub. 2013. "Financing for Development and Climate Change Post-2015." Draft for Discussion. Sustainable Development Solutions Network. http://unsdsn.org/wp-content/uploads/2014/02/130316-Development-and-Climate-Finance.pdf (accessed April 27, 2018).

Saint-Martin, Denis. 2002. "Apprentissage social et changement institutionnel: la politique de 'l'investissement dans l'enfance' au Canada et en Grande-Bretagne." *Politique et Sociétés* 21 (3): 41–67.

Sambo, Luis Gomes, Joses Muthuri Kirigia, and Juliet Nabyonga Orem. 2013. "Health Financing in the African Region: 2000–2009 Data Analysis." *International Archives of Medicine* 6 (1): 10.

Seeraj, Mohamed. 2010. "Why Another Amnesty for Illegal Capital Flight?" *Engineering News*, September 17. www.engineeringnews.co.za/article/why-another-amnesty-for-illegal-capital-flight-2010-09-17 (accessed April 27, 2018).

Seshamani, Venkatesh. 1994. "Structural Adjustment and Poverty Alleviation: Some Issues on the Use of Social Safety Nets and Targeted Public Expenditures." In *Structural Adjustment and Beyond in Sub-Saharan Africa: Research and Policy Issues*, edited by Rolph van der Hoeven and Fred van der Kraaij, 114–25. Portsmouth: Heinemann.

Shepsle, Kenneth. 1986. "Institutional Equilibrium and Equilibrium Institution." In *Political Science: the Science of Politics*, edited by Herbert Weisberg, 51–81. New York: Agathon.

Shepsle, Kenneth, and Barry Weingast. 1982. "Institutionalizing Majority Rule: A Social Choice Theory With Policy Implications." *American Economic Review* 72 (2): 367–71.

Signé, Landry. 2004. "Le NEPAD constitue-t-il une rupture ou une continuité par rapport aux initiatives du Fonds monétaire international et de la Banque mondiale pour le développement de l'Afrique?" Thesis submitted at Jean Moulin Lyon University.

___. 2010. "Innover en politique: les acteurs internationaux, régionaux, et nationaux en strategies de développement économique en Afrique." Dissertation, University of Montreal, Québec.

___. 2011. "The Political Responses to the Global Economic and Financial Crises in Francophone Africa from 1980 to 2010: A Paradigm Shift?" *African Journal of Political Science and International Relations* 5 (3): 179–89.

___. 2013a. "Idées, paradigmes et explication de l'émergence et des trajectoires des stratégies de développement en Afrique." *Revue cosmopolitique* 5 (4): 28–54.

___. 2013b. *Le NEPAD et les institutions financières internationales en Afrique au 2Ie siècle: émergence, évolution et bilan*. Paris: L'Harmattan.

2016. "How to Implement Domestic Resource Mobilization (DRM) Successfully for Effective Delivery of Sustainable Development Goals (SDGs) in Africa: Part 1 – An Innovative Policy Delivery Model." OCP Policy Center Policy Brief PB-16/24. www.ocppc.ma/sites/default/files/OCPPC-PB1623.pdf (accessed April 27, 2018).

2017. *Innovating Development Strategies in Africa: The Role of International, Regional, and National Actors.* Cambridge: Cambridge University Press.

2017. "3 Things to Know about Africa's Industrialization and the Continental Free Trade Area." Africa in Focus, The Brookings Institution. November 22, 2017. www.brookings.edu/blog/africa-in-focus/2017/11/22/3-things-to-know-about-africas-industrialization-and-the-continental-free-trade-area (accessed April 27, 2018).

2018. "Capturing Africa's High Returns." Brookings Op-ed, The Brookings Institution. www.brookings.edu/opinions/capturing-africas-high-returns/ (accessed April 27, 2018).

2018. "Why Africa's Free Trade Area Offers So Much Promise." *The Conversation.* March 26. https://theconversation.com/why-africas-free-trade-area-offers-so-much-promise-93827 (accessed April 27, 2018).

2018. "Africa's Big New Free Trade Agreement, Explained." *Washington Post.* March 29. www.washingtonpost.com/news/monkey-cage/wp/2018/03/29/the-countdown-to-the-african-continental-free-trade-area-starts-now/?utm_term=.5cae605cd14e (accessed April 27, 2018).

Signé, Landry, and Mamoudou Gazibo. 2010. "Innover en stratégies de développement: le Nouveau partenariat pour le développement de l'Afrique." *Revue canandienne d'études africaines* 44 (2): 317–44.

Skocpol, Theda. 1979. *States and Social Revolutions: A Comparative Analysis of France, Russia, and China.* New York: Cambridge University Press.

1985. "Bringing the State Back In: Strategies of Analysis in Current Research." In *Bringing the State Back In,* edited by Peter Evans, Dietrich Rueschemeyer, and Theda Skocpol, 3–37. New York: Cambridge University Press.

1992. *Protecting Soldiers and Mothers: The Political Origins of Social Policy in the United States.* New York: Cambridge University Press.

Smith, Adam. 1971. *The Wealth of Nations.* New York: Dutton.

1976 [1776]. *An Inquiry into the Nature and the Causes of the Wealth of Nations.* Oxford: Oxford University Press.

Smith, Miriam. 2002. "L'héritage institutionnaliste de la science politique au Canada anglais." *Politique et sociétés* 21 (3): 113–38.

Smith, Steven. 2008. "Six Wishes for a More Relevant Discipline of International Relations." In *The Oxford Handbook of International Relations,* edited by Christian Reus-Smit and Duncan Smidal, 725–32. Oxford: Oxford University Press,.

Snoddy, Vanessa K. 2005. *The New Partnership for Africa's Development (NEPAD): Will It Succeed or Fail?* Carlisle Barracks: US Army War College.

Songwe, Vera. 2018. "Africa's Bold Move towards Integration: The Continental Free Trade Agreement." In *Foresight Africa: Top Priorities for the Continent in 2018*, 19. Washington, DC: The Brookings Institution.

Soumare, Amath. 2003. "L'Afrique qui gagne." Paper presented at the Conférence NEPAD Avenir Sciences Politiques, March 13. Paris.

Southern African Regional Poverty Network. 2002. "African Civil Society Declaration on NEPAD." July 28. Southern African Regional Poverty Network. www.sarpn.org/NEPAD/july2002/acs_declaration/ (accessed April 27, 2018).

Steinmo, Sven, Kathleen Thelen, and Frank Longstreth. 1992. *Structuring Politics: Historical Institutionalism in Comparative Analysis.* New York: Cambridge University Press.

Stewart, Frances. 1992. "A Short-Term Policy for Long-Term Development." In *Africa's Recovery in the 1990s: From Stagnation and Adjustment to Human Development*, edited by Giovanni Andrea Cornia, Rolph van der Hoeven, and Thandika Mkandawire, 312–33. New York: St. Martin's Press.

Stiglitz, Joseph. 2002. *La grande désillusion.* Paris: Fayard.

Strange, Austin, Bradley Parks, Michael J. Tierney, Andreas Fuchs, Axel Dreher, and Vijaya Ramachandran. 2013. "China's Development Finance to Africa: A Media-Based Approach to Data Collection." Center for Global Development Working Paper no. 323. www.cgdev .org/sites/default/files/chinese-development-finance-africa.pdf (accessed April 27, 2018).

Surel, Yves. 1998. "Idées, intérêts et institutions dans l'analyse des politiques publiques." *Pouvoirs* 87: 161–68.

———. 2000. "Comparer les sentiers institutionnels: la réforme des banques centrales au sein de l'Union européenne." *Revue internationale de politique comparée* 7 (1): 135–66.

Sy, Amadou. 2014. "Shifts in Financing Sustainable Development: How Should Africa Adapt in 2014?" In *Foresight Africa: Top Priorities for the Continent in 2014*, 25–28. Washington, DC: The Brookings Institution.

Taylor, Ian. 2002. "Commentary: The New Partnership for Africa's Development and the Zimbabwe Elections: Implications and Prospects for the Future." *African Affairs* 101 (404): 403–12.

———. 2003. "La politique sud-africaine et le NEPAD: contradictions et compromis." *Politique africaine* (91): 120–38.

Taylor, Ian, and Paul Williams. 2001. "South African Foreign Policy and the Great Lakes Crisis: African Renaissance Meets *Vagabondage Politique?*" *African Affairs* 100 (399): 265–86.

Taylor, Ian, and Philip Nel. 2002. "'New Africa,' Globalisation, and the Confines of Elite Reformism: 'Getting the Rhetoric Right,' Getting the Strategy Wrong." *Third World Quarterly* 23 (1): 163–80.

Thiabou, Aissatou. 2002. "NEPAD et développement durable." Les Pénélopes. www.medialter.org/article.php3?id_article=3 (accessed April 27, 2018).

Thucydides. 1972. *History of the Peloponnesian War*. Translated by R. Warner. London: Penguin.

1982. *The Peloponnesian War*. Translated by R. Crawley. New York: Modern Library.

Toye, John. 1994. "Stuctural Adjustment: Context, Assumptions, Origin, and Diversity." In *Structural Adjustment and Beyond in Sub-Saharan Africa: Research and Policy Issues*, edited by Rolph van der Hoeven and Fred van der Kraaij, 18–35. Portsmouth: Heinemann.

Tungwarara, Ozias. 2010. "Summary of Findings from the Country Studies." In *The African Peer Review Mechanism: A Compilation of Studies of the Process in Nine African Countries*, 7–22. Johannesburg: Open Society Initiative for Southern Africa (OSISA) for AfriMAP (Africa Governance Monitoring and Advocacy Project).

UNCATD FDI Statistics. http://unctadstat.unctad.org/wds/ReportFolders/ reportFolders.aspx (accessed April 27, 2018).

UNECA (United Nations Economic Commission for Africa). 2012. *A Decade of NEPAD : Deepening African Private Sector and Civil Society Ownership and Partenership*. Addis Ababa: Economic Commission for Africa. www1.uneca.org/portals/nepad/documents/decade%20of%20nepad_ final.pdf (accessed April 27, 2018).

2016. *Africa Regional Integration Index: Report 2016*. Addis Ababa: Economic Commission for Africa.

UN-HABITAT. n.d. "Rabat NEPAD City Project." http://mirror.unhabitat .org/content.asp?cid=2890&catid=219&typeid=13 (accessed April 27, 2018).

2016. *Structural Transformation in Developing Countries: Cross Regional Analysis*. Kenya: UN-Habitat.

United Nations. n.d. "Kingdom of Morocco: Support to NEPAD (Period 2001–2003). www.un.org/esa/africa/support/Morocco.htm (accessed April 27, 2018).

2000. *55/2. United Nations Millennium Declaration*. www.un.org/millen nium/declaration/ares552e.htm (accessed April 27, 2018).

2006. Office of the Special Adviser on Africa. *The Contribution of the Private Sector to the Implementation of the New Partnership for Africa's Development (NEPAD)*. New York: United Nations.

2013. *A New Global Partnership: Eradicate Poverty and Transform Economies Through Sustainable Development: The Report of the High-Level Panel of Eminent Persons on the Post-2015 Development Agenda.* New York: United Nations. https://sustainabledevelopment.un.org/content/documents/8932013-05%20-%20HLP%20Report%20-%20A%20New%20Global%20Partnership.pdf (accessed April 27, 2018).

2014a. *Open Working Group Proposal for Sustainable Development Goals.* July 19. https://sustainabledevelopment.un.org/content/documents/1579SDGs%20Proposal.pdf (accessed April 27, 2018).

2014b. *Resolution Adopted by the General Assembly A/RES/68/309, Report of the Open Working Group on Sustainable Development Goals Established Pursuant to General Assembly Resolution 66/288.* September 10. www.un.org/en/ga/search/view_doc.asp?symbol=A/RES/68/309 (accessed April 27, 2018).

2014c. *The Road to Dignity by 2030: Ending Poverty, Transforming All Lives and Protecting the Planet.* New York: United Nations. www.un.org/disabilities/documents/reports/SG_Synthesis_Report_Road_to_Dignity_by_2030.pdf (accessed April 27, 2018).

United Nations General Assembly. 2002. *Resolution No. A/RES/57/7. Final Review and Appraisal of the United Nations New Agenda for the Development of Africa in the 1990s and Support for the New Partnership for Africa's Development.* New York: United Nations. www.un.org/en/ga/search/view_doc.asp?symbol=A/RES/57/7 (accessed April 27, 2018).

2012. *Resolution No. A/RES/66/293. A Monitoring Mechanism to Review Commitments Made towards Africa's Development.* New York: United Nations. www.un.org/en/ga/search/view_doc.asp?symbol=%20A/RES/66/293 (accessed April 27, 2018).

United Nations Millennium Project. 2005. *Investing in Development: A Practical Plan to Achieve the Millennium Development Goals: Report to the UN Secretary-General.* London: UN Development Programme. http://siteresources.worldbank.org/INTTSR/Resources/MainReportComplete-lowres%5B1%5D.pdf (accessed April 27, 2018).

United Nations Secretary-General. 2003. "Secretary-General's Bulletin." Office of the Special Adviser on Africa. 23 April 2003. ST/SGB/2003/6. www.un.org/en/ga/search/view_doc.asp?symbol=ST/SGB/2003/6 (accessed April 27, 2018).

2014. *New Partnership for Africa's Development: Twelfth Consolidated Progress Report on Implementation and International Support. A/69/161.* New York: United Nations.

Valier, Jacques. 2000. "Pauvretés, inégalités, et politiques sociales dans les tiers-mondes depuis la fin des années quatre-vingt." In *Développement,* edited by François Bourguignon, Daniel Cohen, and Alain Liepetz, 127–56. Paris: La Documentation française.

van de Walle, Nicolas. 2001. *African Economies and the Politics of Permanent Crisis, 1979–1999*. Cambridge: Cambridge University Press.

2005. *Overcoming Stagnation in Aid-Dependent Countries*. Washington, DC: Center for Global Development.

Van der Hoeven, Rolph, and Fred van der Kraaij, eds. 1994. *Structural Adjustment and Beyond in Sub-Saharan Africa: Research and Policy Issues*. Portsmouth: Heinemann.

Ventris, Curtis. 2000. "New Public Management: An Examination of its Influence on Contemporary Public Affairs and Its Impact on Shaping the Intellectual Agenda of the Field." *Administrative Theory and Praxis* 22 (3): 500–18.

Wade, Abdoulaye. 2002. "Le financement entre la recession économique et crise des projets politiques," preface to *Le NEPAD et les enjeux du développement en Afrique*, by Hakim Ben Hammouda and Moustapha Kassé, 9–13. Paris: Maisonneuve et Larose.

Wallerstein, Immanuel. 1974a. *The Modern World-System: Capitalist Agriculture and the Origins of the European World-Economy in the Sixteenth Century*. New York: Academic Press.

1974b. "The Rise and Future Demise of the World Capitalist System: Concepts for Comparative Analysis." *Comparative Studies in Society and History* 16 (4): 387–415.

1983. "The Three Instances of Hegemony in the History of the Capitalist World-Economy." *International Journal of Comparative Sociology* 24 (1): 100–8.

Walter, Riker. 1980. "Implications from the Disequilibrium of Majority Rule for the Study of Institutions." *American Political Science Review* 74 (2): 432–47.

Waltz, Kenneth N. 1979. *Theory of International Politics*. New York: McGraw-Hill.

Weingast, Barry. 2002. "Rational Choice Institutionalism." In *Political Science: State of the Discipline*, edited by Ira Katznelson and Helen Milner, 661–92. Washington, DC: American Political Science Association.

Wendt, Alexander. 1992. "Anarchy Is What States Make of It." *International Organization* 46 (2): 391–425.

1999. *Social Theory of International Politics*. Cambridge: Cambridge University Press.

2001. "Driving with the Rearview Mirror: On the Rational Science of Institutional Design." *International Organization* 55 (4): 1019–49.

Wigboldus, Seerp, Jan van der Lee, Herman Brouwer, and Wouter Leen Hijweege. 2011. *Critical Success Factors in Capacity Development*

Support: An Exploration in the Context of International Coopera-tion. Wageningen: Centre for Development Innovation, Wageningen University and Research Centre. http://library.wur.nl/WebQuery/edepot/174241.

Williamson, John. 1990. "What Washington Means by Policy Reform." In *Latin American Adjustment: How Much Has Happened?* edited by John Williamson, 7–20. Washington, DC: Institute for International Economics.

World Bank. 1989. *Sub-Saharan Africa: From Crisis to Sustainable Growth.* Washington, DC: World Bank.

1990. *World Development Report 1990: Poverty.* Washington, DC: World Bank.

1993. *World Development Report 1993: Investing in Health.* New York: Oxford University Press.

1994. *Adjustment in Africa: Reforms, Results, and the Road Ahead.* New York: Oxford University Press.

1998. *Assessing Development Effectiveness: Evaluation in the World Bank and the International Finance Corporation.* Washington, DC: World Bank.

1999. *World Development Report, 1999/2000: Entering the 21st Century.* New York: Oxford University Press.

2000a. *Can Africa Claim Its Place in the 21st Century?* Washington, DC: World Bank.

2000b. *World Development Report, 2000/2001: Attacking Poverty.* New York: Oxford University Press.

2013. *Financing for Development Post-2015.* Washington, DC: World Bank. www.worldbank.org/content/dam/Worldbank/document/Poverty%20documents/WB-PREM%20financing-for-development-pub-10-11-13web.pdf (accessed April 27, 2018).

2014. "Côte d'Ivoire Set to Raise $1bn Sovereign Bond Next Year." *Global Capital,* October 11. www.globalcapital.com/article/yvxvhtrr3j5m/cte-divoire-set-to-raise-$1bn-sovereign-bond-next-year (accessed April 27, 2018).

World Bank, and United Nations Development Program. 1989. *Africa's Adjustment and Growth During the 1980s.* Washington, DC: World Bank.

World Economic Forum. 2015. "The 13 Fastest-Growing Economies in the World." World Economic Forum. www.weforum.org/agenda/2015/06/the-13-fastest-growing-economies-in-the-world/ (accessed April 27, 2018).

Index